Professional Behaviors and I

Professional Behaviors and Dispositions teaches counselors in training (CITs) how to cultivate counselor competencies and critical thinking skills in support of lifelong professional development. First, CITs will gain a detailed understanding of the professional behaviors and dispositions expected of all counselors. They will then learn how to evaluate themselves for these factors using a universal growth model that promotes holistic, ongoing assessment of oneself and one's relationships. Next, CITs will be presented with concrete tools and activities that they can use to cultivate and retain counselor competencies. Finally, CITs are given a step-by-step guide for creating a professional growth plan they can use throughout their program and their clinical practice. Accompanying this text is a helpful online faculty guide for supervisors to use while working with CITs. Aligned with CACREP, ACA, and ACES standards, this textbook will be useful for all counselors for all Counselors in Training.

Candace M. McLain, EdD, LPC, ACS, is a core faculty member at Walden University in the Clinical Mental Health Counseling Program and has worked as a clinician, faculty and administrator in higher education for over ten years. She is a licensed professional counselor in both Michigan and Colorado as well as an approved clinical supervisor. Dr. McLain served previously as a clinical coordinator, coordinator of assessment and remediation and has served on the ACES Guidelines for Online Learning.

Joelle P. Lewis, EdD, LCSW (CO) is a core faculty member at Walden University in the Clinical Mental Health Counseling Program and has taught in higher education since 2000. She is a licensed clinical social worker in Colorado. Dr. Lewis had a private practice for ten years, specializing in adult survivors of childhood trauma, and was the executive director for a domestic violence treatment program. She also served as the director of a residential treatment center for at-risk adolescents and as a mental health therapist for residential treatment for the chronically mentally ill.

Professional Behaviors and Dispositions

Counseling Competencies and Lifelong Growth

Candace M. McLain and Joelle P. Lewis

Routledge
Taylor & Francis Group

NEW YORK AND LONDON

First published 2019
by Routledge
711 Third Avenue, New York, NY 10017

and by Routledge
2 Park Square, Milton Park, Abingdon, Oxon, OX14 4RN

Routledge is an imprint of the Taylor & Francis Group, an informa business

Library of Congress Cataloging-in-Publication Data
A catalog record for this title has been requested
Names: McLain, Candace M., author. | Lewis, Joelle, author.
Title: Professional behaviors and dispositions : counseling competencies and lifelong growth / Candace M. McLain, Joelle P. Lewis.
Description: New York, NY : Routledge, 2019. | Includes index.
Identifiers: LCCN 2018019683| ISBN 9781138089884 (hardcover : alk. paper) | ISBN 9781138089891 (pbk. : alk. paper) | ISBN 9781315108919 (e-book)
Subjects: LCSH: Counseling psychologists. | Counselors. | Counseling psychology—Vocational guidance. | Counseling—Vocational guidance.
Classification: LCC BF636.64 .M365 2019 | DDC 158.3—dc23
LC record available at https://lccn.loc.gov/2018019683

ISBN: 978-1-138-08988-4 (hbk)
ISBN: 978-1-138-08989-1 (pbk)
ISBN: 978-1-315-10891-9 (ebk)

Typeset in Sabon
by Swales & Willis Ltd, Exeter, Devon, UK

Visit the eResources: www.routledge.com/9781138089891

Dedication

This book is dedicated first and foremost to our amazingly beautiful colleague, friend, and counselor educator supervisor, Marsha Sage. We sat at the Colorado Counseling Association Conference three years ago discussing her desire to publish something in our career together prior to her passing away in 2017. Marsha, we dedicate this book to you. This is your publication as much as it is ours because of all the amazing feedback we have received from you and your students who loved your guidance with them. We also dedicate this book to the numerous CES who tirelessly work with CITs offering all they have, to guide, challenge, and support them in their growth towards optimal competencies, thus positively impacting all clients out there. Finally, we dedicate this work to the numerous amazing students we have worked with over the years who inspired and taught us so much more about ourselves than we could have ever known alone. You are the heroes for your CES and for your future clients to come. Keep up your ongoing growth and development!

Contents

Foreword

In the book *Professional Behaviors and Dispositions: Counseling Competencies and Lifelong Growth*, Dr. Lewis and Dr. McLain exceptionally discuss the importance of the educator or supervisory stance of being a gatekeeper to the profession. They skillfully discuss contemporary implications of these roles by seamlessly integrating a focus on supporting students in dispositional competencies with a discussion of the inherent barriers to gatekeeping, and the importance of consistent terminology used in the context of student remediation that is of value to a variety of mental health counseling professionals. Most importantly, the authors clarify the meaning and application of current CACREP Standards, the current ACA Code of Ethics, and the current ACES Best Practices as they succinctly review historical perspectives transposed with contemporary case examples. I find that the most innovative framework provided by these authors is a much-needed presentation of a model for CES to use with CIT that is grounded in Stages of Change principles and Motivational Interviewing strategies – thus empowering CES to respond to discomfort and difficult circumstances with thoughtful consideration for self and others while they simultaneously assist CIT to cooperate with remediation plans and endeavor to adjust or improve behavior. This book stands as a beacon to all mental health professionals to advocate for the advancement of and excellence in their profession by answering the call from those professionals for a common language, a common purpose, and a model to evaluate and remediate CITs.

Jason H. King, PhD, LCMHC-S, NCC, CCMHC, ACS
Student Development Coordinator in the School of
Counseling College of Social and Behavioral
Sciences at Walden University

Preface

In 2011 I (Dr. McLain) was offered the amazing and daunting responsibility to lead and establish a formal protocol at a local university where I worked, involving creating an admissions process, remediation process, and program assessment process. At the time, I had no idea how beautifully these areas dovetailed to form a synthesized streamlined working machine aimed towards high ethical standards in the field of counselor education supervision. I was 33 years old, recently graduated with my Ed.D. in Counselor Education Supervision and was ready to take on the world. Little did I realize how complex, interesting, challenging, and passionate this appointed task would be for me, both personally and professionally.

As I reviewed all the immense literature I was immersed in, I became completely awestruck by how caring, supportive, humble, and generous my colleagues in CES from around the country were in sharing what they had learned, researched, and created. These experts and mentors in our field actually responded to my emails, questions and desire for ongoing work in our field. Not only was I proud to join a profession of such amicable colleagues, I was invigorated about continuing to learn and develop new processes to meet the needs of Counselors in Training in the field while also gatekeeping and maintaining the ambitious standards of our amazing profession. The more I learned, the more I wanted to know. During this time I was also working directly with CITs who were referred for remediation needs. It was during my third year of engaging in this process that I was promoted to Program Director and started tracking my experiences and asking more questions than were being addressed in the literature. One question I had was about how I felt I was forever changed and had grown, deeply personally and professionally, in the process of supporting supervisees. While serving on the ACES Technology Interest Network Committee I also began asking about how CES could support CITs using remote technology within the remediation process, having it be an even better process for building authentic connections. This is when I began exploring ethical technological tools to help build the rapport and process of Counselor development and support efforts. My colleagues and I presented at ACES and RMACES on these areas and it was a blast. Many CES had ongoing passion, desire and motivation to do more in this realm. Dr. Lewis even completed her dissertation work by looking at how faculty experience working with CIT comportment issues. While attending RMACES, I attended a few presentations concerning development in the counseling field and the room was filled with both educators and supervisors alike. There were more questions than answers and there was a need that I heard from everyone in terms of wanting more guidance and support. During this time, I remember sitting in the conference room while CACREP was leading a presentation on new 2016 Standards. At this moment, while sitting in Park City, Utah, I decided that a manual or book to help support and lead both CES and the CIT on a developmental journey would be fabulous. I fully accepted that it is our responsibility to assess, train, and ensure competencies in the areas of knowledge, skills, and dispositions for our CITs. I had been studying dispositions for years and believed wholeheartedly they were the foundation of all else in a counselor's competency.

At last we could begin teaching and measuring this in our CITs. Over the last two years I have felt more passion and growth in myself as a CES than ever before because of the CITs I had been working with. I was given the wonderful chance to fill an interim Student Development Coordinator position at my university, leading faculty and CITs in professional development protocols, and it was the most rewarding experience of my life because it solidified my experiences of seeing a parallel growth process of CES with CIT. I began to see that in my relationships with CITs who were referred for comportment issues, I was challenged to assess myself and challenge myself in all the areas I was exploring with my CITs. This was profound to me. The more I continue to be open to growth and reflection, the more my CITs engaged readily in the same. It is the feedback from my CITs that encouraged me to write this book because they were reporting to me; although the process they went through was tough, it was amazing and life changing for them with my support. I must laugh because one CIT actually asked me "Have you thought about writing a book or something?" I acknowledge my numerous colleagues, past supervisors, and all my CITs as inspiration in the long hours of research, writing, and application of this material. It is with a most humble and awe-struck demeanor that I present to you the ideology behind this work of *Professional Behaviors and Dispositions: Counseling Competencies and Lifelong Growth*. My hope and faith is that all CES and CITs alike will take this work and use it for their own ongoing growth and development to continue to be the best counselors, educators, and supervisors they can be in the field of counseling to better our clients, our profession, and our entire world towards positive social change long into the future.

Acknowledgments

We would like to make a formal acknowledgment to all those who made this work possible. We start with the amazing publishing team including Anna Moore and Nina Guttapalle of the Taylor & Francis Group. We thank all those who reviewed the work for us, especially Dr. Jason King who has graciously written the foreword and provided ongoing support in this area of research and study, and Dr. David Capuzzi who encouraged and mentored me while also writing an additional recommendation for the book. In addition, we thank the Counseling team at University of Central Florida, including but not limited to Dr. Glenn Lambie, and for their permission, along with that of the Clinical Training Manager, that allows us to share the dispositional features of their assessment research concerning The Counseling Competencies Scale CCS-R. We acknowledge and thank Dr. Diana Hulse and Dr. Tracy Roberts for their permission to offer data and the use of the Corrective Feedback Inventory Revised. In addition, we thank Mr. Pete Walker for his permission to use his 4-Fs Trauma Response Model in our own framework. We also thank Ms. Georgia Rigg, LCSW, for her permission to incorporate the quartered circle for our Universal Growth Model. We thank all those who have studied and continue to study this key area of counselor support. To work with such amazing colleagues offers us ongoing passion in our work in the field of counseling. In addition, we thank the amazing colleagues and our supervisors for encouraging us and offering us the experiences and abilities to support CITs. We acknowledge our friends, families, neighbors, and Higher Power who has put this topic on our hearts as a necessary and deep need within our field of counseling, impacting positive social change to help others long into the future.

Introduction

Entering the field of counseling is a developmental process. As you probably already understand, this is a wonderful, sometimes difficult, ambiguous, and invigorating journey. If you allow the process to unfold and are dedicated to personal and professional growth, you will find the experience marvelous. We, as counselors, have chosen this path for a variety of reasons. Some Counselors in Training (CITs) report that they have always wanted to make *a difference*. Others report that they have always been told they were a gifted *listener* and had an *empathic ear*. Often, CITs report that they are compelled to the helping field due to experiencing their own woundedness. In fact, Barr (2006) did a study that reported that 74% of practicing clinicians in her sample had suffered significant traumatic life events, which led to their clinical career choice and affected their professional life in some manner. The suffering experiences included personal or vicarious exposure to mental health concerns, family conflicts, or abuse and neglect. The famous theorist, Carl Jung (1986), believed in the process of ongoing self-reflection, growth and using our own affliction and past prior woundedness towards becoming a full potential therapist that can help guide others in their own wounding. He coined the term *the wounded healer* to describe the phenomenon of a wounded therapist who had worked through their own struggles, through immense self-reflection, toward ongoing development and growth in having abilities to help others. Arnaud (2017) contended that although the wounded therapist and their personal past struggles are essential in becoming an effective therapist, others believe that the wounded therapist is indeed impaired (p. 135).

It appears there is a fine line between one's ability to pursue ongoing healing and growth and being considered potentially incompetent. Whatever the reason for pursuing a career in counseling, one thing is certain – we are all expected to grow, be self-aware, utilize self-reflection, while maintaining a curious vigor for the process itself. Growth and competency is required, in fact, both by accreditation standards from the Council for Accreditation of Counseling and Related Educational Programs (CACREP) (2016), and by our American Counseling Association (ACA) *Code of Ethics* (2014), in addition to various other mental health professional ethical guidelines. Consider, then, why this process is required of Counselors in Training (CITs). Because ongoing growth is included in so many professional responsibilities, we can embrace the hint of the vast importance of this course of ongoing growth, development, self-refection, and self-understanding. How can we address our own wounded healer background while pursuing growth, training, and competency in knowledge, skills, and dispositions to help others in the counseling mental health field? Even if we do not believe we have any wounds in our background, what are the immense benefits of engaging in this process as CITs? What are the potential consequences if we do not take up the journey?

What if I told you that you have immense capacities and abilities to help others only when you begin to unlock the growth process within yourself? What if I told you it seems scary now, but once you start in the process, and commit to your own growth, you will never want to look back.

Consider the following quote (Anon, n.d.) whose author is anonymous:

> When I was young and free, and my imagination had no limits, I dreamed of changing the world. As I grew older and wiser, I discovered the world would not change, so I shortened my sights somewhat and decided to change only my country. But, it too, seemed immovable.
>
> As I grew into my twilight years, in one last desperate attempt, I settled for changing only my family, those closest to me, but alas, they would have none of it. And now as I lie on my deathbed, I suddenly realize: If I had only changed my self-first, then by example I would have changed my family. From their inspiration and encouragement, I would then have been able to better my country and, who knows, I may have even changed the world.

If you have chosen the journey to become a counselor, you have already committed to deep ongoing growth and change, and we commend you for it. In fact, we are excited for your personal and professional journey and the work you and your CES will do along the way. We do want to offer encouragement within this process as it will be challenging; however, anything worth having never came easily, in my opinion. Trust the process.

Consider this story:

Climbing the Mountain

> I (Dr. McLain) am hiking on a trail up the mountain deep in the Colorado Rockies. I am in a hurry to get to the top for many reasons including the "view" that offers ice blue/purple majestic peaks stretched beyond the bright blue sky, deep evergreen pines, and golden sun sparkling through the sight of endless outlook. I am thinking of my family responsibilities, work, volunteer service, the laundry I must fold. I feel the sense of going, doing, and getting it over with for some odd reason, to move onto the next "thing." I would rather not stop along the way to do the deep, slow reflection of healing work needed. It's painful to stop along the way to do the conditioning work to make it to the summit. When I pause, I feel tightness in my body. Maybe I am afraid if I stop, I won't make it to the top?
>
> I would do much better by stopping along the way to use teachable moments to stretch, grow my muscles, care for my body, take a drink, snack, rest, pray, or self-assess. No, I cannot stop. I am in a hurry to get there, to reach the summit. It may be for my own glory, and maybe even to avoid the here and now imperative self-reflection for my growth. I may likely peter out or be misguided by other hikers trying to reach their own summit without self-care. I may even begin to carry other hiker's bags, or carry hikers themselves up the hill, rushing to hurry to the top, rather than allowing them to carry their own bags, finding their own path. Maybe

I need to unpack my own bag, to take inventory of my supplies for survival, self-care, and thriving in my own journey?

I am focused on rushing to the top. Why am I on this journey to begin with anyway? What does this tree of shade I begin to pass represent to me? Do I ignore it and press on, "no time, gotta keep going to the top!" What about the fork in the trail? I want the fastest way up, go, go get to the top! Who cares about the other paths that lead along a stream, wild roses, or even wildlife such as a beautiful fox or red-tailed hawk, all leading to the top, just not the fastest trail? Did I start this journey with a map to guide me or what have I planned prior to coming on this hike? Do I have resources such as time/food/water or spirituality as a gift and need on my trek? Is it hot, clear weather and what do I do in and with the weather? Keep pressing on and up or self-care and hunker down if rain and lightning hit? Who are the people I meet along the way up and around? Who in my life, my family, truly cares if I make it to the top? Do I say hello? Pass along, stop and chat, and find out what may be ahead, or do I press up and on fast, no time to care? What did I miss by not talking to a hiker? A mudslide, the trail ahead washed out? Do I consult with my map and others or press up and on, no time to care? What was the purpose of this journey again? To reach the top as fast as I can, or to use the trek and journey to the top for lifelong learning, meditation, teaching, understanding about myself, others, and the world I live in? Are you in a rush to get to the top or would you like to enjoy your journey to the top?

References

Anon (n.d.). Start with yourself [quotation]. Retrieved from: www.inspirationpeak.com/cgi-bin/stories.cgi?record=118.

Barr, A. (2006). *An investigation into the extent to which psychological wounds inspire counselors and psychotherapists to become wounded healers, the significance of these wounds on their career choice, the causes of these wounds, and the overall significance of demographic factors.* Retrieved from: www.thegreenrooms.net/wounded-healer.

Arnaud, K. (2017). Encountering the wounded healer: Parallel process and supervision. *Canadian Journal of Counseling and Psychotherapy*, *51*(2), 131–144.

American Counseling Association (2014). *Code of ethics.* Alexandria, VA: Author.

Council for Accreditation of Counseling and Related Educational Programs (CACREP) (2015). *2016 CACREP standards.* Alexandria, VA: Author.

Jung, C. G. (1985). Fundamental questions of psychotherapy. In S. H. Read, M. Fordham, G, Adler, & W. McGuire, (Eds) *The Collected Works of C. G. Jung.* Princeton, NJ: Princeton University Press.

1   Professional Behaviors and Dispositions
What Is PB&D?

This chapter covers a range of experiences Counselors in Training (CITs) face upon entering the clinical mental health field, including the experience of ongoing CIT growth and development and the requirement to continually engage in development and growth. Some CITs may be given a formal growth plan, while others are referred to work on a few areas, and still others choose to do immense growth on their own. Either way, we believe it is ultimately your choice to do the work and growth. In this chapter we also evaluate why many CITs are placed on a *growth plan* and how this is directly related to CACREP (2015) *2016 Standards* of competency in knowledge, skills, and dispositions. Research is shared regarding the most commonly noted areas for CITs requiring a growth plan and we provide a detailed look at how dispositions fit into the research. We believe this data can indeed help those required to do a growth plan, and those who have a desire to learn and grow independently, to understand the expectations of competency.

Furthermore, this chapter offers normalization to CITs, with a developmental perspective and a focus on growth over your entire career. You are all Counselors in Training; by being in your training process you are indeed already professionals, training towards ongoing professionalism in knowledge, skills, and dispositions. PB&D is not a Peanut Butter and Donut sandwich despite that sounding quite interesting. Rather, PB&D stands for Professional Behaviors and Dispositions. "What is professionalism?" "What does it mean for me?" "Why is this so important?" "I can be a professional when I'm at work, but when I am off the clock I can do what I want, right?"

These may be questions or thoughts that many students have had about their career choice. If they are not questions yet, they should be questions pondered and processed as one goes through a clinical mental health program. Professional careers are held to a higher standard than other careers, often with both ethical and legal requirements as well as standards of practice. Counselors have an obligation to do no harm and thus have a higher standard of expectations about how to interact with others and *what to do* 24/7. The scrutiny is higher because of the level of trust in professionals to do what is best when interacting with clients and other professionals.

By nature, a counselor has a power differential with clients; ethical and legal standards of practice take this into consideration for the client's and the public's welfare. Standards are meant to protect others from harm by the counselor, and, therefore, the counselor has a greater responsibility to be aware of the influence they have on clients and supervisees.

These obligations are not only required by programs that are approved by the Council for Accreditation of Counseling and Related Educational Programs (CACREP) (2015), but also for the American Counseling Association (ACA) *Code of Ethics* (2014). In turn, all elements of competency in skills and dispositions are part of Professional Identity in Counseling. Counselors in Training will review their roles and responsibilities of learning and development, while also considering the relationship of the Counselor Educator and Supervisor (CES) within counselor education, who accompanies the CIT and encourages them to be able to change, grow, and develop. This chapter operationally defines the many CACREP and ACA codes that are required for both supervisor and students.

Professional identity development within the counselor is often seen as both an intrapersonal and interpersonal process.

> The intrapersonal process is an internalization of knowledge and skills shared by faculty members and supervisors (e.g., recognizing personal strengths; areas of growth in academic roles). The interpersonal process develops during immersion into the norms of the professional community (e.g., submitting manuscripts for publication, presenting papers at conferences, teaching courses). These two developmental processes co-occur while counselor education trainees are conceptualizing their specific roles and tasks within academia. (Limburg et al., 2013, p. 42)

Within the intrapersonal and interpersonal integration lies the area of not only skills and knowledge, but dispositional competencies as well. There is a deep need for dispositional competency training and ongoing CIT developmental support to achieve professional identity. Professional identity development is imperative from the beginning of your training as a CIT, and throughout your entire professional career. We recognize you are required to have competencies in knowledge, skills, and dispositions. There are multiple resources to assist CITs in developing knowledge and skills. However, the dispositional opportunities to grow and become competent are not as prevalent. Therefore, the focus of this book is on dispositions, considering how much they also impact knowledge and skills as well. It can be argued that we can all learn the knowledge required of the field, and even practice the skills, but how do we gain personal and professional counselor dispositions? In mental health, considering the responsibility of caring for others, with the utmost ethical standards comes intense pressure and a dire need for ongoing self-reflection, desire for growth, acceptance of feedback, and use of critical thinking. Consider the ramifications if this is not taken into consideration within your training.

So, what does all this mean on a practical level?

> I (Dr. Lewis) quite often worked with an attorney some years ago regarding my clients. He was my "go to" lawyer. My sons played soccer with his son. At one of the games, he didn't like a call the referee made against his son, and confronted the referee, yelling obscenities, and actually "belly bucked" the ref! That was the last time I used him as an attorney. My trust in his abilities to maintain control and to act with integrity and respect was severely compromised by that display. Although he wasn't in a courtroom exhibiting these behaviors, to me, it still told a lot about

his character and professional dispositions. Too harsh you say? Maybe. But my obligation was to "do no harm" to my clients, and what if I referred a client to him who set him off? His behavior was unprofessional and public. Understanding that we all require ongoing growth is the first step towards becoming competent as a CIT; however, before we dig deeper into the developmental process, let's operationally define terms towards universal understanding.

Operationally defining terms

- **Counseling as a profession**: "Professional counseling is a professional relationship that empowers diverse individuals, families, and groups to accomplish mental health, wellness, education, and career goals" (ACA, 2017).
- **Counselor Educator Supervisor**: Those who train and enter the counseling field are professionals who are educated in the art of teaching others to be counselors and supervising both at the student and professional level. The education includes a doctoral degree in Counselor Education and Supervision from an accredited university. A CES can have various licensure but also adheres to the ACES *Best Practices in Clinical Supervision* (2011) and ACA *Code of Ethics* (2014) as well as following CACREP *2016 Standards* (2015). In addition, they may shift from roles including therapist, teacher, and consultant (Bernard & Goodyear, 2004). However, the CES is not in the role of giving therapy to the CIT.
- **Student Remediation**: Supporting a student to gain professional competency in all areas, while also maintaining a gatekeeping function for the field of counseling. This may include but is not limited to: retaining the CIT in the program, dismissing them from the program, recommending a leave of absence, transfer to a non-counseling program if warranted, or continued guidance, support, and teaching to reach competence (Foster & McAdams, 2009; Homrich, DeLorenzi, Bloom, & Godbee, 2014).
- **Student Recidivism**: Students who repeat remediation processes more than one time. The changes that were gained may not have been effective enough for long-term changes; thus, the CIT either continues with the same unprofessional interactions, or when they reach one area in competence and another issue arises in a different area.
- **Student Support**: Support that can be done in a variety of ways to assist CITs in their growth process, through remediation, short-term support for life-events, and mentoring or training. Support can include helping with skills, knowledge, or dispositions. Professional development, comportment or remediation is considered a form of student professional support as well.
- **Personal Counseling for Supervisees**: Counseling for Supervisees: If supervisees request counseling, the supervisor assists the supervisee in identifying appropriate services. Supervisors do not provide counseling services to supervisees. Supervisors address interpersonal competencies in terms of the impact of these issues on clients, the supervisory relationship, and professional functioning. (F. 6. c., ACA *Code of Ethics*, 2014.)
- **Evaluation**: Per the CACREP *2016 Standards* (2015), formative evaluation examines the development of professional competencies, with a focus on identifying

strengths and deficiencies and corresponding learning interventions. Summative evaluation focuses on outcomes and is used to assess whether desired learning goals are achieved consistent with a professional standard (p. 45).

- o **F. 9. a. Evaluation of Students**: Counselor educators clearly state to students, prior to and throughout the training program, the levels of competency expected, appraisal methods, and timing of evaluations for both didactic and clinical competencies. Counselor educators provide students with ongoing feedback regarding their performance throughout the training program (ACA *Code of Ethics*, 2014, p. 15).

- o **F. 9. b. Limitations**: Counselor educators, through ongoing evaluation, are aware of and address the inability of some CITs to achieve counseling competencies. Counselor educators do the following: 1. assist students in securing remedial assistance when needed, 2. seek professional consultation and document their decision to dismiss or refer students for assistance, and 3. ensure that students have recourse in a timely manner to address decisions requiring them to seek assistance or to dismiss them and provide students with due process according to institutional policies and procedures (ACA *Code of Ethics*, 2014, p. 15).

- o **F. 9. c. Counseling for Students**: If students request counseling, or if counseling services are suggested as part of a remediation process, counselor educators assist students in identifying appropriate services (ACA *Code of Ethics*, 2014, p. 15).

- **Defining Competency**

  - o **Counseling Knowledge**: Per CACREP, CES are to monitor and evaluate the CIT's knowledge, skills, and professional dispositions towards competency in these areas. In addition, knowledge is defined by Merriam-Webster as "the fact or condition of knowing something with familiarity gained through experience or association, or acquaintance with or understanding of a science, art or technique" ("Knowledge," 2017). It appears that knowledge involves understanding and application, or confirmation of that knowledge, as evidenced by assessment towards optimal competencies by CES.

  - o **Counseling Skills**: Foundational counseling skills at the micro, mezzo, and macro level; these include basic and advanced counseling skills. These skills are also categorized in the field in looking at what are known as "helping skills" according to Neukrug (2016).

  - o **Professional Counseling Behaviors and Dispositions**: Desired traits that were identified by Spurgeon, Gibbons, and Cochran (2012) as "commitment, openness, respect, integrity, and self-awareness" (p. 103, Table 1). Further, the CACREP *2016 Standards* (2015) defined "The commitments, characteristics, values, beliefs, interpersonal functioning, and behaviors that influence the counselor's professional growth and interactions with clients and colleagues" (p. 43).

- **Professional Development Plan**: It appears most professionals hold to the standards of practice such as looking to reliable and valid assessment tools, evaluation processes, developmental remediation action plans, and ongoing assessment protocols that have been working in the field.

- **Professional Growth Plan also referred to as Professional Development Plan, Remediation Plan etc.**: Assessment, evaluation, support, and developmental processes to allow the CIT opportunity to demonstrate competencies in areas of required need, support or growth to fulfil CES Gatekeeping responsibilities and obligation in the field of professional counseling.
- **Student Deficiencies**: Counselor trainees who do not meet professional standard competencies for skills, dispositions, or professional behaviors. The term was implemented to distinguish deficiencies from *impairments*, which could have implications through the Americans with Disabilities Act (Bryant, Druyos, & Strabavy, 2013; Gaubatz & Vera, 2002).
- **Comportment Issues**: "Inability to insightfully understand and resolve their [student's] own issues so that these issues do not interfere with the therapeutic process" (Bemak, Epp, & Keys, 1999, p. 21).
- **Student Professional Development**

  - **Pre-admission**: The period when a CIT investigates the program, profession, commitments, and has understanding, disclosures and consent to understand an agreement to enter the program and the profession.
  - **Goodness of Fit**: assessment from the program and CIT concerning the quality of fit to the specific program and profession based on experience, desire, and ability.
  - **Assessment Through the Entire Program**: Evaluation process per the program of choice, often beginning with admissions process, throughout coursework; may be based on criteria and CACREP standards and objectives and formal and informal assessment process.
  - **Professional Identity Development**: Ongoing commitment from the CIT towards ongoing training, continuing education, and supervision, feedback and assessment. Often includes ongoing developmental growth plan the CIT maintains on their own.

- **Critical Thinking**: Critical thinking is the intellectually disciplined process of actively and skillfully conceptualizing, applying, analyzing, synthesizing, and/or evaluating information gathered from, or generated by, observation, experience, reflection, reasoning, or communication, as a guide to belief and action. In its exemplary form, it is based on universal intellectual values that transcend subject matter divisions: clarity, accuracy, precision, consistency, relevance, sound evidence, good reasons, depth, breadth, and fairness (Scriven & Paul, 2015).
- **Analytical Thinking**: Analytical thinking is a thinking process or skill in which an individual can scrutinize and break down facts and thoughts into their strengths and weaknesses. It involves thinking in thoughtful, discerning ways, to solve problems, analyze data, and recall and use information (Warner, 2014, para. 2).
- **Synthesis**: deductive reasoning; the dialectic combination of thesis and antithesis into a higher stage of truth ("Synthesis," 2017).
- **Due Process**: Providing notice to students and an opportunity to be heard and/or appeal the action being proposed; action being proposed or taken is not motivated by bad faith, ill will, or is made arbitrarily or capriciously (McAdams, Foster, & Ward, 2007); following prescribed procedures to ensure rights are respected and consideration given throughout the process of remediation (Kerl, Garcia, McCullough, & Maxwell, 2002).

- **Professional Identity**: As professional counselors, our identity is multi-faceted. It begins with our professional and personal beliefs, commitments, understanding, and definitions of our roles and responsibilities. We are professionals at all times, and therefore bear a dedication to our profession. There is great responsibility in how we carry ourselves, behave, and the impact we have on others. As professionals, we have expertise that others do not have. This is an ongoing, serious responsibility that is continuous until we retire or pass away.
- **Professionalism**: The act of behaving professionally as indicated by following the ethical and legal standards and codes of the profession, membership in professional organizations, continuing with development of skills, knowledge, and appropriate interactions with others through continuing education, training, and recent research, and holding oneself to a standard above that of a non-professional; maintaining professional boundaries; engaging in self-examination, mitigating assumptions and biases, and conducting oneself in a manner befitting the profession to which the person belongs (ACA *Code of Ethics*, 2014; Bodner, 2012).
- **Gatekeeping**: "The process whereby a counselor or education program intervenes when candidates and students are not equipped with the requisite knowledge, skills, and values for professional practice" (Ziomek-Daigle & Bailey, 2009, p. 14).
- **Gate Slipping**: Counseling student trainees who are deficient in professional competence, yet who complete a counseling program without successfully completing remediation or leaving the program (Gaubatz & Vera, 2002).

Although perhaps overwhelming, take time to familiarize yourself with the terms to consider the many other professionals, entities, and impact involved in your training and supervision growth process. Ponder the numerous professionals with licenses who are currently supervising, teaching, or mentoring you. What might they stand to lose or gain having you under their supervision? Reflect on the definitions and how they may apply to colleagues or other professionals in your life. Consider the impact they may have on those around them, including the impact they may have had on you. As mentioned, professional dispositions, which are a large part of the training process, and impacting skills and knowledge, include "The commitments, characteristics, values, beliefs, interpersonal functioning and behaviors that influence the counselor's professional growth and interactions with clients and colleagues" (CACREP, 2015, p. 47).

In addition, the ACA *Code of Ethics* (2014) added the word "gatekeeping" to the definitions as "the initial and ongoing academic, skill, and dispositional assessment of students' competency for professional practice, including remediation and termination as appropriate" (p. 20).

In considering some operational definitions of the dispositions, we can look to one example from the literature. Lambie, Mullen, Swank, & Blount (2016) presented dispositional categories using the Counselor Competency Scale (CCS); our challenge to you as the CIT is to complete a self-assessment considering the dispositional competencies.

(**Note:** *The Counseling Competencies Scale—Revised©* (CCS-R), developed by Glenn Lambie Ph.D., is available exclusively through *Clinical Training Manager*™, the counselor education software platform developed by Tevera, LLC. For more information, see the Resources Appendix at the back of this book.

Consider your own interactions with your peers, supervisors, colleagues, other students, and clients. How well do you exhibit these dispositions daily?

Competency Standards

- **Professional Ethics:** Competency means you are going above and beyond and using critical thinking within an ethical decision-making model to inform your ethical judgment.

   Think about a time when you had an option to be quiet and get something you wanted or to speak the truth and risk losing it. What did you do then? Now consider, what would you do now?

- **Professional Behavior:** Competency means going above and beyond using emotional regulation, critical thinking, and professionalism in your behaviors.

   Think about a time when you were involved in an emotionally charged conversation with a fellow professional and your feelings were very hurt. How did you handle this interaction? Were you able to convey your authentic feelings while also getting your professional point across in a respectful manner? How might you handle it differently today?

- **Professional and Personal Boundaries:** Competency means going above and beyond demonstrating consistent and strong boundaries with supervisors, peers, and clients.

   Have you worked in a position before where you struggled with maintaining professional and personal boundaries? How did this play out? What did you learn from that experience?

- **Knowledge and Adherence to Site and Course Policies:** Competency means going above and beyond demonstrating consistent adherence to *all* counseling site policies and procedures, including attendance and engagement.

   What are some of the major site policies you have had to follow and reinforce? What were you assessed on as a counselor in training? Have you worked elsewhere and ever found yourself in a position of not following policy or procedure?

- **Record Keeping and Task Completion:** Competency means going above and beyond demonstrating consistently the ability to complete *all* required record keeping, documentation, and assigned tasks in a thorough, timely, and comprehensive fashion.

   What are notable features of record keeping and report writing, documentation and other case management tasks? What are the costs of not completing adequate records in counseling? What are the ramifications of not completing the records in a timely fashion?

- **Multicultural Competence in Counseling Relationships:** Competency means going above and beyond demonstrating consistent and advanced multicultural competencies (knowledge, self-awareness, appreciation, and skills) in interactions with clients, peers, and supervisors.

   What are some aspects of cultural competency that you have addressed in your own training and development over the years? Consider a colleague or client you have worked with that challenged your biases, your worldview, and inspired your self-reflection towards your own growth. What were the top three things you learned from this experience?

- **Emotional Stability and Self-Control:** Competency means going above and beyond demonstrating consistent emotional resiliency and appropriateness in interpersonal interactions with clients, peers, and supervisors.

  Is there a time you were triggered by a colleague, supervisor or client and how did you handle it? How did you handle it in the session, afterwards and in supervision? What did you learn about yourself in this experience?

- **Motivated to Learn and Grow:** Competency means going above and beyond demonstrating consistent and strong engagement in promoting his or her professional and personal growth and development.

  What are the top three professional goals you have for your current professional developmental process for this year? What are your top three dispositional goals you hope to continue to work on this year?

- **Openness to Feedback:** Competency means going above and beyond demonstrating consistent and strong openness to supervisory feedback and implementing suggested changes.

  When you have received feedback in the past, did you experience it as positive, enlightening, critical, or condescending? How do you personally offer feedback to others? What feelings do you experience prior to giving the feedback and after receiving feedback from others?

- **Flexibility and Adaptability:** Competency means going above and beyond demonstrating consistent and strong ability to adapt and ability to read and flex appropriately.

  Consider a time when you were asked to switch up your entire schedule, presentation, job or plan. How did you experience this sudden required change? What are your strengths and weaknesses when it comes to being adaptable or flexible as a counselor in training?

- **Congruence and Genuineness:** Competency means going above and beyond demonstrating consistent and strong ability to be genuine and accepting of self and others.

  Consider a time when someone last told you how they were experiencing you as a colleague, peer, counselor, or boss. Did they use descriptive words such as authentic, genuine, real, down to earth, nonjudgmental, caring, and assertive? How did you measure up to the advanced competency expectations in this exercise? Where are some potential roadblocks or potholes that may influence your professional journey? Deeply consider that all counselors have an ongoing need to work on these areas of disposition towards excellency.

When we are not striving toward optimal competency with our dispositions, we are at risk of *damaging our clients* in their journey. At best, we may impede the client growth process due to our own reluctance to grow, or, worse, allowing countertransference to get in the way. As a CIT, it is difficult to take a client to a place you have not yet been, and, worse, you may try to complete your own healing through the work of the client. How will that lead to ethical and potentially legal consequences? From the literature, it is apparent there are several commonly seen comportment issues in CITs who are referred for remediation or growth plans. According to Henderson (2010), the following themes were found to be the top behavioral indications leading to remediation: "(1) receptivity to feedback; (2) basic counseling skills; (3) boundaries with clients, colleagues, and/or supervisors; (4) openness to self-examination; and (5) advanced counseling skills. Receptivity to feedback was ranked number one overall as the behavioral indicators" (p. 147). What does this mean for you as a CIT?

Case Study

Based on the information below, find as many of the common comportment issues as possible in this case study. Use the check list at the bottom of the case to indicate areas of concern. Mark all that apply (see Worksheet 1.1 in the Resources Appendix). This case is a fictional blended case example.

Jack is a brand-new student in his counselor graduate-level training program. He appears eager to begin the process of training; he shared since his first day of class that he had come from a very traumatic background of abuse, neglect, and suffered ongoingly his entire life from his own addiction problems. He shares with you that he has been working in a substance abuse clinic, working towards his drug and alcohol certification. In his discussions with peer colleagues he was eager to point out that he would make "the best counselor because he understood what his clients were going through." He also submitted work and made comments often without supporting them with any scholarly research or substantiation. In fact, he commented to a peer in class that "life experience is far better than research." In addition, a peer colleague gently confronted him asking "do you think that you are healed enough to also offer boundaries and self-care in your counseling profession?" Jack quickly retorted, "I take pride in my past struggles and no one is perfect." He paused and remarked, "I already know how to counsel; I just need the degree to say I am fit for licensure." The instructor stepped in and acknowledged that everyone has something to learn in the counselor training process and Jack interrupted stating, "I am sure many do, but some of us have already done all of our personal work."

As a fellow CIT evaluating this case, what areas of concern might you have as a professional colleague to Jack? Check all that apply as concerns:

- Grades are below acceptable standards;
- Seems to display uncontrolled emotions;
- Behavior does not meet standards in the profession;
- Concerns about comportment;
- Not demonstrating skills at the required level of competence.

After reviewing the purpose of CIT training, competencies, operational definitions, and offering a case example and identifying the need for gatekeeping in our profession, we also have shared the main reasons CITs find themselves in remediation or having competency issues. As you begin your journey and reflect on your own developmental journey leading you this far, consider starting with a strong foundation.

Strong Foundations

Let us start from the beginning of your CIT process to offer some structure. When you enter the field of counseling, you consent to adherence to site organizational policies and understandings. Counselors in Training understand that they are held to higher professional accountability than some other professions, given the nature of the field. Along with the mental health profession, other professions that are held to high standards include medicine, education, law, and many others when there is substantive risk to an innocent party. Often, during the preadmissions process, admissions process, and CIT orientation, you are also given an immense amount of information about the program and organizational expectations of a CIT, student, etc. This includes assessment, standards, policies, procedures, and expectations. Counselors in Training are often not aware that by consenting, signing, and understanding this agreement you are indeed a *professional* held to the highest, strictest standards. The moment you are accepted into a counseling program you are obligated to follow the ACA *Code of Ethics* (2014).

Due to the nature of the expectations and understanding, we also acknowledge that this, in turn, means the CIT should have a humble, open, desire for learning and growth as they are operating under a variety of faculty and supervisors. The licensure and professional reputation you have is at stake, and you have worked far too hard and long to obtain the dream you had at the beginning of your program. Counselors in Training must consider this immense responsibility, while bearing in mind their own desire toward professionalism themselves. This is where the first response of dispositions comes into play.

Next, CITs enter their coursework and many find the variety of format, content, knowledge, and peer interaction is both invigorating and challenging. Often, CITs report aspects such as: "going back to school after a long break has its challenges," or "I am afraid about the scary process of graduate school, balancing work, family, school, and readiness for this monumental task," or "where will I find time to do all the work expected of me?" We strongly encourage prospective students to evaluate these aspects prior to admission or accepting a clinical position because the *plate of life* can be awfully full for many; taking on a professional developmental process, such as counseling, challenges the CIT personally and professionally on all levels. We often ask prospective CITs to consider taking out a paper plate and dividing it out in terms of time, roles, or responsibilities for the average week. Turn it over and reflect on where would you fit CIT training in on that plate? A visual that I (Dr. Lewis) created for my students started with a dinner plate of mine. On that plate I put multiple things I happened to have in my kitchen, including teabags, an old grater, a brush, salt and pepper, a star cookie cutter, a vegetable peeler, a meat thermometer, a tea strainer, a cheese cutter, a bunny/cabbage salt and pepper shaker set, an orange peeler, a Cape Hattaras NC lighthouse indoor thermometer, a chip clip, a random lid, and a small sauce container. It is enough to fully cover the dinner plate, piled more than one layer high, and demonstrating a very full plate. Each item represents an area of my life dedicated to fulfilling various responsibilities. The teabags represent my selfcare time; the old grater represents that I am responsible for making meals for my entire family on a daily basis. The brush represents my volunteer hour workload at my local church. The bunny salt and pepper shakers represent my current employment obligations, and so on. Consider that the plate now represents your current *busy-ness* of life. If this is what your life looks like right this moment, what will you have to move off that plate, *for a season*, to be able to gain the knowledge, insights, and skills that are needed for your continuing education? You will soon be involved with people's lives. Their lives. This is important. How willing are you to take some of these things off your plate while you attend classes? Enroll into your required field experience? Something must move off for you to focus on your learning, with your future clients in mind. Can you slide through classes without putting your full mind, energy, and all of your investment into your learning? Yes. Will it have an impact on your clients? Yes. You may eventually hurt people if you shortchange yourself in your training.

When I (Dr. Lewis) did my second master's degree, some years after my first, I was convinced that I could do it without changing what I did in my life. I got to the second semester of my work when I realized there was no way I could keep all that I was doing in my life on the plate and just plop a master's degree on top of it all. I thought I could. I had done this before, after all. It wasn't that bad. However, this degree was taking more of my attention and concentration and work than the previous one seemed to do – perhaps because I was older, or my children were at a different age, or just because I had added more to my plate than I realized. So, I decided that, for a season, I would resign as the Worship Team Director and from the Worship Team itself; I would resign from two committees I was on; I would stop having to manage dinner every single night by requesting my husband take care of three nights a week, and that we, as a family, created menus for the week so I could prep more quickly. I also decided that the dust was not going anywhere if I didn't dust every week, and that the kids could now help with dishes and cleanup. I was told that I needed *one half* of my plate empty to fit the master's program on it. So, I tossed out some of the get-togethers with friends and family, nixed the out-of-state visitations, and put off vacations until after the degree – what's two years in the big picture? I kept things like tucking the kids in at night, having our family game night, and set my schedule for school work a week earlier than the due dates so I did not have to feel stressed. I had to prioritize to get the degree done. Yes, there were nights when my husband would take a book off my face as I lay snoozing in bed – dreaming that osmosis of proximity would get the information into my head. Think about it. What can really move aside for a season in your life?

One powerful support for the CIT is a dedicated support system. *Who is in your support system?* We encourage your pursuit of building and gathering people around you who are truly willing to support you, to take the load off you when you need some space, to stand beside you as you grow into the professional you are becoming. These trusted safe folks will be known as your cheerleading team. They will carry you through the tough times and the challenges. Salovey, Rothman, Detweiler and Steward (2000) presented evidence that a positive attitude and healthy emotional responses, including a supportive social support system, improves health, longevity, and immunity to illnesses. Their research found that, even with traumatic events, when the person who experienced the trauma talked or wrote about the event, even with strong negative emotions connected to the recounting, they found a positive effect on their physical health afterwards. In addition, people who gained and continued to use positive expressions of emotions also gained more insight and were less likely to get ill or feel the need to seek medical care. Furthermore, Salovey et al. presented that, generally, those who do not have dedicated support systems seemed to get ill more often and have changes in temperament when degrees of tension increased than those who had strong support systems in place. Contemplate the dispositions of those to be on your cheerleading team? Do you want someone authentic, compassionate, realistic, safe, healthy, wise, peaceful, mature, professional and supportive? Consider the following questions regarding your alignment to counseling as you enter your first course:

1 What compelled you to want to pursue this field and why?
2 What do you believe will be your role, function and duty ethically, legally and professionally to the field? Consider a brief professional counselor identity statement to offer a foundation for your developmental process. "I believe a counselor is xxxx."
3 What are your strengths and ongoing needs for growth for this process or role?
4 What are you most concerned about in your developmental process and why?
5 How are you able to consider your ongoing need for self-reflection, self-exploration, to accept feedback from faculty and supervisors, and to commit to ongoing growth and development?
6 What do you need from your CES and how can they best support you in the process? What do you potentially need from your cheerleading teammates? Who can you call in an emergency, or when you have a time crunch? Who do you trust with your children, pets, or home responsibilities? When will you know it is time to call for help?

Review the American Counseling Association website and find their definition of a counselor, including roles and responsibilities of a professional counselor; deeply consider that in reflection on your answers above (see Worksheet 1.2 in the Resource Appendix).

After completing the above assignments, take the inventory below to identify your own readiness for change in terms of ongoing CIT growth and willingness to accept feedback (see Worksheet 1.3 in the Resource Appendix). Growth inevitably involves change and change often means discomfort for many. Reflect upon the following questions, and score each one on a scale of 1–5, where 1 is: This is not true for me at all; and 5 is: this is totally true for me completely. Where do you land?

1 I am great. Nothing needs to change. I am only here to jump through the hoops to receive my degree and move forward. I am good but thank you. 1 2 3 4 5
2 I know I need to grow and change. I am uncertain if I am ready to embark on what that exactly entails or means, and it is a bit scary but . . . I do know it is necessary at some point for me to be an effective, ethical counselor. I am working on observing who may be safe to explore with, eventually. 1 2 3 4 5
3 I want to be ready for change. I am not sure what that means, but I am willing, and will seek support, ask questions, and prepare myself for that process personally and

professionally. I recognize it will require work, facing my fears, but I want to grow. 1 2 3 4 5

4   I am actively in the process of change. I am humble, receive feedback from colleagues, supervisors, faculty, and use self-reflection, openness and curiosity for learning, and I am eager to continue to progress towards sometimes painful growth and ongoing change. **1 2 3 4 5**

5   I have been involved in change for some time, and I want to continue to engage in it through the knowledge, skills and dispositions required of me. I have a plan for how I will continue to do this using my support network, my personal commitment and through ongoing inquiry for feedback from faculty, colleagues, self-reflection, and from supervisors. **1 2 3 4 5**

Excellent work! Now, depending on the total score, can you tell your own readiness for change and growth? Rate your own readiness for growth and change and deeply consider the benefits and the costs to you to stay still or to embark on this adventure.

The following stages of change were identified by DiClemente, Prochaska, Fairhurst, Velicer, Velasquez, & Rossi (1991, p. 1):

1   Pre-contemplative: self-protective, not ready to change
2   Contemplative: thinking about changing; estimate own readiness to change
3   Preparation: getting ready to make the change
4   Action: making changes
5   Maintenance and Relapse: Monitor and stay on track

If you find you are not ready for change, what can you and your CES do to help assist you towards a readiness for change?

- Deeply consider past times in your life when you engaged in positive change and what helped motivate or facilitate growth for you. What do you stand to gain or lose by not moving through the change progression?
- Consider the benefits and costs to you in your current counselor developmental journey. If you are not ready for change, growth, or to move forward in change, have you considered the following?

  o   Taking a break from your training as a counselor.
  o   Obtaining personal counseling and engaging in even more personal healing.
  o   Is this the right field, profession, and career for you? There are many things that counselors do, from School Counseling to Career Counseling to Clinical Mental Health Counseling, to Addictions Counseling. Outside of counseling, there are avenues such as Social Work, Psychology, Life Coaching, Case Management. Are you in the right place?
  o   Reassessing work–life balance and health.

Consider some activities offered by your CES, such as the following, that can help guide you in your motivation towards change and desire for growth.

- Have you experienced a recent crisis or reason for change that has motivated you, and, if so, what is it?
- If you have had a CIT remediation or development referral, what was the issue you experienced and what are your thoughts about the rationale and requirement you now may have?
- Consider engaging in meaningful connection with rapport building with your CES to discuss what occurred. How might you practice being authentic, receptive, engaged, and curious about your own growth process?
- Bear in mind that your CES is not telling you that you need to change. Rather, they will likely be asking you to offer your perspective on and experience of what happened to lead to the referral for a growth plan, and how you feel about it. Only you can decide when and if you are ready to embark on *change*.
- Consider what led to the requirement for a growth plan.
- What are the anxieties, fears, and consequences at stake?
- What positive strengths do you have in being in this process currently? Share them with your CES.
- Are you feeling one or more of the following about the act of engaging in CIT growth? Check all that apply and share with your faculty:

  o Hesitant (I am confused as to why I am here, what is going on, or why I would need to change anything).
  o Defiant (I am angry, and fear losing control over the process, my profession, my schedule and expectations of what I had planned).
  o Suffering (I feel hopeless about change and overwhelmed by the time and hard work this will take me).
  o Excusing (I have all the answers, and this was not my problem, but theirs).

Feel free to jot down some notes concerning your experience and your deeper reflection on the questions offered above (see Worksheet 1.4 in the Resources Appendix).

After reviewing this chapter, take a moment to consider your own personal definition of a professional counselor and who you hope to be. Include elements such as ethics, the law, worldview, values, etc. Finally, read your program or agency expectations, student manual, and all required expectations of students to ensure you understand exactly what is expected of you and the process of training to become a professional counselor. How might you review the hiking story from the beginning of the chapter now?

> I (Dr. Lewis) believe that the mountains we climb are real. They may not be huge lumps of rock, or formed by a volcano, or tectonic plate movement, but they are challenging, and push us to do more than we ever thought we could do. Our mountains may be conquering a new skill, improving parenting skills, or kicking an addiction. Whatever it is in our lives, we have mountains to climb. I believe that we learn more from our failures than from our successes . . . IF we stop and review the process, look in the mirror to see what our piece of it was, and what it was not. When we find what our responsibility is, then we gain the power to be able to make changes. That is an internal locus of control. Every time we claim an external locus of control, we give away our personal power. When whatever happens to us is someone else's fault, then we have no power whatsoever. We need to claim our own responsibilities and our own power.

Summary

We have reviewed the requirements of CES and training programs in the field of counseling, including but not limited to ACA *Code of Ethics*, CACREP, and program standards towards ensuring CIT growth and development. We have offered operational definitions, standards of practice for CES gatekeeping functions, and offered some definitions of competence as well. Ultimately, we encourage you, as the CIT, to take heart in knowing you can explore and discover a variety of amazing skills, abilities, and growth, once you are ready for the challenge. We acknowledge it is not an easy task, but one that does require energy, reflection, time, vulnerability, and courage. We believe you can do it, with the help of your CES, and, perhaps, even considering personal counseling in addition to your counselor developmental process. Before you move forward, however, you must be committed to change and ready for the process or else it may result in a change that does not stick for you. Once you have built rapport, trust, and commitment to your process, and with your CES, you are ready to begin the next exciting step in understanding, "How do I know I have it?" Taking the step of self-assessment and growth will answer that question for you. Take the invitation.

References

American Counseling Association (ACA) (2014). ACA *Code of ethics*. Alexandria, VA: American Counseling Association.

American Counseling Association (2017). *Professional counseling*. Retrieved from: www.counseling.org.

Arnaud, K. (2017). Encountering the wounded healer: Parallel process and supervision. *Canadian Journal of Counseling and Psychotherapy, 51*(2), 131–144.

Association for Counselor Education and Supervision (ACES) (2011). *Best practices in clinical supervision*. Alexandria, VA: Association for Counselor Education and Supervision.

Barr, A. (2006). *An investigation into the extent to which psychological wounds inspire counselors and psychotherapists to become wounded healers, the significance of these wounds on their career choice, the causes of these wounds, and the overall significance of demographic factors*. Retrieved from: www.thegreenrooms.net/wounded-healer.

Bemak, F., Epp, L. R., & Keys, S. G. (1999). Impaired graduate students: A process model of graduate program monitoring and intervention. *International Journal for the Advancement of Counseling, 21*(1), 19–30.

Bernard, J. M., & Goodyear, R. K. (2004). *Fundamentals of clinical supervision* (5th ed.). New York, NY: Pearson Publishing.

Bodner, K. E. (2012). Ethical principles and standards that inform educational gatekeeping practices in psychology. *Ethics & Behavior, 22*(1), 60–74.

Bryant, J. K., Druyos, M., & Strabavy, D. (2013). Gatekeeping in counselor education programs: An examination of current trends. *VISTAS Online: American Counseling Association,* (51), 1–12.

Council for Accreditation of Counseling and Related Educational Programs (CACREP). (2015). *2016 CACREP Standards*. Alexandria, VA: Council for Accreditation of Counseling and Related Educational Programs.

DiClemente, C. C., Prochaska, J. O., Fairhurst, S. K., Velicer, W. F., Velasquez, M. M., & Rossi, J. S. (1991). The process of smoking cessation: An analysis of precontemplation, contemplation, and preparation stages of change. *Journal of Consultation and Clinical Psychology, 59*(2), 295–304.

Family Times (n. d.). If I had only changed myself first. Retrieved from: www.family-times.net/illustration/Encouragement/201185.

Foster, V. A., & McAdams, C. R. (2009). A framework for creating a climate of transparency for professional performance assessment: Fostering student investment in gatekeeping. *Counselor Education and Supervision, 48*(4), 271–284.

Gaubatz, M. D., & Vera, E. M. (2002). Do formalized gatekeeping procedures increase programs' follow-up with deficient trainees? *Counselor Education and Supervision, 41*(4), 294–305.

Henderson, K. L. (2010). The remediation of students in counseling graduate programs: Behavioral indicators, terminology, and interventions (Doctoral dissertation). New Orleans, LA: University of New Orleans.

Homrich, A. M., DeLorenzi, L. D., Bloom, Z. D., & Godbee, B. (2014). Making the case for standards of conduct in clinical training. *Counseling Education & Supervision, 53*(2), 126–144, doi: 10.1002/j.1556-6978.2014.00053.x.

Jung, C. G. (1985). Fundamental questions of psychotherapy. In S. H. Read, M. Fordham, G. Adler, & W. McGuire (Eds). *The Collected Works of C. G. Jung.* Princeton, NJ: Princeton University Press.

Kerl, S. B., Garcia, J. L., McCullough, C. S., & Maxwell, M. E. (2002). Systematic evaluation of professional performance: Legally supported procedure and process. *Counselor Education & Supervision, 41*(4), 321–334.

Knowledge (2017). In *Merriam-Webster's online dictionary.* Retrieved from: www.merriam-webster.com/dictionary/knowledge.

Lambie, G., Mullen, P., Swank, J., & Blount, A. (2016). *Counseling Competencies Scale, Revised (CCS-R).* Orlando, FL: University of Central Florida, Counselor Education Program. Retrieved from: http://webmedia.jcu.edu/counselingdepartment/files/2016/03/CCS- R-Evaluation.pdf.

Limburg, D., Bell, H., Super, J., Jacobson, L., Fox, J., Christmas, C., Young, M., & Lambie, G. (2013). Professional identity development of counselor education doctoral students: A qualitative investigation. *The Professional Counselor, 3*(1), 40–53.

McAdams, C. R., Foster, V. A., & Ward, T. J. (2007). Remediation and dismissal policies in counselor education: Lessons learned from a challenge in federal court. *Counselor Education and Supervision, 46*(3), 212–229.

Neukrug, E. S. (2016). *Skills and techniques for human service professionals: Counseling environment, helping skills, treatment issues.* Norfolk, VA: Counseling Books, Etc.

Prochaska, J., & DiClemente, C. (1983). Stages and processes of self-change of smoking: Toward an integrative model of change. *Journal of Consulting and Clinical Psychology, 51*(3), 390–395.

Salovey, P., Rothman, A. J., Detweiler, J. B., & Steward, W. T. (2000). Emotional states and physical health. *American Psychologist, 55*(1), 110–121, doi: 10.1037///0003- 066X.55.1.110.

Scriven, M., & Paul, R. (2015). *Defining critical thinking.* Retrieved from: www.criticalthinking.org/pages/defining-critical-thinking/766.

Spurgeon, S. L., Gibbons, M. M., & Cochran, J. L. (2012). Creating personal dispositions for a professional counseling program. *Counseling Values, 57*(1), 96–108, doi: 10.1002/j.2161-007X.2012.00011.x.

Synthesis (2017). In *Merriam-Webster online dictionary.* Retrieved from: www.merriam-web ster.com/dictionary/synthesis.

Warner, J. (2014, February 21). How is critical thinking different from analytical thinking [Web blog post]. Retrieved from: http://blog.readytomanage.com/how-is-critical-thinking-different-from-analytical-or-lateral-thinking.

Ziomek-Daigle, J., & Bailey, D. F. (2009). Culturally responsive gatekeeping practices in counselor education. *The Journal of Counseling Research and Practice, 1*(1), 14–22.

2 Self-Evaluation and Personal Growth
How Do I Know I Have "IT"?

Taking a Look at Self

Everyone enters the field thinking they have "IT" – meaning positive demeanor and counselor competencies in dispositions and behaviors. Often, CITs believe they *just need to learn the knowledge and skills* of becoming a counselor. But, as we talked about already, everyone needs to keep growing, and to know whether they have "IT" or not. Not to mention, having IT includes not only knowledge and skills but also professional counselor *dispositions*. When we look at knowledge, we see that a professional, academic, ethical understanding and information is tantamount to a productive career. For example, what you learn in academic or continuing education training work guides your future in many ways. Learning and practicing skills includes the ability to use foundational counseling skills, the ability to use case conceptualization, the skill of diagnosis, treatment planning, assessment, clinical writing, and documentation. Finally, dispositions include innate abilities or behaviors displayed in reaction to specific events (Facione, Facione, & Giancarlo, 1998). Whether you, as the CIT, are reading this book because of your own personal desire for ongoing growth and development, or if you are being referred for a growth plan by a Counselor Educator Supervisor (CES), you can benefit from the materials we share. The philosophy and purpose behind this book is to provide CITs with the opportunity for growth, with CES challenge and support towards the goal of competence and long-term positive impact in the field of counseling.

This chapter offers CITs an exploration into the reality of counselor dispositions including self-assessment, particularly of CIT insight and receptivity to teachability. Counselors in Training are introduced to exploration of their own worldview, of counselor identity, and, in addition, to several other self-reflective and evaluative growth tools. This chapter builds towards the presentation of our Universal Growth Model (UGM) to help counselors for their life-long growth and development. In addition, a more detailed look at key professional counselor dispositions and behaviors is provided, using one example of a counselor competency assessment tool, the Counselor Competency Scale-Revised (CCS-R) (Lambie, Mullen, Swank, & Blount 2016). (Note: *The Counseling Competencies Scale—Revised©* (CCS-R) developed by Glenn Lambie Ph.D. is available exclusively through *Clinical Training Manager*™, the counselor education software platform developed by Tevera, LLC. For more information, visit: www.clinicaltrainingmanager.com.)

Counselors in Training will be challenged with understanding how to take a 360-degree evaluation of self, using the Universal Growth Model (UGM), while also receiving feedback and insights from their growth team. In addition, we will compare the difference between healthy growth versus a fixed mindset, which is a crucial ability in counseling. Techniques and experiential activities are offered to help you explore what strengths you bring to the table and what areas of ongoing needed growth you may have towards professional identity development. According to the 2016 CACREP *Standards*: "The program faculty conducts a systematic developmental assessment of each student's progress throughout the program, including consideration of the student's academic performance, professional development, and personal development" (CACREP, 2015, p. 4). We hope you will understand that the role of your CES is to assess, teach, monitor, and reassess your competencies as a CIT, which is needed throughout your training. This ultimately means looking out for the profession, clients, and your best interests in becoming the professional you desire to be. The Universal Growth Model presented in this book and created by the authors is a model with a core philosophy that client, CIT, and CES all grow together and, from the model itself, through the process of analysis and work on Self, Relationships, Competencies, and Actualization. We will use this organizational format in describing areas for CIT development. As you can see, this chapter looks at the CIT *Self*.

Some of you are fortunate enough in your training to have curriculum and faculty or mentors who invite you to evaluate your own worldviews, evaluate your biases, use critical thinking, and, simultaneously, to hold your own worldviews. In addition to this process, they may teach you how to do this while conceptualizing, empathizing, and understanding each other's worldviews, while continuing to hone in on your professional competencies as a counselor in training (CIT).

Self-Evaluation in Reflection and Growth Through Competencies

We must examine the significant facets threaded within our CIT identity and CIT philosophy, including character and dispositional benchmarks for counselors. According to Lambie et al. (2016), the dispositions comprise: professional ethics, professional behavior, professional and personal boundaries, knowledge and adherence to site and course policy, record keeping and task completion, multicultural competencies in counseling relationships, emotional stability and self-control, motivation to learn and grow/initiative, openness to feedback, flexibility and adaptability, and congruence and genuineness. We likely will see underlying thematic dispositions we value as we explore and reflect. For example, if you have concluded that your role and responsibility as a counselor is "to do good and help others while adhering to ethical standards of practice," you can see how these attributes or dispositions align with the counseling dispositions noted by Lambie et al. (2016). Another professional may have stated that they valued "ongoing growth and development towards learning," which also aligns with counselor dispositional facets. Now, just because we value a trait, disposition, or feature doesn't necessarily mean we practice it. This is where our ongoing need for self- and other assessments comes in.

There is a powerful example of this in the DreamWorks movie *The Rise of the Guardians* (Joyce & del Toro, Producers, 2012), where Santa Claus, as the lead guardian, attempts to convince Jack Frost that Jack is one of the Guardians. Santa puts on a tough persona during the movie until he shares with Jack Frost the *real* Santa at his *center*, hidden deep inside. Santa discloses this to help guide Jack Frost in finding his own identity as a Guardian and his calling as a Guardian. Santa Claus commented to

Jack Frost that getting to the heart of things indicated that Jack was specifically picked to be a Guardian. And since he was selected, that would mean that Jack had something unique deep down in his very soul to offer. The scene continued as Santa explained what he was talking about when he referred to *the center*. He brought out a set of nested dolls that looked like Santa. The outer doll was very big and intimidating; the next doll was jolly, and the next was mysterious, then fearless and then caring. The very center doll was a swaddled baby. Jack was asked to describe what he saw, replying that the Santa baby doll had large eyes. Santa responded that, yes, he had eyes that were huge because he sees the world with wonder. Santa's worldview is to be in awe of all that he sees and experiences in the world. He sees it all through a lens of wonder. That is his center. Wonder is what he put into the world and ultimately what made him a Guardian. His identity is embedded in his wonder of the world. Jack had to find his own center, or worldview. Consider, what is *your* center?

As professionals, we are mandated to look at ourselves and our worldviews. In addition, we are required to look at counselor dispositions for our own standards of practice. In 2016 CACREP required that, as gatekeepers, we must not only assess and train for skills but also for dispositional features. Therefore, as a CIT, it is your obligation to self-assess and continue your own personal journey through growth to competence. The dispositions are embedded throughout one's worldview, professional identity, and professional CIT philosophy, and also throughout the work of this growth book for you and your CES to explore together.

Where are some potential roadblocks or potholes that may influence your professional journey? When we are not striving toward optimal competency with our dispositions, we are at risk of damaging others and their journeys. At best, we could impede their development. If, as a CIT, it is difficult to take a client to a place you have not yet been, how much more impossible may it be to gain excellence in competency if you yourself are not yet ready? If you have not worked through to reach optimal competency, growth, insight, etc., then you are impeding your own competence. If you are curious and desire ongoing growth and development, the Universal Growth Model may just be what you are looking for to continue your professional development. We will continue to reflect on your worldview, CIT identity formation, and philosophy of counseling while considering how others experience you personally and professionally as we head deeper into the work of "self."

Universal Growth Model (UGM)

Introduction to the Universal Growth Model (UGM)

In introducing the UGM we will use some illustrations as well as various tools that can be inserted into this conceptual framework to understand and conceptualize our personal journey as well as how we interact with others and their personal journey. The premise is that we grow through the model from birth to death, and we have good experiences and bad experiences along the way. Using the base of the quartered circle from Rigg's *Essentials of Psychomotor Therapy and the Healing Circle Model* (2017), we have developed a model of growth that is universal to all counselors, not only to you as the CIT. Furthermore, we have modified it into a model of remediation, adding Bronfenbrenner's work (1979).

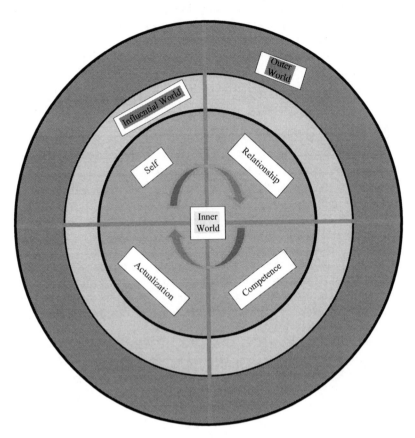

Figure 2.1 Universal Growth Model.

(Modified by the authors with permission from Rigg, 2017.)

Being post-modern thinkers, we included the ecological concept to this model as, indeed, *context is everything*. Strengths are recognized in the correct context. Areas of weakness, when moved into a different environment, become a strength. We are oriented in this profession of counseling with a strength-based perspective, so it seemed natural to put this all together. We are forever influenced by our inner world and experiences, the integration of interactions with those who are near us as well from a global perspective. What happens on the other side of the earth has an impact on us. What happens on our side of this planet influences the other side as well and, further, influences the deepest ocean and outer space. We are inextricably bound together.

We present to you the four-quadrant circle, and start from the upper-left corner. Life begins in the first quadrant, titled Self. This is the beginning of our journey as we strive to make our way around the circle, moving then to the upper-right corner, down to the lower-right corner, and then to the lower-left quadrant. Next, we move back to where we started, in the upper-left corner, and go through the circle time and again. What happens in our lives is that, somewhere along the way, most of us receive a wound of one kind or another. Depending on when that happens and where we are in the cycle, it can create our initial worldview – the lens through which we see and conceptualize the world around us and develop thoughts about self, others and the world. In the Self quadrant, if we receive the nurturing and caring that human babies require, we move steadily through this phase, our needs are met, we are fed, changed, loved. Life is good. As we move clockwise through the entire model we go to Relationship where we notice others in our life. We realize we are no longer symbiotic with mom as one being. We are separate yet in relationship. Dad may be a super fun guy, and grandmas and siblings are there for us to build relationships with, enjoy games, and learn about boundaries and interactions. Sometimes, those relationships are very normal and healthy, and we continue. The next quadrant is about Competence. We begin to understand that we can do some things for ourselves, and that we are good at it. This feels great! We continue to the final quadrant of Actualization in which we make sense of the world, collect our thoughts, and review our place in the world, finding deeper meaning. We clarify our worldview and model of reality. Then, we start again with Self. We continue with building our identity, then move to relationships again, and so on. What frequently happens, however, is that somewhere along the way, something goes wrong in one of the quadrants and we are impacted. When it is in the first quadrant, we may be abandoned or neglected; the second quadrant is frequently about betrayal of the trust we put into relationships; the third quadrant is about feeling empowered or feeling powerless. Feeling powerless can be a devastating thing in our lives, so losing a sense of power over ourselves and our circumstances can alter our worldview. In fact, any of the quadrants can result in the altering of the worldview, or getting "stuck" if you will. In quadrant four, then, we face that reality is changed, we reflect on our reality and realize we can't control it. Sometimes, this leads to being stuck amid chaos, unless we continue the work of self-growth and self-understanding by deliberating doing the work to heal through the quadrant where we got *stuck*. There are people who may have issues in every quadrant, but there is usually an event that initiated the sticking point and that was the beginning of our dilemma and so it needs attention, process and healing to move forward.

Inner, Influential and Outer Rings

As we consider our world through the lens of this model, we also need to determine the effect that our context has on us and others. While the quartered circle model is reflective of our inner journey, that journey does not happen in isolation. Most of us have lives that are visible and interact in some way with the rest of the world. Some may interact more than others, but we are all touched by the world beyond our own skin.

Bronfenbrenner (1979) developed the ecological model, detailing a microsystem, mesosystem, and exosystem of influence, all of which interacts with individuals within the contexts of their environment. The inner (or micro) system is the person and their proximate context. The next system as we move away from the center involves interrelationships between the inner and mesosystems. For instance, the relationship between home settings and school settings for children surely influence each other. If the child's home life is troublesome, they will have a difficult time with their learning tasks at school. Alternatively, the child who may be bullied at school will have a change in how they experience life at home. The two contexts are inextricably connected and therefore mutually interactive. The exosystem, or outer system, may be events that occur in a context that has little physical interaction with the individual, and yet has influence. Hearing of a disastrous event, such as a tornado or hurricane, far away, may still have a person become anxious when storm clouds gather overhead. Despite their having never personally experienced such an event, they are influenced by information about it. Bronfenbrenner's theory was described as: "everything is interrelated and interacts with each other, but to varying degrees and at different times" (Christensen, 2016, p. 24). Likewise, the UGM includes the overlay of the ecological model as the relationships and influences express themselves on each person in significant ways.

The Inner World is where the internal struggles exist, where we are wounded and healed. Like the nested dolls of the Guardian Santa Claus, that inner baby is our core, our center. That is where most of the *action* takes place for the internal work, insight, understanding, and where the motivation to change for good comes from. In addition, the inner world is where your most trusted relationships live. Whether those intimates are human, canine, feline, or stuffed, they are your inner circle of trusted relationships, alive or not. Those are the people you feel the closest to and with whom you share your inner journey. This is truly your inner circle.

The next circle is the Influential World. In this ring are the people who influence you, but to whom you are not necessarily as close as those in the inner circle. For instance, you may have your spouse in the influential circle if there are times of challenge with trust; at other times, your spouse may be in your inner circle. You may have your immediate supervisor in the influential circle if you find that person to be particularly supportive and invested in your growth. You may have family members, coworkers, peers, etc. in this circle, indicating that they offer something to you that helps you function, and you may offer the same to them in one way or another. The people in this ring *influence* your life and you have influences on them as well.

The final circle or ring is the Outer World. These are the interactions with everyone else including neighbors, classmates, teachers, community members, store clerks, vendors, people you see on the street, etc. At that level, there is minimal interaction with you personally *most of the time*. However, things may happen that bring those people closer into your experience. For instance, suppose you see someone on the street slip and fall on the ice. If you are the type of person who rushes to their aid, then you have just brought them closer to your influential circle by having a compassionate social interaction with them. They may not cross the line into your Influential circle, but they are closer than they were before they fell. Others may not rush to help but may continue walking; they may phone for assistance, direct someone else to them, just simply ignore the person on the ground, or may not have even noticed them at all. That keeps them at the outer edge of your outer world, depending on your reaction.

Movement between the rings can be fluid depending on the context of the relationships. Sometimes, you may have someone closer and, at other times, further away. However far away they may be, rest assured that there is still some influence on you regardless of your immediate perception. Many of us believe that the outer circle does not influence us at all. However, whether strong or weak, whether voluntary or not, there is still an effect experienced from those who are in the outer circle. It is easy for us to see and identify the influence of those closest to us. It is also easy to dismiss the influence of those further away, but that may be exactly where an unrecognized effect results in a trigger being tripped, or a bias coming through, or some belief system being revealed. It is critical that we process all layers and continue to be open to our perspectives and reactions changing. The process requires analyzing, critiquing, digging into the inner ring of you and who you are, which requires deep thinking; that's critical thinking. Recognizing that many of our behaviors are long-standing, but we always have a choice to change our behavior, and that is often a requirement of becoming a professional. In reviewing Bronfenbrenner's model applied to our UGM, we see a deep need to establish a foundation of critical thinking as a fundamental skill we use to synthesize and apply everything in the growth process.

Critical Thinking

Before entering the process of self, and hence all other quadrants, critical thinking must be viewed as a foundational skill throughout the entire model. According to Ahuna, Tinnesz, and Kiener (2014), critical thinking is the one constant for success in this ever-changing world. In fact, Ahuna et al. (2014) stated "Judgement requires critical thinking skills, including evaluation of data, recognition of various viewpoints, and mindful formulation of solutions" (p. 1). Counselors in Training can always benefit from ongoing support and challenge in critical thinking skills. Often, developmentally, critical thinking can take time to build in the counselor developmental process. In addition, Tumkaya, Aybek, and Aldag (2009) noted that "the affective side of the issue [of critical thinking] is still being neglected. Critical thinking dispositions and perceived problem-solving skills are important factors for determining educational needs of students" (p. 57).

We see the overlap of counselor dispositions with critical thinking dispositions such as self-reflection (thinking about one's own thinking), cultural competencies, ethical reasoning and judgement, as well as many others. As mentioned, critical thinking has been defined as requiring discipline and active pursuit towards growth. For example, Elder (2007) commented that critical thinkers symbolize a theory of Socrates: lack of scrutiny of our own lives makes us unworthy of life; if everyone refuses to self-assess, the consequence is an indiscriminate, unfair, and perilous planet. In evaluating critical thinking, we see an underlying theme of dispositional qualities that embody the critical thinker and, although unsure of which must come first, it is evident dispositions and critical thinking are intertwined.

We begin by sharing with you, the CIT, that critical thinking cannot be divorced from dispositions in any shape, way, or form. Critical thinking most often involves identifying, evaluating, and constructing arguments, ideas, or theories. Regarding reasoning, the critical thinker offers the ability to infer a conclusion from one or multiple premises. This dynamic of finding one or multiple conclusions to a problem also resembles the work our CITs do in case conceptualization, diagnosis, and ethical decision making. Using critical thinking requires examining logical relationships among statements or data, while also learning how to integrate creativity as well. You use critical thinking while integrating your worldview, counselor identity formation, philosophy of counseling and just about everything else within your professional developmental process. Wade (1995) identified the eight characteristics of critical thinking for you to consider as a CIT. To help encourage you in this area, you may see your CES incorporate the critical thinking characteristics within growth and development assignments.

Critical thinking is:

- Asking questions
- Defining a problem
- Examining evidence
- Analyzing assumptions and biases
- Avoiding emotional reasoning
- Avoiding oversimplification
- Considering other interpretations
- Tolerating ambiguity (Wade, 1995)
- Dealing with ambiguity (Strohm & Baukus, 1995)
- Metacognition (Jones & Ratcliffe, 1993)

When we, as counselors, are indeed operating using critical thinking, we begin to see ourselves developmentally moving from dependency on our CES to self-directness; as adult learners, we also draw upon our reservoir of experience for learning. Adults are ready and eager to learn, assume new roles, desire to solve problems, and apply new knowledge immediately (Knowles, 1980). To understand how to apply critical thinking skills we can use an example with you from the book by Martel (2002) and the movie *The Life of Pi* (Netter, Lee, & Womark (Producers), 2012). We suggest you view the film or read the novel in its entirety while taking notes along the way (see Worksheet 2.1 in Appendix 1).

The story begins with a writer interviewing a man from India named Pi. The writer asks him to tell him his life story. Pi tells him the story of his childhood, family life, their family zoo, love, explorations of identity and individuation, and his family's relocation from India to Canada on a ship that is wrecked. He describes horrific yet beautiful experiences along the way. Pi goes on to tell the writer about his quest for survival on a lifeboat, stranded with several animals, then being left to survive *alone on a boat with a tiger*. Alternatively, he has a slightly different story about what happened in the lifeboat that he reportedly shared with the authorities. The story of his survival and deep profound meaning in life culminates with a question to the viewer and yourself at the end: "Which story do you prefer?" and then we ask you as the CIT, *why?*

After you have watched the movie, answer the following questions:

- How did you experience the film? What emotions did you experience throughout the film?
- What were the most difficult parts of the movie for you? Why?
- List all you can see in the film that applies to ambiguity, critical thinking, cultural diversity, and theories in counseling.
- From the Life of Pi, which story do you prefer? Why? Which is the correct story? Which story is Pi's? Why does it matter?
- How did the ending resonate with you?

This work can be developmentally tailored into several areas of CIT training, such as:

- Application to theories of personality coursework.
    - Consider case conceptualization and list all the potential theories offered within the work, and how you see the theory playing out within the context of Pi and his family members.

- Application to professional orientation and discussion of social and cultural areas of competency.

  - Consider all the various religious and spiritual connections and how you experienced them, your personal biases, worldview, and how they may apply to clients you work with.

- Applied to Association of Spiritual, Ethical, and Religious Values in Counseling (ASERVIC) Spiritual Competencies and evaluation of spirituality in counseling.

  - What are the spiritual competencies to consider that apply to the work?

- Applied to grief and loss, crisis and trauma coursework, and training.

  - What diagnostic criteria or symptoms did you see? What are the themes of grief and loss and trauma? How might you work with someone who has experienced something such as this?

- Applied to practicum, internship, and beyond in application to working with immense issues surrounding ambiguity, supervision, case consultation, etc., including consideration of counseling theories.

  - How can the narrative approach in counseling offer the characteristics necessary for critical thinking? Consider diagnosis, assessment, case conceptualization, ethical decision making, cultural competencies, spiritual competencies, and other tasks as a clinician.
  - What possible theoretical applications did you pull from the film? Give examples of those areas you connect to theory and why.

In addition to assessing your critical thinking skills using this experiential activity (see Worksheet 2.2 in Appendix 1), you may be interested in exploring measurements that are tailored toward assessing critical thinking. One example is the *California Critical Thinking Dispositions Inventory* (CCTDI) (Facione et al., 1998). In addition, consider *The Problem Solving Inventory* (PSI) (Heppner & Petersen, 1982) or others that your CES may recommend as well.

If a CIT or CES sees the need for ongoing critical thinking development, there are many opportunities to continue to grow this valuable skill. The beauty of considering critical thinking as a foundational aspect of your professional development is that critical thinking involves all areas of the UGM throughout your entire life, both personally and professionally. In fact, as mentioned, it has been known for a long time that there are cognitive aspects of critical thinking, but, more recently, the focus of importance in education has also been on the affective or dispositional aspects of critical thinking (Tumkaya et al., 2009). Throughout our years in researching counselor competencies, we have come across themes and activities embedded in the UGM that directly correlate to assessment, practice, and competencies in counseling skills, knowledge, and dispositions. According to the work of Tumkaya et al. (2009), there is support for a dispositional theory looking at components of intellectual behaviors such as ability, sensitivity, and inclination. These facets are addressed in the quadrant and work of *Self*, in addition to *Relationships, Competencies*, and *Actualization*. Moreover, these dispositions or tendencies to behave in certain ways often include a tolerance to ambiguity, a willingness to suspend judgement, and being open-minded, truthful and analytic; in short, it includes a willingness to engage in critical thinking (Beyer, 1987). In summary, you may be delighted to find themes of these features and attributes throughout the UGM.

Summary

This chapter sets the stage for you to be ready for the UGM process by considering your desire for growth and change while implementing critical thinking. The quadrants are in each of our lives. Whatever the quadrant where the person is stuck, that is the prevalent one that needs attention first in order to move forward to the other quadrants. When that issue is resolved, there may be more areas to work on, depending on the person's life experience. We all have a theme in our lives that drives our perceptions and actions. How my circle interacts with yours can be quite a journey of discovery for both of us. However, as we begin to understand ourselves, and others, better, we can find the path that encourages us to hold hands and walk together. That's what the beauty of this model is all about.

The Self Quadrant

The Johari Window

The Johari Window is a conceptual self-awareness activity created by Joseph Luft and Harry Ingham in 1955. It is a tool for giving and receiving feedback, improving communication, and assisting in interpersonal effectiveness. We encourage the implementing

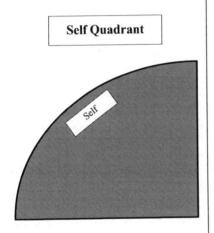

Self Quadrant

Self

The quadrant of *self* invites us to explore our own motivations, actions, reactions, leadings, and history. This is where the journey begins; we must know ourselves first. Knowing our strengths, areas for growth, instinctual responses, etc., all helps us to grow as individuals who are seeking a healthy life, and healthy interactions and relationships with others. In addition, we seek to know ourselves to achieve healthy abilities, and to obtain an ongoing healthy process of self-actualization. CITs are required to self-explore and assess their own worldview, cultural identity, biases, and values. These are fundamental required tasks of the CIT to prevent biases and values being imposed on clients.

The process of reviewing self also helps in cultivating a process of self-discovery towards cultural competencies, thus maintaining high ethical standards.

In this quadrant, for this book, we will be exploring self by using:
- The Johari Window
- Stages of Grief and Loss
- The Wounded Healer
- Trauma/Stress Model of Counselor Development
- Disarming Triggers
- Transactional Analysis as a Tool
- Cultural and Spiritual Reflection
- Self-Care Stress Management
- Defining Worldview and Counselor Identity
- Myers Briggs Type Indicator
- Conflict Management Style

Figure 2.2 Self Quadrant.

(Modified by authors with permission from Rigg, 2017.)

of the tool to explore the various aspects of self, including: The Open Self, The Hidden Self, The Blind Self, and the Unknown Self (see Table 2.1 below). The goal of using the Johari Window is to increase the Open and decrease the Hidden and Blind areas through self-awareness. The more we engage in meaningful relationship, the more we share safely. When CITs explore these parts of themselves, it may include evaluation of personal thoughts, behaviors, and their impact on others. Hence, this impacts the CIT's ability to work with clients to engage in meaningful connection and their self-growth as well. Self-reflection is imperative because the inability to do so may lead to detrimental consequences including countertransference for you as the CIT. Van Wagoner, Gelso, Hayes, & Diemer (1991) found several themes that were known to help minimize countertransference: "We theorized the existence of five interrelated factors: (a) self-insight, (b) empathic ability, (c) self-integration, (d) anxiety management, and (e) conceptualizing ability" (p. 412). We recommend CITs use the questionnaire and answer the questions as offered online as one example of applying the activity. In utilizing the Johari Window there are a couple of strategies that can be employed. You can find the Johari Window exercise online (See the link in Appendix 2). You, or your CES, may wish to employ one or more activities to consider in your work together:

1   The CES and the CIT take the assessment, answer the questions, and then consult after exploring and expressing what came up for them. Next, they can offer insights to each other about what they have experienced. A journey into the Open Window may be informative; sometimes we may share information that the other person was unaware of, which may impact known and hidden areas for either the CIT or the CES.

Table 2.1 Johari Window example

	Known to Self	*Not known to Self*
Known to Others	OPEN What are things I know about myself and share with others? I am a mother of two children, I am a professional Counselor Educator and Supervisor who specializes in addictions work, I believe in CBT as my foundational theoretical orientation, I like gardening, and have a good sense of humor and have leadership qualities. (**Consider the image of an open window.**)	BLIND I have been recently told by others that I appear stressful, anxious and rigid in my work and supervision. (Consider the image of a window with wooden blinds on it.)
Not Known to Others	HIDDEN My fears. Fear of failure, fear of letting others down, fear that my CIT knows more than I do, fear of others knowing my religious convictions, political affiliations, beliefs about gun policy, abortion, etc. (**Consider the image of dark-out curtains over the window.**)	UNKNOWN I am unsure, but willing to learn more of my unconscious biases, and I know I need to do this by being authentic and in relationship with supervisors, colleagues, and other professionals, including using feedback from clients and my CITs. (**Consider the idea of having a window you did not know existed in your home.**)

2 You as the CIT can take the assessment and complete the questionnaire with additional reflective questions such as the following:

   a What was it like completing the questionnaire?
   b What new insights did you find in the process?
   c What emotions came up for you while completing the questionnaire?
   d How will you continue to work towards moving things from hidden or unknown to known?
   e How will this process help you long term in your professional development? Then, finally, explore and summarize with the CES as support.

The CES can implement a "Worldview" assignment with you by considering the Johari Window reflection as a way to open self-exploration and self-understanding (see the Worldview assignment below).

3 In addition, you as the CIT can explore a novel, film, or song and analyze it to explore aspects of the Johari Window through self-reflection and self-understanding.

Review a few questions considering the window chart above.

Open: What are some things you know about yourself, and that others know about you as well? Consider adding items to the square (professional aspects, personal, common things you openly share with others about yourself, and you can include gifts, strengths or even weaknesses).

Hidden: What are some things about yourself you know but keep hidden from others (fears, dreams, politics, religious beliefs, weaknesses, convictions, biases)?

Blind: What are some things you may not know about yourself, but others do know as this comes in the form of feedback from others around you? Remember, to fill this window and reach insight and growth, you must be vulnerable to allow others to know you and offer the feedback.

Unknown: These are things you do not know about yourself, and others may not know as well. This is the future and can be filled by building authentic relationships with others (see Worksheet 2.3 in Appendix 1).

Summary

The Johari Window offers a first look at self-assessment towards movement in being able to consider and maintain a curiosity for ongoing self-reflective works, even during referral for ongoing growth needs that may include: assessment concerns, remediation, professional development work and even grief and loss. When processing this activity with your CES you can benefit from building rapport and empathy through self-disclosure and authenticity in the assignment. We recommend CITs use the questionnaire and answer the questions as offered online as one example of applying the activity.

Stages of Grief (Kubler-Ross)

Receiving news that you are being offered a *remediation* or *growth plan* can be experienced as grief and loss. Sometimes even receiving feedback that you experience as hurtful can lead to grief, or a sense of questioning yourself and your own competencies. Counselors in Training often appear to go through their own stages of grief, which can be supported in work with a CES. Kubler-Ross (1969) offers the stages of grief including: Denial, Anger, Bargaining, Depression, and Acceptance (DABDA). A CIT can go through these same stages when confronted with concerns expressed by faculty/supervisors or program administrators, both in the academic realm and clinical area as well. The CIT may start at any given stage or skip around from stage to stage. Consider how you may have recently experienced grief or loss in your own counselor developmental journey.

Often CITs may begin with denial.

Case Study

The CES contacts the CIT regarding a concern. The CIT denies it:

"Hi, Sally. This is Dr. ____, I have some concerns . . . ."

Denial: CIT: "What?? I DID not do that! You must be mistaken."

CES: "Well, let's look at the concerns expressed."

Anger: CIT: *Internally thinking*: "I cannot believe this is happening. It's like everyone is against me and doesn't want to see me succeed. Who do these people think they are? Well, it's not my issue."

Bargaining: CIT to CES: "So, if I make the changes, can I still pass the class?"

Depression: CIT: *Internally when they realize they have a remediation plan*: "I don't know what I'm going to do . . . my whole life plan depends on this degree! I can't lose everything!"

Acceptance: CIT to CES: "Okay . . . maybe I can learn something about myself if I listen to what is being said and make changes that are real. After all, it will make me a better counselor, and that is what I want."

Consider as the CIT:

- Can you relate to Sally? If so how?
- Can you relate to the CES? If so how?
- What are your personal reflections after reviewing the example?
- How might CIT and CES benefit from such work together?

Grief and loss is a process that you can manage as you are required in your counselor developmental process to let go of the old self in exchange for becoming someone new – a healthier version of who you were. This may be the first time you are experiencing something this intimate, scary, and perhaps painful in terms of change of self. Many CITs may never have received genuine, authentic, corrective feedback from a mentor, authority, or someone deeply committed to the care of their developmental process. The process, albeit difficult for some, can be an exploration of reflecting on parts of the self that have been hidden. Consider the Johari Window as an illustration and assignment that helps in uncovering the hidden and unknown aspects of self. Discovering parts that are hidden to the self may be liberating and yet sad for some. The question of discovery may also provoke the question of whether you are ready for change. Have no fear though, you are not alone in this process as your CES seeks to support you along the way. In addition, CITs sometimes opt on their own to go to personal counseling to work through existing issues for their own healing and growth. This is a healthy and encouraged practice as you seek to help others in their healing process. It is the wise counselor who maintains contact with their own counselor throughout their career.

- Take a moment to consider if you are indeed in one of the stages of grief and loss as per Kubler-Ross's (1969) model (see Worksheet 2.5 in Appendix 1).

  Denial, Anger, Bargaining, Depression, Acceptance.

- If you are in grief and loss, which stage are you at?
- Who is your support person as you explore this process?
- What do you stand to lose or gain as you enter the process?
- How have you endured and worked through other examples of grief and loss in your life?
- What assets and strengths might you lean into to help you?
- What roles do your CES, colleagues, and mentors play to support you?

It is important to note that the stages of grief are not necessarily completed in a linear fashion. Some people may move straight through the process, others may go forward, back, jump over, etc. What is significant is not *how* we go through the stages, but *that* we do. Many may be familiar with this process depending on personal life experiences. Our life experiences are part of who we are. Despite the challenges in our lives, the totality of the experiences is part of what makes us who we are today. I would not change anything in my life because, having gone through my life experiences and survived and thrived, I am who I am. However, we also have the obligation to work through those things that we have experienced as our reactions to some of those experiences may continue to influence our dispositions and behaviors. Therefore, wisdom tells us that we must review our personal journey.

Wounded Healer

After completing a self-reflection activity such as the Johari Window and the evaluation of our Stages of Grief and Loss, it is important for CITs to conduct a Wounded Healer self-assessment as well. As mentioned, many counselors go into the field due to their own experiences and worldview of wounding or trauma experiences in hopes of helping others and, hence, either using clients to work out their own *stuff* or by continuing their own growth by finding meaning in helping others to move past pain towards healing and success. Carl Jung wrote the following passage, presented in *The Collected Works of C. G. Jung* (1985):

> The analyst must go on learning endlessly . . . it is his own hurt that gives the measure of his power to heal. This, and nothing else is the meaning of the Greek myth of the wounded physician. (p. 237)

Sharp (2017) shared that, according to the legend of the Greek doctor Asclepius, he recognized his own wounds first and established a sanctuary at Epidaurus where others could be healed of their wounds. Anyone who sought to be treated allegedly needed to go through a method of cleansing and healing themselves first. This process likely included a cleansing bath to purify the soul, spirit, and body. In addition, a need to sleep after purification was likely because cleansing taxes the body and soul. The Jungian theory appears to suggest that healing can only take place if the counselor is in an ongoing relationship with their unconscious. Otherwise, he or she may identify with the *healer archetype*, which is a form of self-increase and may have the potential to be harmful to others as it makes the entire process of therapy about boosting the counselor. This could potentially lead to negative countertransference as well. In other words, it appears that without going into our own healing, we run the risk of making others suffer and making the clinical experience about ourselves, which can be damaging and unethical.

According to Jung, a wounded healer is a term that refers to a counselor who is compelled to treat clients because the *counselor* is wounded. Consistent with Barr (2006), 73.9% of counselors and psychotherapists report some type of personal life wound, which led to their career choice of counseling (para. 9). Many of these wounds included categories of abuse, family life as a child, personal mental health struggles, social issues, family life issues as an adult, bereavement, traumatic events, other mental health concerns, and life-threatening physical illnesses.

It appears from Jung's teachings that the wounded healer can be used as a healing agent or can be detrimental to both client and therapist. If we evaluate this theory looking at CITs, we see that it is likely many CITs may also come from a wounded healer background; the CITs may be exhibiting similar phenomena with their clients. For wounded healers, corrective feedback could be interpreted as a crisis and may be a more painful experience for those who identify as wounded healers. In fact, Kerr (1993), in his work *A Most Dangerous Method*, shared that Jung had a psychotic breakdown in his late 30s to mid-40s. He reportedly suffered immense depression, anxiety, disorientation, suicidal ideation, and was, for a time, unable to function; yet, he later emerged a new man, more whole, conscious, better balanced, and psychologically aware. Within the experience of our own woundedness, regardless of what it is, we can come out of it positively transformed, as Jung did, which can benefit many clients, or we may be at risk of damaging ourselves and others. The question is, do we come from wounding with the desire to *cure others* to try to feel better for *our* wounding or trauma, or do we work through our own healing first, or ongoingly, and then address helping others from a place of desiring altruistic support to our fellow human beings? Do we come from a position of wanting to empower others to see them become their own hero? Consider the following questions and process with your CES.

Woundedness

1   Part of my worldview as a CIT involves being hurt by people or experiences.
2   Part of my desire to enter the counseling helping profession is to help others because I understand personally the experience of pain, suffering, and injury.
3   I feel a deep desire to contribute to this profession, to give back what was offered to me when I have struggled.
4   Although I have personal life wounding, I have and continue to work through those first-hand experiences.
5   I believe my own history of wounding can and may influence the counseling work I do with clients; therefore, it is important to continue to monitor, work on, and seek ongoing close supervision and consultation.
6   My work or drive to become a helping professional is my entire focus and identity to "help others."
7   Helping others makes me feel good and needed. I enjoy "fixing" a problem for people.
8   I have been known to respond unprofessionally before, especially when I felt "triggered" by something that caught me off guard.

(See Worksheet 2.6 in Appendix 1.)

So, now that you have decided you want to be a wounded healer who is continuing to work on your own healing, to empower clients to be their own hero, what does it mean? Consider wounding, and the several types of wounds many counselors have endured throughout their lives. Maybe you have endured a difficult childhood, abuse, neglect, or other traumas. Perhaps you were involved in an accident, diagnosed with a medical issue, or have witnessed something horrific. Often wounds can come from a traumatic experience.

Trauma/Stress Informed Model of Counselor Development

As reported, many CITs state when entering the field of counseling that they are doing so due to their own wounding and therefore want to become healers themselves. In addition, students who enter the field admit they often have trauma in their background and are eager and passionate to make a difference in the field to help others (Brown-Rice & Furr, 2013; Gaubatz & Vera, 2002). There is a growing trend for trauma-informed education and trauma-informed teaching in this current culture; so, we leave it up to the CIT to consider how they wish to do some personal and professional work themselves as it impacts their professional development and competencies in the counseling field. Your CES will not work directly with your wounding, past trauma, or issues, but know this: it is your responsibility to continue to do any needed work while pursuing your counseling professional developmental process. Your CES can support you regarding your stress responses, as long as you are willing to use self-reflection and desire growth and feedback. That may include your own personal counseling work in addition to professional development work alongside your CES.

Awareness of the reality that we live in very different times where there are more apparent crises, traumas, and disasters is pivotal in understanding how we approach education and professional development. Often, the graduate training experience of counseling can be triggering to CITs as the content explores academic understanding of clinical mental health. For example, when you are asked to complete crisis and trauma intake, you may read a case study about a young girl sold into the sex trade and you must come to terms with some of the horrible traumatic realities that our clients often face in this world. To add to this are the various worldviews, life experiences, and emotional or psychological responses CITs often progress through as they grow and develop as counselors. As noted in the literature by Barr (2006), counselors often go into the field with their own woundedness and those who are still working through their wounding often find they are still processing and healing within their counselor developmental growth. Because of the extensive training requirements and ambitious standards of competency required for the field, these dispositional aspects are likely to surface at some point. It is also important to understand that previous trauma or current stress cannot be left out of the developmental nature of counselor development, especially when considering feedback, remediation and assessing of dispositions.

Many CITs may have done quite a bit of work on their past experiences before starting the educational journey toward professional counseling. Many may even feel that the effects of their past are no longer intruding in their current lives. However, that is the way triggers work; they are unexpected and beneath the surface of awareness. Even current events can encroach on your counseling experience with clients. Stressful events, past or present, appear at the door to your office, enter, and unceremoniously plop themselves in your office and interfere with best intentions.

A few areas often reported in remediation concern cases include examples such as the following. (Note: names are altered. Cases are based on real-life examples but are masked and altered to protect identities.)

Case Studies

- Jenna is referred to remediation due to her inability to demonstrate foundational counseling skills, immense anxiety, stress, and lack of communication with faculty and supervisors at her Field Experience site. She reports going through a messy divorce that included interpersonal partner violence, having a child with special needs, and attempting to work full time while in school. Jenna remarks, "I just simply cannot get my stress load under control and I know it has caused me to make unethical poor mistakes."
- Sam is referred for a remediation plan due to unprofessional communication within the class with peers and faculty, and an ethical violation at his Field Experience site. He reports having lost his mother and father at a young age and working two jobs since the age of 16. He was also reported for academic integrity issues due to submitting falsified hours for his field experience work and admitted "I work two jobs and couldn't get the hours in; I was just so stressed and anxious about finishing on time I thought it was the only way."

As you can see, many ethical violations occur when CITs are stressed or operating out of reactions to their stress load. It impacts not only your professional standing and future, but also clients and the profession at large as well. Deeply consider how stress, if not managed, can be dangerous in our field. Consider your reactions to stress.

- Do you tend to bend the rules? Justify your actions based on a time crunch?
- Convince yourself that your workaround for due dates is okay because you don't know what else to do? Do you understand that those are all ethical violations?

If you cannot trust yourself, it is even more important to be open, accountable, and humble. Bringing the dilemma forward will often allow your faculty, supervisors, or CES to help you problem-solve. Remember, your professional licensed supervisors do this for a living and have probably seen more challenges to complete programs than you can imagine; you are only doing this one time. There may be resources that can help you complete the expectations of the program and the profession with your ethics intact. Ethics are real, and they have consequences when they are not upheld.

As CITs report an experience of a trauma background or current life stressors that are impeding their professional development, the main phenomenon or experience may be one of a *trauma response* or *stress response*. In addition, depending on the CIT's own personal prior exposure to crisis and trauma, or where the CIT is in their own work and what they have been doing with clients, they may also have experience of vicarious trauma (Perlman & Saakvitne, 1995). Some aspects to consider regarding stress include the definition of stress, coined by Hans Selye in 1936, who defined it as the imprecise reaction of the physical figure to any requirement for adjustment (Rosch, 2017). Stressors can be considered from many facets such as biological, psychological, or social. Rosch (2017) says that the closest Chinese character to signify stress is written as two characters, meaning crisis; the two characters represent the words *Danger* and *Opportunity*. Growth often can come from crisis, and that is the beauty of all the challenging work we do personally in this very process of self-growth. In addition, this is the foundational premise for Post Traumatic Growth models.

The phenomenon called Post Traumatic Growth is a theory that has been examined for more than 30 years, exploring how suffering sometimes produces strengthening and growth (Tedeschi, Calhoun, & Groleau, 1995). D. C. Faber, in his *Faber Post Trauma Growth Model* (2012), demonstrated an alternative perspective on viewing the traumatic experiences in our past, not as creating deficits in the person, but, with resilience, the traumatic experience may be reframed into growth opportunities. The trauma survivor can demonstrate that some of the tools required to navigate trauma, particularly combat experience, can be turned into points of growth (Faber & Gray, 2012). This model was developed by Faber after returning from Afghanistan and trying to reintegrate into his rural family life. Through his own struggles, his resilience, his ability to see not only what he was doing but also how his actions were affecting his family and others, he developed this model that helps combat-experienced veterans readjust to life after coming home. It did not seem to be an issue whether the combat experience was 50 years ago or last week; there was healing to be had in this process. Through his work presenting his model, he also noticed that this could be an effective strategy for other types of trauma experienced by men, women, and children. It was through his journey that he was able to offer options to others that could invite them to resume their place in society without feeling they were broken pieces of their former selves. Research is supporting the lived experience of Faber. Harris et al. (2006) stated: "Dealing with the aftermath of trauma is a substantial cognitive-emotional task that can reveal personal strength and new possibilities" (p. 27). It is through that lens that Post Traumatic Growth (PTG) occurs.

We combine these theories to understand that you as a CIT can reach your fullest potential within the remediation/professional growth process as we as CES seek to use our role, responsibilities, and the relationship with you to its fullest in the gatekeeping function, while assisting in the role as educator and supervisor, thus bringing forth immense growth. However, this means your CES is in the delicate role of Counselor Educator and Supervisor, and operates within roles such as teacher, evaluator, supervisor, and sometimes *educational* counselor. This means you may be required, of your own accord, to also seek *personal* counseling as your CES seeks to stay within their boundaries and roles of supervision. Finally, we acknowledge that despite the often-negative associations with stress, some amount of stress is not only healthy for individuals but also required for growth. Be sure to know that, as you embark on this part of your development, your CES is there for you along the way.

Some CITs come into their training program having worked long and hard on their own healing process. Others have not. Some may not believe there is a need for any healing. Some believe they have done so much healing that they may not need any more. Regardless, many CITs may respond to the requirement of a CIT development plan with a stress response mode of "fight, flight, freeze, fawn" (the 4-Fs) (Walker, 2014) when faced with extreme stress. One thing is certain, it is beneficial for any CIT embarking on self-growth or a growth plan of any kind to understand their faculty and supervisors are there to help, support, and teach them about competencies, while also fulfilling their professional roles as gatekeeper. It is wise for the CIT to understand and frame the relationship as such and recognize that the CES is on their side. Some CITs may not receive the CES feedback well, especially in those initial stages, but we encourage you to consider the intent of your CES and your personal benefit relating back to the Unknown box in the Johari Window. I want to share with you a personal story about when I was 16 years old and in need of coaching support.

One example that comes to mind regarding the concept of CES mentoring support is when I (Dr. McLain) had a track and field coach years ago who always gave us the workout routine. I was a sprinter and ran the 100-yard and 220-yard dashes, so when he instructed that we had to run three-mile fartleks, I was upset with him because, in my mind, "I am a sprinter! Why do I need to do all this long-distance training!?" After huffing and puffing and complaining, I realized my coach wasn't asking me to do the dreaded fearful long-distance training alone, he was joining me. He was joining me in the hardship of training. He did this in many practices, and knowing that my coach was willing to run alongside me in the tough long-distance strength training made me respect him and realize I did need to do what he expected of me in gaining endurance, even though I did not understand it at first. He never gave us a free pass to not train, but he did join us on the run. In fact, I ended up winning over 17 medals that year due to the immense training he had me do to prepare for the sprints in the track meets.

We encourage you again to utilize the meaningful connection with your CES while leaning into the process of growth by simply working towards building a rapport with them. In the process of building a rapport with your CES, keep in mind their role and intention is to support and challenge you for your own good. Keep in mind your own personal tendency to respond from a stress response as indicated by Walker (2014). In the example above, I was angry and resentful initially, then I realized it was for my own growth and benefit. Although some CITs may not respond from one of these perspectives,

Table 2.2 Stress responses with negative characteristics within the CIT training response. (Modified by the authors with permission from Walker, 2017.)

Fight	Flight	Freeze	Fawn
Irritated	Panicky	Dissociative	Co-dependent
Controlling	Rushing/Worrying	Hiding/Isolating	People pleaser
Anger	Driven/Compulsive/ Perfectionistic	Achievement phobic	Doormat
Entitlement	Micromanager	Spaced out	Social perfectionism
HOW TO *Potentially* RESPOND	HOW TO *Potentially* RESPOND	HOW TO *Potentially* RESPOND	HOW TO *Potentially* RESPOND
De-escalate and focus on rapport building, foundational skills, empathy, trust and meaningful connection	Consider grounding techniques, meaningful connection and accountability through meetings, person centered techniques, etc.	Consider grounding techniques and helping bring the CIT to current awareness of here and now and connect to meaningful connection	Consider ways to challenge and support through creative assignments, meaningful connection and use of immediacy and metaphor
Tap into The Strengths of:	Tap into The Strengths of:	Tap into The Strengths of:	Tap into The Strengths of:
Assertiveness	Disengagement	Acute awareness	Love and Service
Boundaries	Healthy Retreat	Mindfulness	Compromise
Courage	Industriousness	Poised Readiness	Listening
Moxie	Know-How	Peace	Fairness
Leadership	Perseverance	Presence	Peace-making

we encourage you to consider if you do. Often people can respond to triggers of stress with one or more of the following stress responses.

First and foremost, we recognize not all CITs will respond with one of these stress responses; however, we encourage you to consider your potential or tendency, if it applies, to lean into the positive strengths of each and to use self-reflection in helping your process to be one of growth and edification. Keep in mind that being authentic within the CES relationship concerning your tendency to respond out of one or more of these areas in your growth process is critical so they can assist you with authentic, honest communication, and with meaningful connection towards growth.

- Which stress response style do you most relate with? Share, when you are ready, with your CES.
- Which positive strengths for each response do you recognize in yourself?
- What other aspects come to mind as you reflect on the model, theory and phenomena of stress response, especially considering perhaps your current work in your counselor developmental process?
- What, in addition, might be helpful to share with your CES concerning your responses and how to move forward in growth and development?
- How might your trauma/stress response be your responsibility to manage while working on other areas of your professional development?

(See Worksheet 2.7 in Appendix 1.)

Walker further explained that we have these responses instinctively due to variances in our own personal trauma, abuse, neglect, birth order, and genetics, which may lead us toward a specific 4-F survival instinct. The beauty of Walker's model is that not only can we reflect deeply and consider our own ongoing need for growth, but that there are also positive features of the 4-Fs to consider in our behaviors and personalities as CITs. This work can be time-consuming but offers an abundance of empowerment once insights are gained.

The healthy route is to undergo the difficult and time-consuming work towards continuing to heal our own lives using authenticity, assessment, and relationships, while evaluating our own ongoing counseling dispositions. For example, I (Dr. McLain) often offer an assignment in teaching diagnosis where students must indicate potential biases they may have when working with clients. I cannot tell you how many students normally report "I have no biases." Soon they are all involved in heated discussions exhibiting that they are clearly triggered in the assignment discussion prompt. I relay to students that we all have biases. Some are hidden, some are unknown, and some are known to us, although we hate for anyone to know about them or to think we have them. Think back to your Johari Window and make the connection. Often, biases may expose a trigger previously unrecognized. A trigger is any emotional reaction to an event, comment, context, or interaction, indicating that there is more work to be done to disarm the trigger. Disarming a trigger can be accomplished by reflecting, considering, and working through any unfinished business we may have.

Disarming the Stress/Trauma Trigger

One technique I (Dr. Lewis) like to use to identify the source of the trigger is a three-step process that can be shared with clients. Consider the emotional response that was just experienced. Identify the feelings that are associated with the reaction. Then:

1   Think about the **last time** you felt this same emotion. Who was there, what were you doing, what did you see, what did you hear, what did you smell, how did you feel? Identify the emotions and check out all five senses as you process and reflect on the context. Make notes in a journal or on an electronic or paper notepad.

2   When was the **first time** you felt this way? Again, process through your senses and context. Look at the similarities and the feelings. Which feelings seemed to align with which events? Look for themes, commonalities, conclusions you may have come to as you review this occurrence through the lens of the event in #1.

3   When was **the time before that**? Typically, a person will identify the "first" time as somewhere in their early teens. Through experience, many people identify that the true first time was earlier in childhood, and the teenage experience was repeating the pattern. So, go back to the time before that. What was going on? What do you remember about the situation? What were the thoughts and conclusions you came to at that point in time? And process through all that happened at that point, which may reveal a long-held belief that was probably not the truth. You have found your center, and you can now disarm that trigger. As you process through the thoughts, memories, events, emotions, and beliefs, you may be able to find a new understanding of who you are. (See Worksheet 2.8 in Appendix 1.)

Once the error of *kid logic* is revealed, and the event is viewed through an adult perspective, a new understanding is gained, thus disarming that trigger. The process may need to be repeated frequently depending on the triggers that a person has; however, the key is the emotional reaction, particularly emotions such as anger, hurt, or fear. One visualization that may be helpful is to imagine a closet full of nicely wrapped gifts. We know what is in each box, and could, if needed, open each one, review it, and then replace it in the closet. It's not that we pretend the boxes are not there; it's that they no longer control our behavior. They are stored well in the closet, neatly wrapped in bright paper and pretty ribbon, and no longer need to be something we trip over.

Even when we, as the CIT, have an excessive personal emotional response as we seek to deescalate anger, anxiety, fear, etc., we realize we can categorize it, put it on the back burner to handle later, and stay present in the here and now with the client; they need us to remain unbiased, fair, and yet authentic with them without allowing *our* triggers to hijack their experiences and needs. Put the box under the chair and pick it up later to explore after the client has left. Explore it, manipulate it, dig into it, and once you have evaluated all of it, put it in the closet. This is also the process to use in working with your CES. How do we recognize we may be reacting to a trigger?

- When we are triggered we may appear: Impatient, intolerant, defensive, frustrated, argumentative, feel personally attacked. In addition, some CITs report feeling compelled to hang on to these emotions during a call or meeting and even long afterwards.

- Triggers provide us with information. It is data. It is getting our attention: "Hey! You have something to resolve here!" Recognize it as an invitation for curious exploration, not a condemnation. It is information for your good. If you choose to use it in a healthy way, it can move from the hidden or unknown area of the Johari Window to the known.

- Triggers are normal; we all have them. The question is what do we do with them, and what is our reaction or response to them, and are we acting professionally and responsibly in response to them?
- Triggers are often an indicator of ongoing needed growth in an area of our own development, personal, professional, or both.
- Modeling emotional and relational stability within our professional relationships can help others to pursue the same.

The question regarding our handling of triggers is: Do we lose our professional boundary, or do we self-reflect, consult, use the Johari Window, and work on the issue within ourselves for ongoing professional growth? Can we find someone who is ethical, trustworthy, willing to be honest, yet accepting and safe for us to explore our own ongoing healing and growth with? Might this person be your faculty or supervisor who has taken on a professional commitment to challenge and support you towards your ongoing professional development under their licensure and training? Who do you have in your professional and personal life that may be the safe, trustworthy colleague, mentor, supervisor, etc. to bring issues to when necessary?

Let's explore a case example of a potential trigger:

Case Study

Stacy is a (fictional blended) CIT who was working with a client "Angie" in her Practicum experience. Stacy had grown up in an alcoholic, abusive home with a father who would become out of control once he began drinking, which was every weekend. After work on Fridays he would hang out in the bar with his buddies from work, and usually come home singing Irish ballads very loudly. That was the cue to the family that the weekend had begun. There was no respite for Stacy and her siblings since school was not in session.

Stacy listened to the almost exact same story from Angie, except the client's father would sing Italian opera. Stacy felt a very familiar feeling in the pit of her stomach, the client faded out from her vision, and the voice of the client sounded like the *Peanuts* character Charlie Brown's mother talking, "Waa waa waa waaaa wah." She could feel herself being dragged back in time. Although she fought it, she seemed powerless to get back to the session with the client. The client had just unknowingly tromped on Stacy's trigger.

Let's imagine you are her site supervisor, and you know what has just happened to Stacy. To protect the client, you step in and bring the client's session to a good ending. Now let's imagine you are Stacey and you are visiting with your site supervisor. To protect the client, and to continue to grow in your counselor developmental process, what do you need to do?

How would you respond? What emotions come up for you when you imagine yourself in this situation? What do you think Stacy needs to hear for her own growth and other clients' safety? Do you see it? The emotional reaction? Time for Stacy to process and disarm that trigger!

Walker (2013) listed *positive* characteristics for the 4-F responses, which include:

- Fight: Assertiveness, Boundaries, Courage, Moxie, and Leadership.
- Flight: Disengagement, Healthy retreat, Industriousness, Know-how, and Perseverance.
- Freeze: Acute awareness, Mindfulness, Poised readiness, Peace, and Presence.
- Fawn: Love & Service, Compromise, Listening, Fairness, and Peacemaking (p. 106).

The positive characteristics, or strength-based responses, are helpful and supportive to the growth of the CIT as processing through the characteristics for the most prevalent responses can help the CIT see themselves not as broken, but as *survivors* with value. There is the side of our responses that may make authentic interactions more challenging. We'll review this by continuing the case study below, but let's look at the other side of this coin.

Walker (2013) identified the following as the detrimental responses we demonstrate:

- Fight: . . . Explosive, Controlling (Enslaving), Entitlement, Type-A, Bully, Autocrat, Demands Perfection, . . .
- Flight: . . . Panicky, Rushing or worrying (Outrunning pain), Driven-ness, Adrenaline junkie, Busyholic, Micromanager, Compelled by perfectionism, . . .
- Freeze: Dissociative, Contracting, Hiding (Camouflaging), Isolation, Couch Potato, Space case, Hermit, Achievement-phobic, . . .
- Fawn: Codependent, Obsequious, Servitude (Groveling), Loss of self, People-pleaser, Doormat, Slave, Social perfectionism, D.V. victim, Parentified child (p. 108).

The detrimental reactions can stifle any level of communication or interpersonal relationships because they are *reactive*. It is certainly possible that we carry many of these markers, but the point is to look at the one most prevalent in our own behaviors, and then develop a process for moving away from the negative toward the positive to have healthy interactions with others.

Let's continue to explore as if you, as the CIT, are triggered while engaged in client work: Being an aware wounded healer, we can recognize when our trigger is tripped with a client or your CES; we are upset, irritated, and can then consider which reaction we are naturally leaning towards, and we can gain control of ourselves with grounding. Begin by simply making a one-word note for yourself so you remember to go back to this moment when you have time for self-reflection and then can take it to supervision. This is not the time, as your client needs you. Attend to the client by reflecting a feeling, which will always take the focus off you and put it back where it needs to go: on the client. Stick close to all your foundational skills. That is a surefire way of getting out of yourself and back in the room with the client, and it must be done at the initial stage of your reaction. Focus on the client. Listen to what they are saying. Reflect the feeling and pay attention to whether you are on point or not. Some reflections may be what you are feeling; if it matches the client, then fine. If not, adjust and try again. The client will tell you if your probe was a miss or not. They will say, "Well, kind of" or "In a way". . . and then will correct you as long as you let them. Then, try again, "Oh I see . . . it wasn't that you were angry as much as you were confused?" It is like shooting darts; you must adjust how you throw the dart to hit the bullseye. Stay with the client by focusing on them. Remember, you wrote down a one-word note so you can go back at the right time and process this, and you must.

Now, you are alone and not rushed. Begin by taking a deep breath. An example of how I (Dr. Lewis) walk through my triggers is this:

Recall the incident. Recall the feeling I had just before my trigger was tripped. What was I feeling? Irritation and an acute sense of failure seem to be the most prevalent emotions in the moment and I am definitely reacting to that by gritting my teeth, taking shallow breaths, and feeling angry. I'm going to take the time to work through the steps. Unclench my jaw, take a deep breath, relax and blow out the stress.

When was the last time I felt this way? Perhaps it was with a colleague who stated that my methodology was wrong and theirs was correct, insisting that I needed to follow their directives. Aha. I can still remember the event! We were in the office break room, the coffee pot was making noise as another pot filled drip by drip, someone had a half-eaten piece of cake on the table, the noise coming into the room was from multiple people typing in the office, and someone was laughing with a high-pitched laugh. How did I feel? I felt . . . like I didn't really know anything and had not a single lucid thought to contribute. I felt powerless and stupid.

Okay. When was the first time I felt that way? I remember a teacher in 8th grade who was making fun of me in front of the whole class. At the end of the class he threw a trash can at me out of his own frustration. I was humiliated. Ohhhhh.

So, when was the time before that? I remember coming home from school. I am the youngest of four siblings. I was so excited to share something new that I just learned in school and told my big sister. She responded with, "Everybody knows that! How dumb can you be?!" I remember the feeling of just being deflated. In my mind, I knew I must be stupid. Found it! There's the trigger. I get it. . ..

Now that I know what it is, what do I do with that knowledge? The next step is to look at the original situation with grown-up eyes. How did this experience help me grow into the professional that I am today? What did I learn from that journey? Well, I learned that I was not stupid, but I was four years behind her in school. So, she knew the information four years before I did; of course, she would not be impressed. What did I learn from my 8th grade English teacher? Grown-ups look stupid when they lose control. I also learned that it wasn't such a big deal how we got to the answers; it was more important that we got there. Okay. Was I right to feel inadequate with a colleague? No. But I was allowing myself to be intimidated and I embraced the "less than" perspective. Paraphrasing Eleanor Roosevelt, no one can make you feel bad about yourself without your permission. Now, I wonder what may have been different if I pushed my agenda harder. I'll never know; but, it could have been amazing. So, back to the current situation. I have a better understanding of my triggers, my responses, and my efficacy as a professional. I am not intimidated, scared, shamed, or anything else. I can listen to good ideas and I can present my ideas with confidence, and perhaps we can combine ideas into something incredible! What may get in our way of working through this ourselves? Perfectionism is often an issue.

Are CITs susceptible to being mistaken? Absolutely. That is something we are not only susceptible to but should embrace. Using critical thinking, explore the perspectives of others who were present. Did the perfectionism change anything? If not, then it is now a useless commodity; something that is simply in the way of rising to your full potential. Kick it out. Perhaps one can look at other organizations and leaders to explore the human right to make mistakes. Consider this quote from John Wooden, the hall-of-fame basketball player and coach: "If you're not making mistakes, then you're not doing anything. I'm positive that a doer makes mistakes" (Wooden, n.d.). Making mistakes can involve vast learning, especially if one acknowledges the mistake, takes ownership of it, learns from it, and rectifies the mistake by growing (Anderson, 2013). There are multiple ways of encouraging ownership of the right to make mistakes, including some rite or ceremony reclaiming imperfection. Consider how the *adult* was overcompensating and taking over, not allowing that inner child to function, make mistakes and learn from them; to fall off the bike and get back on. Some people write a letter to their "perfectionism" and thank it for keeping them safe, but now they can do that on their own, so "goodbye ol' buddy." If it sneaks back, then you can say "Hello, Old Friend . . . I'm doing OK, so you can go back to sleep/Hawaii/Pluto," (i.e., to wherever you sent it when goodbyes were said). As we continue to explore interactions, consider adding in the tenets of Transactional Analysis (TA) (Berne, 2011), with the goal of getting communication to be adult to adult.

Transactional Analysis as a Tool for CIT Self Awareness

Transactional Analysis (TA) was created by Eric Berne in the 1950s, defining ego states in interactions as Parent, Adult, and Child (Berne, 2011). As a communication model, the best form of communication is to have an adult-to-adult conversation as a dyad. When speaking adult to adult, emotions are controlled and communication is understood well by both parties. In contentious personal interactions, the direct communication may rarely be seen. The illustration developed by Berne shows the four basic communication patterns of interactions. Consider two people who may speak and respond in three basic styles: Parent, Child, and Adult. The best combination is Adult to Adult; that is when the exchange is honest, forthright, straightforward, and informational. Defensiveness or bossiness are absent. Another combination is Parent to Child, which is basically what it sounds like. When one person begins to act like a child, the other may quite unintentionally step into the parent role to correct the child. The opposite is also true, in that the one who begins to tell the other what and how to do something, which is parental, drives the other person to act like a child. In addition to those structures, there may also be the Child to Child and the Parent to Parent communication styles. Both of those are manifested by either throwing fits or tantrums together, whining, complaining, pouting, defending, i.e., "I won't, I won't, and you can't make me!" or "You're not the boss of me!" The Parent to Parent is when both people are trying to run the show, tell each other what to do and how to do it, and even condemning one another, such as, "You never do anything right!" "I don't do it right? Who just messed up the checkbook?!"

How does this work as a professional counselor? When your client is acting like a child do not be seduced into being the parent. Allow that client to sit in it and resist the urge to rescue the client. Express empathy, using foundational counseling skills without taking the feelings away from the client. Immediacy is your best skill during this time and keeps you present in the here and now with your client, which also keeps you in the

Adult mode. You can say to your client, "I hear a lot of pain in your voice right now. I'm feeling very sad that you have been hurt, and I'm feeling like I need to rescue you. I'm wondering if, right now, you are feeling powerless?" You kept your conversation Adult to Adult and aimed to help empower the client rather than rescue them. You allowed your client to feel their own feelings, while providing the labels they may need to understand more about themselves in their deep reflective work.

The same can happen with actual children and adults. The parentified child has quite literally taken on the role of *parent* while the adult continues in their role of dependent, incapable, unreliable, and unaccountable child-like adult. The child who has become the parent can get quite used to that role and can have a difficult time giving it up. For instance, some foster children may come from those dynamics in their birth homes, and then struggle in foster homes when they are being asked to give up the role of parent and just be a kid. They don't know how. They feel rejected. They need to be taught how to play, let go, and relax.

Often, CITs have a variety of roles and responsibilities and may be working with clients at the same time as they are under supervision of a CES. In that relationship, similar techniques apply. How can you be open to hearing what your CES is saying without the negative 4-Fs? Keep in mind that, as we have discussed, working in growth or remediation processes can be time-consuming, exhausting, and deeply stressful for CITs, and sometimes for the CES as well. To ensure we are mitigating bias, triggers, and are in a good place to begin our ongoing training of self-assessment, we want to explore our own existing tools and self-understanding.

Here are some self-exploratory questions integrating all we have learned so far:

- Coping skills: How do we measure up to the preaching and teaching we do to our clients about self-care?
- What are your negative coping tools? Do you run to the fridge whenever you are stressed, smoke, drink alcohol, or use other substances to self-medicate?
- What negative coping strategy do you go to first?
- What are your stress responses? Do you usually lean to fight, flight, freeze or fawn?
- Do you find you create stress and, if so, do you do it to soothe yourself using these negative strategies?
- Distractions or avoidance? Do you avoid dealing with a situation? Do you distract yourself with a coping strategy? Is it negative or positive?
- Are you open to change? Are you willing to self-assess? Are you able to truly hear and incorporate feedback?

This process is moving you toward a more authentic congruent life and, therefore, leading towards healthy relationships with others.

Multicultural and Spiritual Connections

Whenever we work with others we must always consider our own worldview, which includes elements of culture and spirituality. Multicultural awareness, and how it impacts our interpersonal and intrapersonal interactions, is not only related to our worldviews and spiritual beliefs, but also how our experiences inform those interactions. We also need to be aware of how our actions and interactions are experienced by the other person, through their cultural lens. Knowing ourselves, and then under-standing how others experience us and understanding our influence on other people, is critical to investigate to avoid countertransference. We are obligated to explore our own thoughts, views, biases, behaviors, etc., as professionals. This includes reviewing our own "cultural competencies" as per the ACA *Code of Ethics* (2014) as well as the ACA's *Multicultural and Social Justice Counseling Competencies* (2015).

We certainly would not ask you as the CIT to do something we were not willing to do ourselves as your CES, and we want to demonstrate the importance of lifelong growth especially in this area. Therefore, it is crucial that we look at how and what we do in our own lives. Socrates said that the unexamined life is not worth living. Wiersbe (2002) went on to say, "Yet, few people sit down to weigh seriously the val-ues that control their decisions and directions" (p. 96). This quote shows that our self-examination is necessary and requires our attention as much as it is imperative for the CIT. Furthermore, Wiersbe also stated: "Self-evaluation can be a dangerous thing, because we can err in two directions: (1) making ourselves *better* than we are, or (2) making ourselves *worse* than we really are" (p. 112). This sobering thought brings us the knowledge that we need to balance our own assessment, gain input from other sources, and share our thoughts with trusted others to be sure we are being realistic in our exploration. Our perceptions must be clear when we look in this mirror. For those who remember fun houses where there was a hall of mirrors that made a person look tall, short, fat, skinny, etc., we want to be sure we are not distorting the truth of who and what we are when we review our own actions and orientation. Cultural competency is a part of the counselor's ongoing growth and development throughout our lives and we are all in need of ongoing self-assessment, feedback from others, and newfound learning within the realm of knowledge, skills, and dispositions. Often I have students ask me at the beginning of their counselor developmental journey "what does cultural competency have to do with my dispositions?" I share with them that it has everything to do with it. Our ability to self-reflect can help us acknowledge our biases and our desire for ongoing growth can inspire vulnerability to share authentically with others to reach new understanding in our sometimes-distorted worldviews. Our ability to receive feedback, even if tied to a culturally painful realization, allows us to then use that experience and be ethically better counselors in the field.

Consider how hidden biases may find their way into your work as a CIT, with your CES, and with your clients. One example was one I (Dr. Lewis) ran across with an internship class long ago. The CIT was presenting a case example and video of a session with one of her clients. The issues were identified by the CIT as being a lack of self-esteem and the inability of the client to advocate for herself and her needs, resulting in depression. The entire class jumped on that bandwagon, almost vilifying her husband as being insensitive and demanding. The client seemed to shrink smaller and smaller as we watched the video, and, had she been present for the discussion, surely would have disappeared beneath the floorboards. Here's the missing information: the client was a first-generation Latina from Mexico. In her culture she was meeting her cultural expec-tations. The students were imposing their individualistic perspective on her, which, had it continued in that vein, no doubt would have ended in divorce and isolation for this Latina woman. As I inquired about her cultural identity, the class seemed to take in a collective sharp breath. They had, indeed, imposed their biases on this client, and in the spirit of wanting to make the client like them, they had completely missed the issues the client was seeking help for to begin with. Beware the hidden bias.

Multicultural competency includes our awareness of our own cultural influences, and the ability to hold those natural perspectives at bay while stepping into the client's reality. We must suspend our interpretations so we can see the issues through the client's lens. We must meet the client where *they* are, and not drag the client to where we are. Many people are hurt by well-intended clinicians who make the claim that they have no biases, perhaps because they do not want to appear to be insensitive to the experiences of others. However, in that denial, we have inadvertently created a schema that says, "since I have no biases, I am multiculturally competent." Nothing could be further from the truth as that state of denial actively blocks any understanding of the other person's world. As a result, we are impotent in being able to connect to that client as the need to maintain denial supersedes our ability to join the client in their reality.

This exercise is profoundly needed from time to time as our lives are full of additional experiences that bring forth new opportunities to explore, reflect, and see where we may be mistaken and need to pay attention to our competencies. As mentioned, the ACA posted the *Multicultural and Social Justice Counseling Competencies* (2015) with objectives for counselors that should be considered. The areas include: Counselor Self-Awareness, Client Worldview, Counseling Relationship, Counseling and Advocacy Interventions. Consider that multiple documents repeat the need for the counselor to be self-aware; this is significant as the lack of self-awareness ultimately has a strong potential to harm the client, the counselor, and the profession. To continue ongoing self-awareness, we need to put ourselves in culturally diverse situations and relationships with others for ongoing feedback. We recommend you become familiar with these competencies throughout your professional development while also actively engaging in relationships with those who are diverse. In addition to cultural competency, we acknowledge the need for all counselors to consider spiritual competencies as well.

Connecting spiritually, if applicable in your development, is a huge asset for the work you will do in the future. While we do not present our own views or opinions about spirituality, when the client brings it up we can explore their beliefs with them and how they may use those beliefs as a resource during trying times. It is evident that, despite not bringing in your spiritual or religious beliefs, they may in fact still contribute to your worldview, theoretical orientation, and hence your client conceptualization. Being aware of what you believe is imperative to avoid bias. If you do hear the client asking to include their personal spiritual or religious self in the therapeutic relationship, it can be a strong rapport-building opportunity and potential support as well.

The same is true in supervision. When you, as a CIT, can explore spirituality, there is a faster and deeper connection when you connect your beliefs to the supervision process. Imagine that you just got some sad news in the internship class and believe all is at risk and your life is over. You may be convinced that all is lost; you are inconsolable, thinking that you would not ever be able to complete the internship and graduate, and, because you are nearly at the end of your doctoral degree, there is a special sting to the entire experience for you. Using the Transactional Analysis (TA) communication model, you, as the CIT, can step into the Adult role and avoid slipping into the role of Child to seek comfort, justification, sympathy, etc., from your CES. Using the Adult voice and inflection, comment to your CES about needing a moment to think. Is there strength for you by using your beliefs to help calm down and instill the hope in you? If so, then you are free to move on to being solution-focused, able to develop a plan and put it into action. Also, as a multicultural experience, we need to understand the central characteristics of different faiths and belief systems. The technique here may also work with future clients, while you, as the CIT, must ensure you are following criteria from the Association of Spiritual, Ethical, and Religious Values in Counseling (ASERVIC) Spiritual competencies, as well as the Multicultural Competencies as indicated by the ACA *Code of Ethics* (2014) and the ACA's *Multicultural and Social Justice Counseling Competencies* (2015). Furthermore, consider a biopsychosocial spiritual perspective of your own needs as well as applying those paradigms to future clients. Whether you are in the position of CIT, eventually a CES, or from the client's stance, considering a belief system or not, we can reflect to others the strengths held in those beliefs.

The ACA *Code of Ethics* (2014) states that a core professional value of the ACA is "honoring diversity and embracing a multicultural approach in support of worth, dignity, potential, and uniqueness of people within their social and cultural contexts" (p. 3). The purpose of the Association for Spiritual, Ethical and Religious Values in Counseling (ASERVIC) Competencies is to support and enhance the multicultural spiritual standards of the profession. We recognize that the ASERVIC Competencies include elements of the counselor's understanding of the differentiation between religion and spirituality, while also having a foundational understanding of a variety of beliefs held by individuals, major world religions, agnosticism, and atheism. In addition, the counselor is expected to recognize "that a client's beliefs, (or absence of beliefs) about spirituality and/or religion are central to his or her worldview and can influence psychosocial functioning" (ASERVIC, n.d., p. 1). This means that the counselor must have self-awareness and self-understanding regarding their own spiritual or religious beliefs, or lack thereof, in terms of their own worldview. Consider the following Spiritual/Religious Self exploration questions in terms of your worldview and its impact on your clients and counselor developmental process:

1   What are your spiritual or religious attitudes, beliefs, and values concerning humanity, life, death, emotional and psychological health, diagnosis, treatment, and well-being?
2   How does your religious and spiritual life, or not having one, impact your counselor developmental process?
3   What are your attitudes, beliefs, and values about integrating counseling and mental health with spirituality and religion?
4   How do you evaluate the influence of your spiritual or religious values and beliefs on the work you do with clients and supervisors?
5   What are your limits to understanding clients' potential spiritual or religious perspectives and needs? Who can you consult or seek supervision from to help support you?
6   What are models of spiritual or religious development and how might this impact the human growth experience?

Further, consider the stress response using the 4-Fs, Fight, Flight, Freeze, or Fawn, regarding spirituality and religion in counseling: which was the *go to* coping strategy for you as you considered the applicability of spirituality? If the person is a runner, they may choose the Flight response and may implode into a powerless mass, unable to do anything to resolve the internal conflict. Someone whose default to stress is Flight may lean toward utilizing all coping resources available, including a strong faith, spirituality, or attachment to one's higher power. They are able to develop a plan to manage the issue, utilize coping resources, and then to put it all into motion to arrest the melt-down. On the positive side of the 4-Fs, they have the strength to persevere and seek homeostasis and health. By tapping into that characteristic, staying in Adult mode, and gradually stifling the negative 4-Fs, you can indeed prevail, and very quickly, and create healthy solutions. This one way to connect and process as a CIT and practice another way to react to the initial stimulus while using the cultural or spiritual belief system as the vehicle.

As we finish with self-assessing and exploring stress and trauma responses, we cannot help but consider the following: as we continue to heal, work, and grow in these areas of ongoing personal and professional growth, how might we mitigate the heavy stress of simply becoming a counselor? Often CITs are in a graduate training program and working in field experience, while also working full-time jobs, with a family, and other "life" responsibilities. Working on stress can be stressful. Hence the need for evaluating and creating self-care and stress management plans to help us long term in the profession.

Self-Care and Stress Management

Considering our discussion of life stressors, and stress or trauma response inclinations, we also must take heed to understand that stress management, or self-care, is a pivotal part of a CIT's process. Lack of stress management or self-care can impact dispositional competencies immensely, as offered earlier with a few CIT case examples. In fact, many of the dispositions are interconnected with self-care, such as professional behaviors, boundaries, emotional stability, and self-control (CCS-R, Lambie et al., 2016). According to the literature, when students do not take care of themselves in a variety of ways, they begin to make poor choices and slip in ethical integrity. In fact, self-care strategies appropriate to the counselor role are noted in the standards as well (CACREP, 2009, Section II, *Standard* 1. d.; CACREP, 2016, Section II, *Standard* 1. k.).

It is well known that working in the field of counseling poses a higher level of stress, including potential for vicarious trauma and burnout, considering the high number of clients seen, long work hours, and the ethical/legal emotionally charged situations counselors face (Moore & Cooper, 1996). Sapolsky (2004), in his extensive research on stress, stated "The first is that if you plan to get stressed like a normal mammal, dealing with an acute physical challenge, and you cannot appropriately turn on the stress response, you're in big trouble" (p. 15). In other words, without the stress response, our blood pressure can drop and we can easily go into shock since we need our bodies to turn on the stress response cycle to save our lives sometimes. Next Sapolsky stated "If you *repeatedly turn on* the stress response or if one *cannot turn off* the stress response at the end of the stressful event, the stress response can eventually become damaging" (p. 15).

Now, take the last section on trauma response and understanding of the wounded healer, and then apply that to this section on our stress responses, self-care, and the ability to implement intentional stress management and self-care. We recommend counselors find a valid and reliable self-stress assessment to gain a sense of their own personal stress levels and to be able to plan towards mitigating the negative effects of stress, keeping in mind that good things are considered stressful as well as challenging things. We present one model of stress management called the *Albee Incident Model* (Albee, 1982).

Within the Albee Incident Model there is a focus on primary prevention, community issues, systemic change, marginalized populations, and psychoeducation for emphasis. In terms of applying the model to CITs, we see that it can easily be used as a prevention tool due to its focus on individual change and the evaluation of stressors in the CIT training process, and it can be of value in any developmental growth process.

The first step is to consider implementing the stress assessment to understand if your stress is dysfunctional or if it is within the normal guidelines of health. The model asserts that there are organic factors in stress and these are divided into our coping skills, self-efficacy, and support. If we reduce the numerator factors such as organic factors, stressors, exploitation, and powerlessness, and increase our ability to cope, to find higher self-efficacy, seek additional supports, and gain personal empowerment, we are less likely to suffer negative aspects of stress and can cope more easily (Albee & Gullotta, 1997; Lewis, Lewis, Daniels, & D'Andrea, 2010). To equip CITs with a structure towards a stress management plan, they can evaluate the following factors from the Albee Incident Model:

Organic Factors: Genetics, environmental factors, substances, toxins, nutrition, disease.

- Consider factors that you may experience that are working against you such as medical conditions, preexisting conditions, genetic aspects, smoking, substances, toxin exposures, healthy diet or nutritional concerns, etc. These can work against you as biological stressors.

Stress: As mentioned, according to Selye (1936), stress is the body's response to demand for change (Rosch, 2017).

- This also includes *Distress*, which is considered bad stress, and *Eustress*, which is considered good stress. There is also acute stress and chronic stress. How we handle stress, i.e., being able to turn off the stress response cycle as mentioned by Sapolsky (2004), is pivotal.

Life events: consider our unique reactions to stress based on our worldviews, perceptions, and the meaning we place on these events.

- There are several sources of stress, especially for the CIT. Remember that "plate of life" activity we mentioned in Chapter 1? Reflect on your own plate while considering the following:
  - How much control or autonomy do you have in daily life? The higher the autonomy, the less stress is normally experienced.
  - Competitive type A personality? May be prone to higher stress levels.
  - Perfectionistic tendencies? May be tied to higher stress.
  - How well do you handle change?
  - Biopsychosocial aspects of stress to consider in your personal and professional life.
  - Consider taking a stress evaluation test to score your stress levels.

Coping Skills to Help Mitigate Stress on your Plan

SELF-CARE

- Consider a biopsychosocial spiritual self-care plan of things that you need to help take care of yourself.

  - Biologically – consider physical aspects such as diet, exercise, sleep hygiene, medications, supplements, vitamins, minerals, water intake, massage and physical aspects of stress management.
  - Psychologically – consider personal counseling, meditation, progressive relaxation, mindfulness, yoga, etc. (some of these are biological and psychological and spiritual).
  - Socially – consider your support. Friends, family, loved ones, colleagues, consultant supervisors, and community surrounding you as support. Consider attachment within the deep meaningful relationships that you have that are safe, and edifying.
  - Spiritually – consider if you have a faith, belief in a higher power, social cultural facets of spirituality, and prayer, meditation, etc.

- Forgiveness, acceptance, mindfulness, which are also Dialectical Behavioral Therapy (DBT) concepts, to help let go of things that cannot be controlled (Linehan, 2014).
- Competency, as we touch on later, too, leads to increased coping (Kenkel, 1986).

SELF-EFFICACY

- Consider building self-identity formation.
- Self-acceptance.
- Sense of competency (see the bike metaphor (Worksheet 2.11) and self-efficacy).
- Values, worldview ideas, thoughts, and beliefs can serve as a support against stress outside in the "world."

SOCIAL SUPPORTS

- Friendships, family, community.
- Sense of belonging, valued, meaningful connections.
- Meaningful contributions to something.
- Support from members in your social circle for your choice to engage in the counseling training process and encouragement in your growth process.

Summary

If you, as the CIT, take the time to review your own personal woundedness, stress responses, and then assess your overall stress levels, you can create a stress management self-care plan that can easily be implemented, both during your training and long into your professional future. Counselors are more vulnerable to higher levels of stress given the nature of their work; by using the Albee Incident Model, the CES can work with you to create a self-care plan that meets your unique individual needs, while also offering a long-term supportive plan. To continue to move forward as you learn to self-care and cope with life's challenges and stressors, now consider your conceptualization of the world as you lean into understanding your own counselor identity process.

Worldview

About 12 years ago, I (Dr. McLain) was flying with my 18-month-old daughter to visit family. I had learned early on to pack plenty of toys, crayons, and, of course, "Grandma's" brand of chocolate-chip cookies. We had our bag of cookies ready so that, when my little cherub awoke, I could bribe her into quiet, peaceful submission until we landed. I had been comfortably sitting by an older woman who was reading in the aisle seat. I had hoped my daughter would sleep until the landing so as not to disturb her, or anyone else for that matter. I happened to look for our bag of cookies when I thought it was about time for my daughter to wake from her nap. It was nowhere to be found. Annoyed, I fidgeted in my seat, looking in all three purses, bags, etc., to no avail. Suddenly, the woman sitting next to me opened our bag of cookies and literally started chomping down on them in front of us! A hundred thoughts and potential comments went through my brain as I saw my daughter's eyes start to flutter open with wide-eyed anxiousness. "Oh great!" I thought, no cookies and the lady next to us is eating them all when we needed them! I was about to confront the lady sitting next to us as she finished off the cookies, but my daughter distracted me by pointing out the window asking why the clouds were so thick. A few moments went by and we prepared for landing and I distracted my baby with toys as I sat grumpy in my seat. I am not sure why I didn't confront the woman except, I suppose, it was fate. As we landed and everyone began to exit the plane, there in the seat, under my daughter, was her bag of cookies. The same cookies the woman was eating as she must have had her own bag of the exact same cookies. Thank God I did not yell at her because, despite my thinking she was a selfish cookie thief, I was wrong . . . and my worldview was then shifted from what it had been prior to finding the "truth" that was hidden to me during the plane ride.

That is an example of a person's worldview and how quickly it may change when confronted with a different paradigm. Worldview is a philosophy of life or a conception of the world. It is defined by the following three sources as:

"A comprehensive conception or apprehension of the world especially from a specific standpoint" ("Worldview" (Collins), 2017).

"A person's world view is the way a person sees and understands the world" ("World View" (Collins), 2017).

"A person's worldview will determine his/her attitudes towards life and death. They also provide a worldview – a way of discerning right from wrong, good from bad" ("Worldview" (Merriam-Webster) 2017).

So why is a worldview imperative for CIT training? In terms of having an orientation to where we begin, it is foundational to understand each of our unique, culturally diverse worldviews. For example, I immediately assumed the woman sitting next to me had stolen my daughter's cookies. I was forming a biased judgment based on what I saw, how I had experienced others, and, likely due to past experiences, perhaps some of which I didn't even recall in that moment. This experience was the way I viewed the world. Is the world safe? Are people assumed to be honest, good, and truthful? When we interact with others we naturally experience an integration or collision of worldviews. To establish a counselor professional identity, we first must define and understand our own worldview. Next, we see how worldview influences us and how our life experiences influence our worldview. Consider the following in application to self-understanding and worldview.

- Everything you create is a self-portrait. Consider poetry, writing, art, home reno-vation projects, hobbies, music, teaching, parenting, ideas, values, etc. that are communicated in numerous ways.
- Everything you have experienced contributes to the formation of your worldview, including suffering, celebrations, experiences of "otherness," etc. and how this relates to your desire to be a counselor.
- Nature/nurture: What comes first, the chicken or the egg?
- Everything you say and do is a representation of who you are and of your world-view; every reaction you have projects your worldview into the world.
- Does your behavior always represent your worldview accurately?
- What if your worldview is skewed?
- Our worldview is constantly changing and evolving based on continuous personal life experiences.
- Consider how your personal worldview influences your conceptualization of fac-tors covered in the first sections of this chapter.

Now try this worldview activity. Draw a circle on a piece of paper representing your world or use the blank quartered circle in Worksheet 2.9 in Appendix 1. You may benefit from using a paper plate as a circular visual guide as well. Now divide the circle in half both vertically and horizontally. Next, label each section in turn "biological," "social/cultural," "psychological," and "spiritual." Engel (1977) identified a biopsy-chosocial model which was integrated into our Universal Growth Model through the application of the quartered circle template (Rigg, 2017). For each of these categories, consider the following examples of one's thoughts, ideas, beliefs, biases, values, experi-ences of self, others, and the world.

Biological: Ideas, Values, Thoughts, Beliefs

The Biological worldview includes ideas, values, thoughts and beliefs about our selves: our own body, self in addition to the human body, sexuality, birth, disease, medical, genetics, medicine, treatment, nutrition, science, origin of life, death, etc. An example of Biological worldview: "I believe that mental illness has a genetic factor."

Social/Cultural: Ideas, Values, Thoughts, Beliefs

The Social/Cultural worldview includes ideas, values, thoughts and beliefs about our own lives, in addition to their application to others in terms of: Family, com-munity, culture, ethnicity, biases, tradition, prejudice, privilege, socioeconomics, politics, government, freedom, moral and ethical standards. An example of Social/

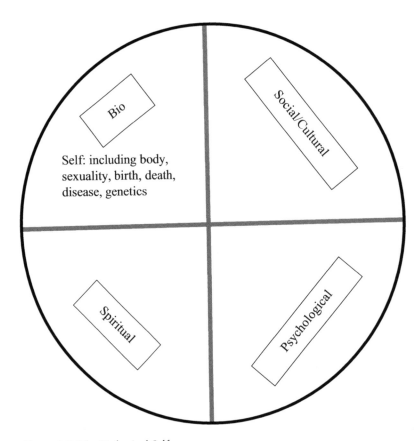

Figure 2.3 The Biological Self.

(Source: modified by the authors with permission from Rigg, 2017.)

Cultural worldview: "I believe that all people are born into privilege and prejudice of some nature; without connecting with others, we will never dispel injustices we have experienced."

Psychological: Ideas, Values, Thoughts, Beliefs

The Psychological worldview includes ideas, values, thoughts and beliefs about our own psychological thoughts, feelings, ideas, fears, concerns, anxieties, passions, understandings. Also, about the brain, cognitive, affective, science of the mind, dreams, thinking, behaviors, morality, ethical standards, etc. An example of Psychological worldview: "I believe that a child growing up in a home with authoritarian parents will most likely rebel."

Spiritual: Ideas, Values, Thoughts, Beliefs

The Spiritual worldview includes ideas, values, thoughts and beliefs about a Higher Power, religion, spirituality, relationship with God, creation, identity, life, death,

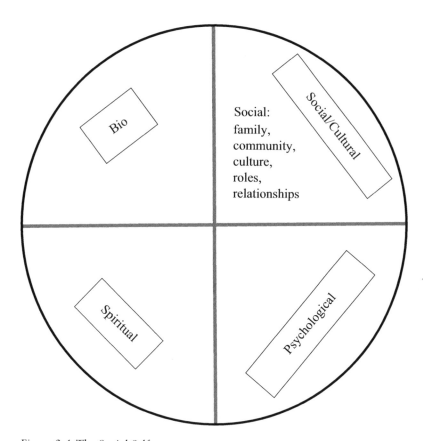

Figure 2.4 The Social Self.

(Source: modified by the authors with permission from Rigg, 2017.)

human condition, meaning, purpose in life, ideas about good, evil, freedom, moral and ethical standards. Spirituality, or a relationship with a Higher Power of any kind can be a deep and meaningful part of identity, including counselor identity, and impacts all the work with clients in the future. According to the Association of Spiritual, Ethical and Religious Values in Counseling (ASERVIC), we, as counselors, should pay attention to the value of considering spiritual facets of life (ASERVIC, 2018). An example of Spiritual worldview: "I believe that Jesus Christ came, lived, died for all humanity's sins and that, because of this, there is hope and healing for all who believe in Him."

Additional Activities to Consider Worldview

(See Worksheet 2.10 in Appendix 1.)

- After attending or experiencing a life rite of passage such as a birth, death, marriage, etc., reflect on any new integration of values, beliefs, experiences, etc., that may contribute to a new understanding. Compare and contrast the changes and consider how you have changed your view following the event.

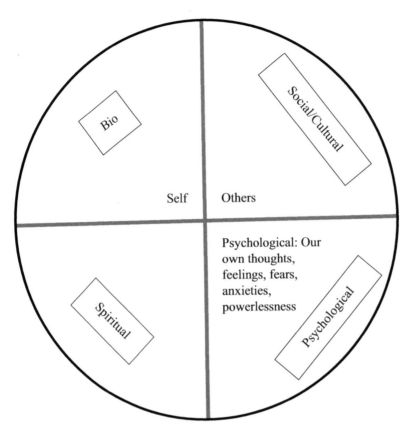

Figure 2.5 The Psychological Self.

(Source: modified by the authors with permission from Rigg, 2017.)

- Review old movies/music that you listened to or watched from various developmental stages. Review Erikson's stages of development (Erikson, 1963) for significant junctures in your development. How do those modalities strike you today?
- Consider a current headline in the news. What do you believe about the news event/article and why? Explore what others who hold opposing beliefs about the headline think and consider where are they coming from. Why do they hold the belief they have?
- Choose to have a conversation with someone who has a completely opposite point of view than yourself on a subject matter. Challenge yourself to stay present in the moment, listen for clarity in their understanding of the topic, and take notes pointing to the three main themes of what they believe and why. Afterwards, ask them if you captured an accurate understanding of what they believe.

Learning to Drive a Car Metaphor 1

Learning a monumental task early on in life can offer us a glimpse into reflection on our experiences in the world that, in turn, lead to our worldview. Consider when you first learned to drive a car. Here is one example:

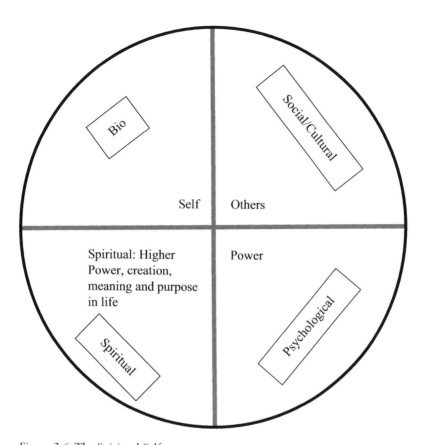

Figure 2.6 The Spiritual Self.

(Source: modified by the authors with permission from Rigg, 2017.)

I (Dr. McLain) was 15 years old and living on a rural farm of 25 acres. My dad was always working on old cars and trucks, and my grandparents even had a heated garage with a full drive-on hoist to work on cars. From an early age I was aware of cars, but, alas, when my dad relayed to me "it was time to learn to drive a car," I panicked. I suppose it was the blatant reality of responsibility that scared me most. The idea of breaking the car, crashing it, hurting someone or myself was most frightful to me. Next was the thought of my father teaching me. Yikes. He had little patience and was always right. How could I learn in such an environment! I was already petrified of "messing up," let alone with him as my "teacher!" At any rate, I allowed him to go with me on my first drive. He yelled, screamed, and ordered me, with a hint of frustration and impatience in his voice the entire time. Finally, I was able to master the task enough for him to say, "you'll be fine in driver's training." When no one was around, I took the 77 Impala out in our field and learned to really drive; then I began driving short distances down the road to my friend's farm and that is how I learned to drive! How funny because, as I relay this story, it reminds me of when my cousin taught me to snowboard in Breckenridge, Colorado, for the first time around the age of 19. I was hoping to get off the ski lift and just take my sweet time learning to balance on the board slowly coming down, say, a green or blue hill, but, NOPE! He attempted to lead me down

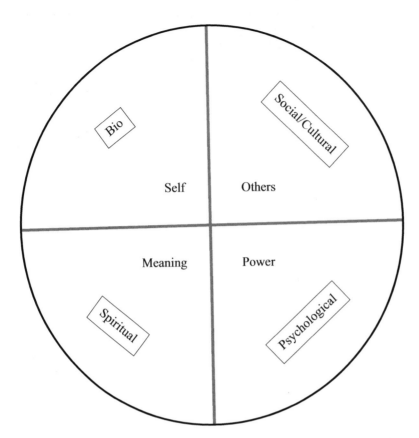

Figure 2.7 The Whole Self.

scary steep black runs while yelling at me the entire time. I remember thinking how frightening it was that I was on such steep runs and could barely stay on my snowboard, let alone fly down while his anger and rushing me was intolerable. Once again, I could sense the frustration, impatience, and annoyance with my horrible skill level at snowboarding, and, of course, being trained by a cousin who was "a professional" didn't help! Funny, I learned back then that just because you are an expert at something doesn't mean you're a great teacher at it! Well, truth be told, I attempted to take breaks, rest my knees (from falling nonstop), and wanted him to go down without me so I could be alone and get the feel of it while watching others around me. It wasn't until I was left alone, to observe, practice, fall, and make mistakes without immense scrutiny, that I mastered my way down the hill, staying on the board. Now I was having fun!

So, as you think back to either learning to drive a car or learning a fascinating tough sport of some kind, what comes to mind for you? Consider my responses to the following questions as an example to guide you.

• What does *my* (Dr. McLain's) learning to drive and ride a snowboard story mean to me?

I see a theme in both stories of my needing to learn alone without pressure, impatience and hurrying. I see that, in both examples, I was fearful and it was compounded by my own fear of failure. I think it was a cycle of being given critical, condescending, feedback while under pressure, and being assessed in a non-supportive way. I wasn't told what I was doing "right," just everything I seemed to get "wrong." I knew what I was doing wrong without being told so, I figured, I could learn on my own. I think I took this with me all the way to graduate school because often I was afraid of being "on the spot" in front of others when trying to perform. Perhaps I assumed my teachers and peers would do the same as my dad and cousin had, and I just wanted to be alone to learn despite that being impossible in clinical mental health. I was finally able to challenge my worldview when I encountered instructors who were supportive and took their time in teaching me. My worldview pointed towards feedback as being scary, negative, and performance having to be pressured and perfect without room for any mistakes. I also learned early on that because someone is a *master* at something does not mean they are a good teacher of it. It made me want to truly understand how to be a good teacher.

- Who were the key players involved besides myself?

  In my story, my dad was involved in the learning to drive a car and my older male cousin was involved in the learning to ride a snowboard. I have since noticed that it can be more difficult for me to accept feedback from older males in positions of authority. In learning something scary, the world was a scary place, and my belief was there were no gentle teachers, perfection was demanded, and failure was to be feared more than anything else.

- What ideas, thoughts, and feelings might I have about this experience as it relates to others, myself, and the world?

  I have come a long way since these two learning experiences, but I see how these experiences demonstrate an existing worldview (thoughts, ideas, beliefs about self, others, and the world) and how they have also contributed to the altering of my worldview. Ironically enough, processing, reflecting and healing through these experiences has shifted my worldview again! I see that perhaps my dad and cousin had good intentions to teach me, but my learning style and needs did not match their teaching style and, for me, I need a safe, slow, gentle space where mistakes and imperfection are welcome to help me learn and grow to be the best I can be. From these experiences I also have incorporated this notion into my own counselor teaching and supervisory philosophy.

Learning to Drive a Car Metaphor 2

I (Dr. Lewis) looked forward to learning to drive and gaining freedom in the process more than anything else in life! That was the major transition to being mature. At least, it was in my mind, and in just about any other teenager's! When it was my turn, all my siblings were out of the house. My oldest brother was on his own and married, and the next two were out of state at college. My middle brother had worked in a garage, and found, I believe, a 1952 Mercedes Benz 150 SL convertible to restore, and he had done an awesome job! He left it at home for our mom to use, and since it had a stick shift (four on the floor! How lucky can one teenager get!?), that was the vehicle my mother wanted me to learn on, saying "If you can drive a stick, you can drive anything." After what seemed forever of "finding my wheels," as she said, by driving back and forth to match my front tires with where she was standing, without running her down, and doing the same for the back wheels, we started venturing. My mother is a teacher. She generally has some pretty good tolerance, and, by then, I at least knew how to steer from the surreptitious practice done with friends and one time with a "dirty old man school bus driver." Outside of Philadelphia, PA, there were lots of hills. She drove me to one that went straight up into heaven. It had to be close to a 90° angle, with a crossroad at the bottom and a stop sign. I had to wait for the crossroad to be clear, and then make it up that huge hill with a stick shift. I gunned that engine when it was clear, let the clutch out, and flew up that hill. I noticed in the corner of my eye that my mother was trying desperately to get her door open and jump out of the car! To this day, that vision makes me laugh! I think she was more scared than I was, and ready to bail out! Once we got to the top, I found a place to turn around, and then had to go back down. She taught me to use the gears to help me slow down, and in our Rocky Mountains I use the same technique to this day for mountain driving. I never went back to that hill, and I'll bet she didn't either. One and done was good enough. What's the theme? O, help me, but it is Admiral David Farragut's exclamation in the Battle of Mobile Bay (1864) in the Civil War: "Damn the torpedoes, full speed ahead!"

My mother continued to support me as I ran headlong, with the accelerator to the floor, into various careers and opportunities that seemed to appear in front of me, like that hill. I didn't have any idea where we were going, or why, but I followed the road until the hill was in front of me. That's how I wound up doing so many fun and exciting jobs that challenged me and helped me grow in the breadth of experiences. From being a law enforcement officer to an entrepreneur, my life's journey has been replete with exciting options, which often stretched me to the very limits of my abilities.

- What does *my* (Dr. Lewis) learning to drive story mean to me?

  I had new insights as I wrote this story. My mom and I went on many adventures and made some exciting discoveries. She had the knack of getting lost for about an hour, driving around and we would discover some new part of our world together. She gave me my spirit of adventure and I learned not to panic when I was lost. I would find myself in about an hour. She gave me the courage to step into new contexts and see what I could discover. I often use the terminology that life is an adventure, and I think that's where I got that from. We also had a rather symbiotic relationship for some years, where I could actually feel her pain. As an adult, I was able to individuate, but, as a child, I was a cling-on with my mom. She knew everything there was to know, from the obvious to the obscure, and I loved learning from her.

- Who were the key players involved besides myself?

  Obviously, my mom was a big part of this story and was clearly a key player. However, my mom was not always predictable. Our relationship has changed dramatically because she is deep into Alzheimer's at her over 90 years of age. She still knows my voice and my laugh, which is a good thing. The relationship that was at times contentious, has become, more often than not, a love fest on the phone with each other. However, there are times when "hot and cold running mother" shows up, and I am instantly transported to that child who was so confused about "what was wrong with mom?" She had a streak, and, as my beloved stepdad said, "a mean left hook" when that persona took over. So, navigating the unknown may have been a key to my tolerating ambiguity. Another key player was my biological dad, who I did not meet until I was 21 years old. His absence in my life played a role in my relationship with my mom, for I always knew she had loved him deeply before he betrayed her trust. I was often accused of being "too trusting" of others. My first husband once said that one day, that it would come back to bite me, and it was he who took the first bite. I learned that I had a choice: to trust or not to trust. I chose to trust first; unless I was proven wrong, I would see the best in people before I would look for the worst.

- What ideas, thoughts, and feelings might I have about this experience as it relates to others, myself, and the world?

  I did embrace the life as an adventure option, which tends to give me a positive outlook on life. Having been called a Pollyanna, who always looks for the good in people and in situations, I see that my perspective has been a lifelong one. I love to learn new things and tend to seek them out. I am trusting until proven wrong, and then I am done with that situation or person. While I can forgive, I don't need to expose myself to toxicity. These and other experiences, relationships, and opportunities all shaped my worldview. While my earlier naiveté has been matured, my basic view is that the world is an exciting place to be and a dangerous place, but perseverance and hard work will get me through whatever is placed before me. The challenges can be conquered, and my survival rate is high. Well, so far, anyway!

  (See Worksheet 2.11, Riding a Bike or
  Driving a Car, in Appendix 1.)

As an additional worldview activity try the "How I learned to ride a bike" metaphor. Think back to a time when you were younger and learned to ride a bike. What was that experience like for you and who helped you? Did anyone watch and cheer you on? What are the three most significant things that stand out in your memory about this experience? How did you feel after you mastered it? Consider how this experience applies to other things you have learned to master in life and describe the similarities or differences in the experience. How did this experience shape aspects of your worldview or values, your ideas and thoughts about self, others and the world? (Use the same worksheet, Worksheet 2.11, Riding a Bike or Driving a Car.)

1 Consider exploring your worldview with your CES by considering art, literature, film, or music, or examples from Chapters 2 and 5.
2 Consider asking your CES to share other examples from a biopsychosocial and spiritual perspective as well.
3 Finally, consider integrating aspects of critical thinking in evaluating your ability to use the metaphor while exploring your worldview.

Discovering a Personal CIT Identity

If worldview informs everything we think, believe, and do to some degree or another, then how might worldview impact your counselor identity statement? A counselor identity statement can be a statement about who you are as a counselor. It often includes professional and personal beliefs, commitments, understanding, and operational definitions of role and responsibilities. Often, one of the first assignments a CIT has is to consider what inspired them to want to be a counselor and to pursue this training. Some common responses from CITs may include:

- I have always been drawn to helping others;
- I am often told I am a good listener;
- People say that I have empathy and understanding;
- I have a personality that seeks to know about people and to help them discover things about themselves;
- I believe in online or in-seat education/training;
- I believe that technology has pros and cons and must be used with caution and great responsibility;
- My friends all come to me with their problems and say I should be a counselor.

Here is a great place to start with your CES, to reflect yourself on why you specifically chose the field of counseling, and to reflect on your natural gifts and tendencies towards the role of counselor. In this be sure to explore the following and share with your CES:

1 What is the function, role, and mission of the clinical mental health counselor?
2 What licensure, training, and credentials must a counselor have to be ethically able to work as a professional in the field?
3 What is the difference between a counselor and, say, a social worker, psychologist, or life coach, and why?
4 Who are some of the founding fathers and mothers of the clinical counseling field and what are the core foundational philosophical elements that have helped form the counseling field?
5 What is the American Counseling Association? What benefits are there to joining?
6 What is the Council for Accreditation of Counseling and Related Educational Programs (CACREP) and why do they matter?
7 How does my original mission for pursuing this field align with my research on the preceding questions? (See Worksheet 2.12 Why Counseling? in Appendix 1.)

McLeod (2014) wrote:

> According to Jung, the ego represents the conscious mind as it comprises the thoughts, memories, and emotions of which a person is aware. The ego is largely responsible for feelings of identity and continuity. Like Freud, Jung (1921, 1933) emphasized the importance of the unconscious in relation to personality. (Paras 6–8.)

The unconscious part of our identity comes through our creativity. Unconsciously, when we create anything – a meal, a piece of art, a poem, an idea, or even a conversation – it is often the result of unconscious definitions of who we are. The ego is the part of the personality that is conscious. In considering our own worldview and counselor identity, it is important for a CIT to take a moment to consider the following questions.

- Review your personal beliefs and values (worldview) from this chapter.
- What are your personal attributes/strengths?
- What are the current roles in which you serve? Mother, father, husband, wife, advocate, teacher volunteer, etc.
- Why did you enter the field to begin with? Here, it is important to explore what led you to becoming a counselor, and to believing this was your calling or the fulfillment of your dream, including how this ties into your worldview.
- Reflect on the mentors and influences that helped shape your experiences. Who was the most influential teacher or mentor you had throughout your life?
- Explore the personal goals that you have for yourself and how you can contribute to social change in mental health/counseling.
- Where do you personally fit into the role of counselor, the field and your responsibilities as a CIT?

(See Worksheet 2.13 Review and Reflect, in Appendix 1.)

Steps to Creating a CIT Identity Statement

Now we look at how to construct your foundational draft of your Counselor Professional Identity Statement. Remember that this will grow and change throughout your career but this can help you in your foundational developmental process.

1 **Defining Your Role**: Student, intern, practitioner—and your audience (who are you serving?).
2 **Defining Who You Are**: The credentials you have or the ones you hope to obtain. Consider developmentally where you are at currently in your process. Student, intern, CIT, graduated and accruing hours, licensed, licensed and seasoned, supervising, etc.
3 **Defining What You Do**: Each field has a unique title and perspective. For instance, counseling is a "professional relationship that empowers diverse individuals, families, and groups to accomplish mental health, wellness, education and career goals" (Kaplan, Tarvydas, & Gladding, 2014, p. 366). Mellin, Hunt, and Nichols (2011) remarked that "scholars have argued that counseling can be distinguished from related vocations because of its development, prevention, and wellness orientation towards helping" (p. 140). Furthermore, Burns and Cruikshanks (2017) stated that "normal development, prevention, wellness advocacy and empowerment are unique hallmarks of counseling" (p. 69). By looking at other professions, such as Social Work, Psychology, etc., find out what makes the identity you embrace unique, and what the perspective is for that viewpoint.
4 **Defining Where You Work**: Clinical Mental Health Counselor, Rehabilitation Counselor, School Counselor, Career Counselor, etc. A counselor's identity can include cultural aspects such as their geographic region, setting, community, etc.
5 **Defining Your Focus of Practice**: What is your current or future scope of practice? Drug and Alcohol, School Counselor, Trauma specialist, etc. Define the services you want to offer in your role and perhaps the population you hope to serve. Clinicians and CITs must know their state laws, board requirements, certification/

licensing standards of practice, etc. for any state in which they may wish to practice. Consider ongoing opportunities for specialized training including continuing education, research projects, presentations, and even field experience serving in the area chosen. What population do you serve?

6   **Defining Your Orientation**: What unique attributes, skills, and specialist competencies do you have or may need? Which theoretical perspective(s) do you embrace or are curious to explore in more detail?

7   **Defining Why You?** First, you may need to begin by establishing credibility. Some ideas include graduating from CACREP program and reviewing the standards, ascribing to the ACA *Code of Ethics* (2014) standards, advocacy, honor society membership, additional continuing educational training, supervision, or experience, and evaluating the other ACA areas of competencies.

Activities for CIT Identity:

- Identity statement paragraph;
- include elements of worldview;
- include ethical standards and decision-making guidelines;
- include roles/responsibilities as a counselor;
- include larger social cultural aspects.

(See Worksheet 2.14 in Appendix 1.)

Philosophy of CIT Identity

The word philosophy originates from the Greek term *philosophia*, which, literally translated, means a love of wisdom. To love wisdom, we must be awake, asking questions, and thinking actively with critical and creative thinking. Consider the song from the band Twenty One Pilots, written by Tyler Joseph for the song *Car Radio* on the album *Regional at Best*: I will describe what I gather from the song each time I hear it. Faith is important to the songwriter and to me and there is the idea of being awake in the world with faith and there is also the contrast of being asleep in the world or dead while walking around and living here. We have a choice to make, to be fully alive and awake or to be walking zombies. For me, having faith means having to be awake and being awake involves thinking, feeling, and fully being. It involves creating art, painting, singing, or even writing this book. The songwriter in this case is making a statement that in his music he is adamantly attempting to get us all to wake up and think! And so he is not ashamed in being authentic, needy, and even hysterical to convey the passion he has for us all to wake up and think. We can analyze his worldview from this and even my own worldview in noting common themes of important value such as:

- Faith
- Cognition
- Feeling alive
- Ability to reason
- Passion
- Freedom of artistic expression
- Responsibility to fellow humanity to share truth and help others.

Activities for Philosophy of CIT Identity

- According to the summary above, what other things might the songwriter, myself, or you value or believe in our worldview and philosophy of life?
- How might you relate to these words or compare and contrast them to your own worldview ideas?
- Choose your own favorite poem, short story or song and consider the lyrics and words and how they represent your own worldview, philosophy of living, or even counselor identity traits.
- Consider how worldview, philosophy of life, and beliefs and understandings in counseling, education and prior supervision may impact your CIT philosophy and identity statement.
- In a statement or two, what is your philosophy of counseling? What is a counselor and their purpose? What is your personal belief in your role and responsibility to clients in the field?
- What is your philosophy concerning the online format and the use of technology, or bricks and mortar schooling?
- In a statement or two, what is your philosophy of life? One example is "Hakuna Matata" which means "no worries."

(See Worksheet 2.15 in Appendix 1.)

Summary

In summary, evaluating our worldview as CITs while integrating it towards understanding one's counselor identity and philosophy of counseling is a pivotal foundational starting point for taking responsibility for your own professional development. At the end of the day, it is only you as the CIT who is responsible for ensuring you learn the skills, knowledge and dispositions necessary to be competent, ethical and to excel in your work within the field. Next, we will discuss additional self-assessment tools towards helping your personal and professional self-exploration process.

Myers Briggs Type Indicator

The Myers Briggs Type Indicator (MBTI) is a great self-assessment tool that CITs may also benefit from. In addition to the basic MBTI, there is a Conflict Style Analysis, which can provide useful understanding of features of the personalities and how they may interact in a setting, written by Damien Killen and Danica Murphy, available from CPP publishers (Killen & Murphy, 2003). In applying the purpose of the MBTI, the CIT can learn about their communication preferences in order to understand how to work well with colleagues, peers, faculty, and supervisors alike. What appears to be random variation in our behaviors is in fact orderly and consistent due to the scientific ways in which individuals prefer to use their perception and judgement.

The CIT must be aware that the assessment is looking at perception and judgement, which aligns with our foundational worldview and core underlying philosophy of counseling. A CIT should review their worldview information prior to exploring the MBTI as this can be most helpful. There are 16 distinctive personality types that result from the interactions among the preferences that an individual operates from given their worldview, personality, and tendencies towards these preferences.

Consider where you are in your counselor developmental journey in terms of what to apply. Those CITs who are near to taking the Career Development class may benefit from taking the full MBTI as it is often required for coursework. In addition, if you have already had the Career Development course, reviewing your formal results from the assessment may be a fantastic way to explore, self-assess, reflect, and add additional assignments towards self-understanding as well. Finally, if you are a postgraduate, you may have taken the assessment and can consider reviewing your results in supervision as a terrific way to initiate a new level of developmental understanding with the existing data.

If you would like a fun quick way of applying this assignment you can also use the human metrics Jungian Typology assessment (see Appendix 2: Resources), which is free online, or seek the full MBTI if you have access to this.

After you have taken the assessment, you can go over the following areas of discussion:

- What are your preferences and percentages? Explore the summary reflection in the assessment tool with your CES.
- What are the type descriptions that go along with your results? Do you agree or disagree, and why?
- These are all preferences and there are no right or wrong types or combinations. However, what do you see as your greatest strengths and potential weaknesses in terms of communication in evaluating and reflecting on your type?
- What are some key indicators to keep in mind after reviewing your type?
- What are some thoughts about who you work with daily considering your type?
- How might your data and the descriptions help you better understand yourself?
- How might you combine this activity with others such as the Johari Window, worldview exploration or others to reflect further and deeper on your self-growth?
(See Worksheet 2.16 Applying MBTI in Appendix 1.)

In addition to understanding your preferences, you may also enjoy exploring your ability to manage conflict and to consider how you navigate these areas in your current world.

Conflict Management Model

Conflict management model research and assessment may be a beneficial tool for CITs to consider reviewing as well, particularly the unique work of Thomas and Kilmann (1977) and their *Conflict Mode Instrument*. The instrument is available on the official website, with a limit of one assessment per person or it can be purchased. The focus is to complete an assessment that will identify which of five possible styles the person taking the assessment has when dealing with conflict. The results have a range of high to low importance in relationships, and high to low importance of goals. The five styles are as follows and may be represented by the corresponding animals:

- high assertive/low cooperative: Competing win–lose (Shark);
- low assertive/high cooperative: Collaboration win–win (Owl);
- low assertive/low cooperative: Avoiding lose–lose (Turtle);

- low assertive/high cooperative: Accommodating lose–win (Teddy Bear);
- center of the model: Compromising: partial win–partial lose (Fox) (this is the ideal conflict style and one that many aim to achieve). (Thomas & Kilmann, 1977)

The application of this model is helpful when working with other individuals, and helpful when working with groups or teams. Using this model to understand the basic styles of those who are involved in conflict may be helpful as CES and CITs are working to resolve issues together.

Summary

Looking at Self is the first step to understanding if you have IT, meaning the ability to build, grow, and be competent in professional behaviors and dispositions. The topic may have left you with even more questions by the end of the chapter and that is actually wonderful! The reality is, your CES is assessing you, giving you feedback, and helping assist you in your growth process so, as long as you remain eager to learn, desire growth, and are able to utilize your self-assessment tools and hear and implement feedback, you will succeed. In Chapter 3 we will review how this supervisory relationship can assist you as we explore the next quadrant of Relationships. Keep in mind that these tools are valid throughout your program and lifelong professional development as you self-assess and continue to receive assessment from others as well.

Application

Growth is always a choice. We must determine our commitment to change and growth, and, perhaps by looking into the future a bit further, we can see the advantages in front of us. You are in this profession because something drove you to it; you have a desire to help others, perhaps based on how much you were helped. This is a heavy mantle to wear as the risks are high. Should there be a fixed mindset, meaning that you are convinced that you have nothing new to learn, then your longevity in the profession may be severely compromised. Is it possible for you to embrace opportunities for healthy growth? What does that look like? It is our (the authors') opinion that the most critical paradigm to embrace is one in which continuous growth is sought after, and it occurs.

Being open to opportunities for growth means that we must embrace our humility. We must believe that there is more for us to learn, more skills to hone, more insights to gain, and that the combination of all those things will result in our expertise, efficacy, and deep understanding as we mature in the profession. What are the risks if we have a fixed mindset? The potential for everything from harming clients to losing a license we have spent a lot of time and money gaining is possible. When we have choices to make, do we make the right choices? Are shortcuts more important than gaining the true understanding of our craft? These are questions to consider each and every time you have a conundrum in front of you.

I (Dr. Lewis) have had the pleasure of walking in a meditative labyrinth, which allowed me to focus my thoughts about what the best course of action was for a particularly puzzling situation. Generally, it all comes down to the bottom line: how will this benefit others, the profession, and me? How will it harm others, the profession, and me? Consider carefully before making a decision that may seem a quick fix, but that you truly know in your heart it is wrong. Yes, as humans, we can quite readily justify our choices; however, inside of us, we know right from wrong. Don't take the easy way as that generally leads to another similar choice, and then another and, before you know it, you have stepped so far out of the professional boundaries that, when confronted, there is no justification.

One of my professors had been the Executive Director of the licensing entity in that state. Ironically, I had him for an ethics class. He commented that, in his research, the typical offender in mental health was a middle-aged male who had been in practice for 20 years. I had to puzzle that out; why would that be? It was because he got comfortable in his own world of justification. He stopped reading the ACA *Code of Ethics* every six months as recommended. He walked so far out of the labyrinth, and justified every step away from the circle, that by time he realized where he was, it was too late. He lost everything, and, sometimes, he even went to prison. And it all started with one decision that pushed the ethical boundaries. I used to tell my children that a huge mess started with one thing out of place. Don't take that one step over the line.

References

Ahuna, K. H., Tinnesz, C. G., & Kiener, M. (2014). A new era of critical thinking in professional programs. *Transformative Dialogues: Teaching and Learning Journal* 7(3), 1–9.

Albee, G. W. (1982). Preventing psychopathology and promoting human potential. *American Psychologist, 37*(9), 1043–1050.

Albee, G. W., & Gullotta, T. P. (1997). *Primary prevention works*. Thousand Oaks, CA: Sage Publications.

Ambiguity (2017). In *Merriam-Webster's online dictionary*. Retrieved from: www.merriam-webster.com/dictionary/ambiguity.

American Counseling Association (ACA) (2014). *Code of ethics*. Alexandria, VA: American Counseling Association.

American Counseling Association (ACA) (2015). *Multicultural and social justice counseling competencies*. Alexandria, VA: American Counseling Association.

Anderson, A. R. (2013). Good employees make mistakes: Great leaders allow them to. *Forbes*, April 17. Retrieved from: www.forbes.com/sites/amyanderson/2013/04/17/good-employees-make-mistakes-great-leaders-allow-them-to/#1367f604126a.

Association for Spiritual, Ethical and Religious Values in Counseling (ASERVIC) (2018). *Competencies for addressing spiritual and religious issues in counseling*. Retrieved from: www.aservic.org/resources/spiritual-competencies.

Barr, A. (2006). *An investigation into the extent to which psychological wounds inspire counselors and psychotherapists to become wounded healers, the significance of these wounds on their career choice, the causes of these wounds, and the overall significance of demographic factors*. Retrieved from: www.thegreenrooms.net/wounded-healer.

Berne, E. (2011). *Games people play: The basic handbook of transactional analysis* [Kindle edition]. Retrieved from: www.amazon.com/Games-People-Play-Eric-Berne-ebook/dp/B005C6E76U/ref=sr_1_1?ie=UTF8&qid=1514049297&sr=8-1&keywords=Games+people+play.

Beyer, B. (1987). Practical strategies for the teaching of thinking. Boston, MA: Allyn and Bacon.

Bronfenbrenner, U. (1979). *The ecology of human development: Experiments by nature and design*. Cambridge, MA: Harvard University Press.

Brown-Rice, K. A., & Furr, S. (2013). Preservice counselors' knowledge of classmates' problems of professional competency. *Journal of Counseling and Development, 91*(2), 224–233.

Burns, S., & Cruikshanks, D. R. (2017). Evaluating independently licensed counselors' articulation of professional identity using structural coding. *The Professional Counselor, 7*(2), 185–207, doi: 10.15241/sb.7.2.185.

Christensen, J. (2016). A critical reflection of Bronfenbrenner's development ecology model. *Problems of Education in the 21st Century, 69,* 22–28.

Compassion (2017). *Merriam-Webster's online dictionary.* Retrieved from: www.merriam-webster.com/dictionary/compassion.

Council for Accreditation of Counseling and Related Educational Programs (CACREP) (2015). *2016 CACREP standards.* Alexandria, VA: Council for Accreditation of Counseling and Related Educational Programs.

Decety, J., & Ickes, W. (Eds) (2011). *The social neuroscience of empathy.* Cambridge, MA: The MIT Press.

Elder, L. (2010). *Richard W. Elder: Biographical information.* Retrieved from: www.critical thinking.org/files/Richard%20Paul%20Biographical%20Information.pdf.

Engel, G. L. (1977). The need for a new medical model: A challenge for biomedicine. *Science, 196*(4286), 129–136.

Erikson, E. H. (1963). *Childhood and society.* New York, NY: W. W. Norton & Company.

Faber, D. C., & Gray, M. J. (2012). Evaluation of a program designed to facilitate understanding of veterans' post-combat adjustment and reintegration: Pilot study of the Faber Post-Trauma Model. *Journal of Depression and Anxiety, 1*(4), 1–4, doi: 10.4172/2167-1044.1000121.

Facione, P. A., Facione, N. C., & Giancarlo, C. A. F. (1998). *The California critical thinking disposition inventory.* San Diego, CA: Academic Press.

Gaubatz, M. D., & Vera, E. M. (2002). Do formalized gatekeeping procedures increase programs' follow-up with deficient trainees? *Counselor Education and Supervision, 41*(4), 294–305.

Harris, J. I., Erbes, C. R., Engdahl, B. E., Tedeschi, R. G., Olson, R. H., Winskowskiu, A. M., & McMahill, J. (2010). Coping functions of prayer and posttraumatic growth. *The International Journal for the Psychology of Religion, 20*(1), 26–38, doi: 10.1080/105086100903418103.

Heppner, P. P., & Petersen, C. H. (1982). The development and implications of a personal problem-solving inventory. *Journal of Counseling Psychology, 29*(1), 66–75.

Jones, E., & Ratcliff, G. (1993). *Critical thinking skills for college students* (Report No. R117G10037). Washington, DC: Office of Educational Research and Improvement. Retrieved from: https://files.eric.ed.gov/fulltext/ED358772.pdf

Joyce, W., & del Toro, G. (Producers), & Ramsey, P. (Director) (2012). *The rise of the guardians* [Motion picture]. Glendale, CA: DreamWorks Studio.

Kaplan, D. M., Tarvydas, V. M., & Gladding, S. T. (2014). 20/20: A vision for the future of counseling: The new consensus definition of counseling. *Journal of Counseling & Development, 92*(3), 366–372. Retrieved from: www.counseling.org/docs/default-source/20-20/2020-jcd-article.pdf?sfvrsn=2.

Kenkel, M. B. (1986). Stress-coping-support in rural communities: A model for primary prevention. *American Journal of Community Psychology, 14*(5), 457–478.

Kerr, J. (1993). *A most dangerous method: The story of Jung, Freud, and Sabina.* New York, NY: Random House.

Killen, D., & Murphy, D. (2003). *MBTI conflict management program.* Mountain View, CA: CPP, Inc.

Knowles, M. (1980). *The modern practice of adult education.* Englewood Cliffs, NJ: Prentice Hall.

Kubler-Ross, E. (1969). *On death and dying: What the dying have to teach doctors, nurses, clergy & their own families.* New York, NY: The Macmillan Company.

Lambie, G., Mullen, P., Swank, J., & Blount, A. (2016). *Counseling Competencies Scale, Revised (CCS-R).* Orlando, FL: University of Central Florida, Counselor Education Program. Retrieved from: http://webmedia.jcu.edu/counselingdepartment/files/2016/03/CCS-R-Evaluation.pdf.

Lewis, J. A., Lewis, M. D., Daniels, J. A., & D'Andrea, M. S. (2010). *Community counseling: empowerment strategies*. Belmont, CA: Brooks/Cole.

Linehan, M. M. (2014). *DBT Training manual*. New York, NY: The Guilford Press.

Luft, J., & Ingham, H. (1955). *The Johari Window. A graphic model of interpersonal awareness*. Proceedings of the Western Training Laboratory in Group Development. Los Angeles, CA: University of California.

Martel, Y. (2002). *Life of Pi: A novel*. Toronto, Canada: Vintage Canada.

McLeod, S. (2014). Carl Jung. *Simply Psychology* [Website]. Retrieved from: https://simply psychology.org/carl-jung.html.

Mellin, E. A., Hunt, B., & Nichols, L. M. (2011). Counselor professional identity: Findings and implications for counseling and interprofessional collaboration. *Journal of Counseling and Development, 89*(2), 140–147, doi:10.1002/j.1556-6678.2011.tb00071.x.

Moore, K., & Cooper, C. (1996). Stress in mental health professionals: A theoretical overview. *International Journal of Social Psychiatry, 42*(2), 82–89.

Netter, G., Lee, A., & Womark, D. (Producers), & Lee, A. (Director) (2012). *Life of Pi* [Motion picture]. Los Angeles, CA: 20th Century Fox.

Nouwen, J. J. M., McNeill, D. P., & Morrison, D. A. (1983). *Compassion: A reflection on the Christian life*. New York, NY: Doubleday.

Paul, R., & Elder, L. (2013). *Critical thinking exam*. Tomales, CA: The Foundation for Critical Thinking. Retrieved from: www.criticalthinking.org/data/store/store_393734382.800x800.jpg.

Perlman, L. A., & Saakvitne, K. W. (1995). *Trauma and the therapist: Countertransference and vicarious traumatization in psychotherapy with incest survivors*. New York: NY: W. W. Norton, doi: 10.1080/00029157.1996.10403354.

Rigg, G. (2017). *Essentials of psychomotor therapy and the healing circle model*. Greeley, CO: Author [self-published].

Rosch, P. J. (2017). *Reminiscences of Hans Selye, and the birth of "stress"*. Weatherford, TX: The American Institute of Stress. Retrieved from: www.stress.org/about/hans-selye-birth-of-stress.

Sapolsky, R. M. (2004). *Why zebras don't get ulcers* (3rd ed.). New York, NY: Henry Holt and Company.

Sharp, D. (2017). *Jung lexicon: A primer of terms and concepts*. Sausalito, CA: Psychceu.com. Retrieved from: www.psychceu.com/jung/sharplexicon.html.

Strohm, S. M., & Baukus, R. A. (1995). Strategies for fostering critical thinking skills. *Journalism and Mass Communication Educator, 50*(1), 55–62.

Tedeschi, R. G., Calhoun, L. G., & Groleau, J. M. (1995). Clinical applications of posttraumatic growth. In S. Joseph (Ed.) *Positive Psychology in Practice: Promoting Human Flourishing in Work, Health, Education, and Everyday Life*. Hoboken, NJ: John Wiley & Sons, Inc. Retrieved from: https://ptgi.uncc.edu/wp-content/uploads/sites/9/2015/01/Tedeschi-et-al-Joseph-Ch-30-Clinical-applications-of-PTG.pdf.

Thomas, K. W. & Kilmann, R. (1977). Developing a forced-choice measure of conflict-handling behavior: The "MODE" instrument. *Educational and Psychological Measurement, 37*(2), 309, doi: 10.1177/001316447703700204.

Tumkaya, S., Aybek, B., & Aldag, H. (2009). An investigation of university students' critical thinking and disposition and perceived problem-solving skills. *Eurasian Journal of Educational Research, 36*, 57–74.

Van Wagoner, S. L., Gelso, C. J., Hayes, J. A., & Diemer, R. A. (1991). Countertransference and the reputedly excellent therapist. *Psychotherapy, 28*(3), 411–421.

Wade, C. (1995). Using writing to develop and assess critical thinking. *Teaching of Psychology, 22*(1), 24–28.

Walker, P. (2014). *Complex PTSD: From surviving to thriving.* Lafayette, CA: Azure Coyote Publishing.

Wiersbe, W. W. (2002). *Be joyful: Even when things go wrong, you can have joy.* Colorado Springs, CO: David C. Cook.

Wooden, J. (n.d.) *BrainyQuote.* Retrieved from: www.brainyquote.com/authors/john_wooden.

World View (2017). In *Collins online dictionary.* Retrieved from: www.collinsdictionary.com/us/dictionary/english/world-view.

Worldview (2017). In *Collins online dictionary.* Retrieved from: www.collinsdictionary.com/us/dictionary/english/worldview.

Worldview (2017). In *Merriam-Webster online dictionary.* Retrieved from: www.merriam-webster.com/dictionary/worldview.

3 How to Exhibit Key Counselor Dispositions

How Do I Get "IT"?

The "IT" is those professional counselor dispositions and skills we talked about in the last chapter, which focus on self-reflection and that are cultivated through relationships. This chapter offers an entire section of various activities and assignments to help promote flourishing counselor dispositions within relationships. As a CIT, you are encouraged to reflect on your results from the assessment tools provided earlier in the book while integrating your findings into the activities offered below.

Relationship Quadrant

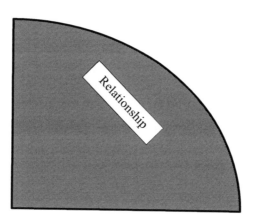

The quadrant of relationship invites us to explore our own relationships, both professional and personal. It can be argued that it is through relationships that we learn, assess, and grow, and gain insight into ourselves not otherwise captured from only within ourselves. In this quadrant, for this book, we will be exploring relationships through:

- Foundational Skills including Empathy (Carkhuff Scale)
- CCS-R Foundational Skills
- Pretzel Model of Triple Parallel Process
- Corrective Feedback Inventory
- Stages of Change (Motivational Interviewing)

Figure 3.1 Relationship Quadrant.

(Modified by the authors with permission from Rigg, 2017.)

Foundational Skills Including Empathy

We believe the foundational counseling skills include but are not limited to: empathy, paraphrasing, clarifying, attending, non-verbals, summarizing, being curious, asking open-ended questions, making a connection, challenging, and even deeper skills such as advanced empathy, feeling reflections, and use of metaphor, all of which are essential keys to building a meaningful connection with your CES and clients in your developmental work. Furthermore, recognizing the parallel process that occurs in relationships will set the stage for your work with your clients. Within this quadrant of relationships, we recommend the CIT spends time reviewing how to build these skills towards meaningful relationships. You may have already had skills training, and, if so, you can tap into those skills from previous coursework, books, etc. Another option may be to use the following assessments and activities to explore, assess and practice foundational skills.

As mentioned, the CCS-R (Lambie, Mullen, Swank, & Blount, 2016) is one of many counseling competency assessment tools created to assess foundational skills competency, professional behaviors, and dispositions. (**Note:** ⁺The Counseling Competencies Scale—Revised© (CCS-R) developed by Glenn Lambie, Ph.D. is available exclusively through Clinical Training Manager™, the counselor education software platform developed by Tevera, LLC. For more information, visit: www.clinicaltrainingmanager.com).

Your program or agency may utilize a different counselor assessment tool or protocol; however, many of the core foundational skills and dispositions are likely to be similar. We consider the relationship part of the quadrant of the Universal Growth Model a lynch-pin, where we must be willing to self-assess our own foundational skills while also looking at how to grow. When you meet with your CES for consultation, supervision, or mentoring in your ongoing growth or for a remediation plan, you must be able to exhibit these attributes to bond, connect, and allow for growth to occur. These skills will transfer to your work with your clients in the future. Some of these key foundational skills of importance include the following.

Nonverbal Skills

Nonverbal skills include: body language, eye contact, voice tone, rate of speech, use of silence. Are you, as the CIT, connecting, listening, making connection with non-verbals to demonstrate an ability to hear and apply feedback? Are you interested in growing? Do you send the message you are eager to learn and care deeply about the process? What are your nonverbals saying about your willingness to do this work as you approach the relationship with your CES, supervisor, or mentor? Are you projecting a willingness to be vulnerable and honest?

Encouragers

Encouragers include: both minimal encouragers and door openers, such as "say more" or "tell me about that." Here, your CES may use this skill with you, but you too can ask for more information to glean new understanding about your own development. This is part of building relationships and encouraging further introspection. The openness to listening to what the person is saying and not thinking about your answer while the other person is talking is key for counseling, and for relationships overall. When CITs get stuck in their own heads when listening to the CES or to a client, communication is compromised severely. Don't deceive yourself either; the client knows you are in your own head. The key is to pay attention to everything the other person is saying, take a breath and a moment to consider what they said, and then ask them to clarify questions for greater understanding. That sends messages to the person that not only includes the fact that you are indeed listening, but also that what they have to say is important to you, that you are open enough to hear without immediately defending your position, and that you are willing to put your biases aside to attend to them.

Questions

Closed-ended questions are only to be utilized as needed; open-ended questions are critical to the development of the relationship with your clients and with your CES. Avoid double questions when trying to form your thoughts. Stop, think, and then speak. Again, your CES may use open-ended questions with you, but you too can ask for more information as needed and as appropriate. Be curious and seek clarification if things are not clearly understood, or the depth of understanding is not what you would like it to be.

Paraphrasing

Basic content reflection is paraphrasing; you are saying back to the person, in your words, what they just told you. Take note of how your CES is modeling this foundational skill as you share your story, process, feelings, and experiences in supervision. There are several reasons for paraphrasing, including showing that you understand what they are saying and establishing empathy and connection with each other. Note that the connection you have with your clients is just as critical as your connection with your CES.

Reflection of Meaning and Reflection of Feelings

Again, take note of how your CES uses this skill as you seek to practice it yourself in skills training. Practice this skill so that you are accurately reflecting the feeling as well as the meaning of what your client is saying. Do you really understand them? Have you been able to put your thoughts away so that you can truly *attend* to what your client is saying? Now, note how your CES is doing that for you. Consider how much they listened to you without interrupting. How much have they reflected to you, demonstrating that they understand what you are saying and feeling? Reflect on how easy that made it for you to continue to talk, and, perhaps, even to begin to trust them. That's what you want to be able to do.

Summarizing

Summarize the content, feelings, and behaviors, and the influence they may have on the future. You and your CES may also use this skill as you seek to find meaning in your growth or remediation process. Then practice this skill so that you are digging deeper to reflect a feeling that may be there, though the other person may be minimizing the feeling. For instance, let's suppose your client says that something that happened to them was "scary;" you may respond with: "You were terrified!" The client will correct you if you go too deep or not deep enough. If the client says, "Well, sort of" or "kind of" then you know that you missed the mark. Try again, "Oh, not terrified, but shocked!" Again, they will correct you if you shot too high or too low. Listen and keep trying until you get the "Yes!" from the client. Then, you both know you are on target with each other. It's like shooting darts. You are trying to get a bull's eye, but that takes adjusting your position, throw, wrist movement, release, breathing, etc. before you can consistently hit the center ring. Keep throwing until you hit the mark. The connection you gain is worth it. Do you quit after one throw and a miss? Do you get caught up in getting it *right*? That's something to rearrange as the process of reflecting is part of the relationship building for strong rapport. Don't give up and leave your client out in the cold; shoot to hit it right within three to four throws.

Advanced Reflection of Meaning

This includes values and core beliefs, taking the whole context to a deeper level. The advanced reflection of meaning that goes this deep is often where the very significant work is being done. You are connected to each other, trust each other, and respect each other; the reflections are taking you to the heart of the issues. This may also come toward the end of a growth experience or toward the end of a remediation process. Often CITs can find this in the reflection of the entire process.

Confrontation

This includes the counselor challenging the client to recognize and evaluate inconsistencies. Confrontation is not about fighting or arguing with the other person. Your CES may illustrate this skill with you in a non-conflictual manner. You will feel challenged and supported simultaneously. Lean into this work as this is where newfound insights can often occur. Again, you may also find mirroring and modeling from your CES, so you can also learn to elicit these responses with clients. You may be confronting an inconsistency; you may be helping the client to stop to hear what they just said. There are multiple ways to ask questions that challenge the supposition of the other person's position.

Goal Setting

A counselor collaborates with a client to establish realistic, appropriate, and attainable goals that are specific and clear. Often you and your CES will create goals for your ongoing competency and growth together. This parallels the work you will do with clients.

Focus of Counseling

A counselor focuses or refocuses a client on the therapeutic goals set through their collaborative efforts. Your CES will likely help keep you focused on your educational goals towards competency through ongoing growth work or remediation plan work.

Facilitating a Therapeutic Environment

A counselor exercises accurate empathy and care; a counselor is present and open to the client and a counselor expresses appropriate respect and unconditional positive regard. Pay attention to how your CES models this as well, as you seek to understand how to reciprocate in meaningful connection to your CES, and eventually to your clients, colleagues, etc.

Consider the following assessment and reflective activities to refine your foundational skills:

- Review a role-play video session to gauge your foundational skills.
- Consider investing in an educational technology tool such as *Acclaim* (see Appendix 2: Resources) that offers you the ability to save videos that are encrypted, and receive feedback from supervisors and faculty alike that is confidential.
- Review your prior techniques, skills, or course assessments to reflect on areas of strength and areas of needed growth in foundational areas.
- After meeting with your CES, ask for an observation or assessment of a video or transcription to inquire about feedback on your skills.
- What are additional ways to grow, assess, and practice your skills towards optimal competencies? (See Worksheet 3.1 in Appendix 1.)

Carkhuff Empathy Scale (Empathy as an Attachment Tool)

Empathy is a necessary component in the human relationship in order to form meaningful connections. Empathy is included in the foundational skills, but we take special note to consider assessing, reflecting, and continuing to work on empathy skills and the phenomenon of ensuring trust, connection, and rapport for the rest of our lives. Empathy involves perspective taking, which can be cultivated, modeled, and taught if lacking. In fact, one might argue that empathy, perspective-taking, and mindsight (Seigel, 2009) all work together to build healthy, secure attachments within meaningful relationships. This notion of the connection of empathy and perspective-taking impacts everything, including cultural competencies, assessment, diagnosis, and the deep meaningful connection. For example, Coke, Batson, and McDavis (1978) believed in a model of empathy that included mediation, which is understanding the perspective of a person in need. They believe gaining understanding increases empathic emotion, which in turn increases helping. In turn, perspective-taking is also a characteristic of critical thinking. Critical thinking is an important feature of many areas of development including perspective-taking and empathy; and we will continue to address critical thinking in this text. We recommend a model of building empathy and perspective taking within the UGM, which involves the self, relationship, competency, and actualization processes, initially at a micro level. Here is an example.

Case Study

Four-year-old Sam left the grocery store with his dad. They were buckling up in the car when Sam realized, with great fear, that he left his dirty, stained, tattered "Special Blankey" inside! He cried out to his father, "Daddy! Blankey is inside the store!" (1. precipitating event or feeling).

Dad responded with understanding and perspective-taking (2.) to his little boy realizing how important Blankey was to him. Dad may not care for an old dirty blanket. Some parents may want to "lose" such a ragged appendage. Instead, dad responded (3.), "Oh no, ok, it's going to be ok. I know you love Blankey so much and worry about him. We will go back inside and find him, ok buddy?"

1 Is the precipitating event, behavior, or emotional feeling expressed by someone?
2 Is the ability to perspective-take and put ourselves in the other person's shoes while assessing the situation and tapping into the emotion and experience of the other person present?
3 Is the ability to respond accordingly with empathy, care, and compassion demonstrated?

(See Worksheet 3.2 in Appendix 1.)

You may not be able to always "fix" the problem, like dad and Blankey, but the point is that you are connecting to the experience, need, perspective, and position of the other person from their viewpoint and not your own. This, in turn, even if Blankey was lost forever, builds attachment.

Empathy is pivotal and goes hand in hand with critical thinking, perspective taking, and mindsight (Seigel, 2009). This valuable and much-needed ability is crucial in understanding the human experience and, hence, relationships in general, and this is well documented in the research on attachment theory. Your CES will model and teach these concepts while offering experiential activities to help guide you. However, you too must be open and willing to explore and practice these components as they are essential to the work of building meaningful connections with your CES, and your clients. So, many of you reading this may be asking, what is the difference between sympathy and empathy? Great question! Here is an example using metaphor. Sympathy is putting yourself in someone else's shoes, but you know they are indeed not your shoes and you will be able to take them off at any moment; furthermore, they are hurting your feet and there is a blister forming. Whereas empathy is putting yourself in those shoes and being able to experience what the other person is feeling, affectively and cognitively, as if the shoes were indeed owned by you.

Carl Rogers, a humanistic person-centered therapist himself, believed empathy to be a foundational requirement for connecting with the client in order to work towards healing and growth. "The popularity of Rogers' use of empathy during the 20th century eventually led to the development of a popular five-point scale to measure empathy, known as the Carkhuff Scale" (Neukrug & Schwitzer, 2006). This assessment can be a way for your CES to assess you or for you to self-assess your own empathetic skill level (see Worksheet 3.2 in Appendix 1).

Here are the paraphrased levels and examples, based on Carkhuff's Empathy Scale (Carkhuff, 1969, pp. 174–175).

Level 1

The counselor's verbal and behavioral responses do not meet the needs of the clients or take away from the client's experience significantly.

An example of this may be when a counselor dismisses a client with a verbal or nonverbal cue, causing the client to shut down and stop expressing their experiences. At this level, the exchange may be – Client: "I was frightened." CIT: "And you really had no reason to be frightened, now did you?" We have all experienced this interaction before. Consider a time when you were attempting to be somewhat vulnerable with someone and they became disinterested or, worse, judgmental. You do not feel your needs were dismissed, but you felt hurt that the person dismissed and judged your experience. Your CES can formally and informally assess you as the CIT in a variety of ways including observation, self-reported experiences, role-play examples, and even through case exercises.

Level 2

The counselor responds to the client's feelings in a way that subtracts from the client's expression of experience or feelings.

Perhaps at a less intense level than Level 1, but still the CIT is unable to add to the safety, connection, awareness, communication, and understanding of the client. The example at this level is – Client: "I was frightened." CIT: "You were worried."

Level 3

The counselor responds to the client in an interchangeable manner so as not to add any depth or breadth of feelings to the client's experience but meets them exactly where they are at in their communication and conveyance of feelings.

This is an example of the CIT exchanging evenly with the client's experience, so they have no deeper awareness, meaning, or connection than what they started with. They match the other person's level. The example continues – Client: "I was frightened." CIT: "You were frightened."

Level 4

The counselor adds notably to the client's expression of feelings or experience and adds a deeper level of awareness and meaning for the client to utilize, one that they would not have had alone.

Here, the client experiences something new, meaningful, aware, and connected, having more than what they came into the conversation/experience with. There is a new understanding, connection, and insight because the CIT has expressed the feeling on a deeper level. An example may look like this – Client: "I was frightened." And the CIT responding with, "You were terrified." The response takes the feeling to a deeper level.

Level 5

The counselor's response adds significantly to the client's self-understanding and connection to deeper meaning and feeling. This awareness offers the client even more depth and breadth to self-understanding and thus fosters a deep meaningful connection to the counselor.

Using the example above, the Client says, "I was frightened." The CIT may respond at this level with a comment of: "You were horrified and thought you were going to die!" That response goes to a deeper meaning than what the client was expressing initially and may bring a deeper understanding to the client as they wrestle not only with danger but also with mortality.

Often it is in the deeper empathetic exchange with clients that we see the phenomenon of connecting in meaningful ways. One of my favorite examples of this is in using metaphor with clients. If the CIT can connect to the client in such a deep, meaningful way that the client not only feels the CIT truly *gets* them, but they also feel a new deeper sense of connection, awareness, growth, and insight than what they came in with, the awareness is profound. One way to offer more advanced empathy in the reciprocal relationship of CIT and client is through metaphor. The CIT can introduce a metaphor that the client can deeply connect with while then beginning to make their own ongoing meaningful connections, which can provide abundant empathetic connection.

In addition to empathy, there are several other dispositional foci to consider in your work with your CES in the developmental process. After reviewing the Carkhuff Empathy Scale, consider your own self-assessment or feedback from others concerning your empathic resonance skills. If this is an area you want to work on, consider the following.

1   Pay close attention to your CES and their own demonstration of empathy as you work together towards your common goals of competency and success in counseling.
2   Consider empathy training techniques and skills while paying attention to the emotional and cognitive types of empathy.
3   Consider the types of empathy including cognitive and affective. Which do you struggle to exhibit and why?
4   Consider videotaping role-play skills sessions, including empathy examples your CES may suggest, to offer opportunities to initiate, practice, and execute deep empathic understanding and review for learning.
5   Consider a short story, poem, fairytale, or lyrics from a song to explore, evaluate and process in terms of recognizing each character's perspective and potentially what they are experiencing and feeling. Process this with your CES to gauge your understanding and ability to connect to the emotion of others in the art and relationship with your CES.

(See Worksheet 3.3 in Appendix 1.)

Empathy is an invaluable foundational skill that is needed for being in relationship with others. Empathy involves critical thinking, perspective taking, and the ability to demonstrate compassion, care, and foundational skills such as immediacy and feeling reflections. It is recommended that you, as the CIT, consider that skills, professionalism, and dispositions go hand in hand in your professional development and can therefore be included within the professional developmental process.

Meaningful Engagement with Your CES as Support (Pretzel Model)

The UGM is an on-going, continuous developmental model that impacts your work as a CIT and hence your CES and clients. We offer a look at the "Pretzel as a Triple Parallel Process" model when considering your relationship and growth with your CES, and how it also impacts your clients. The basis of counseling is a wellness model (AMHCA *Code of Ethics*, 2015), and it encourages and expects changes and growth for *all* involved. Because of that perspective, this model has multiple applications and a singular outcome: positive change. Envisioning your CIT growth and change impacts a bigger systemic change and has social and cultural implications as well as implications for knowledge and daily practice in relationships. As mentioned, Bronfenbrenner's (1979) model of micro, mezzo, and macro changes that occur in the system is applicable here, as demonstrated by the inner, influential, and outer rings in the UGM. As one system interacts with another, movement is felt throughout all of them, as demonstrated in Newton's Cradle, which is a set of suspended metal balls transferring energy through the middle balls and making the two end balls move back and forth one at a time. The energy is transferred so only the two end balls show movement.

The Pretzel as a Triple Parallel Process

Imagine you are viewing a three-ring pretzel in your hand. There are three circular sections and they meet in the middle in a knot. This is the vision we had for this process. Keep that image in mind as we discuss this Triple Parallel Process.

As discussed, Bronfenbrenner's ecological model impacts many layers of a societal cultural system. In the same way, the triple parallel process assists in the growth or detriment of everyone involved. Therefore, it is imperative CITs take their professional growth seriously, and lean into the supervision offered when in training and beyond. Initially, Sumerel (1994) viewed the parallel process as countertransference by defining it as behavior demonstrated by the clinician who reflected the problems of the client within the supervisory relationship interactions. Later, it appears that Searles (1955) discovered the phenomenon of parallel process, distinguishing it as more than transference or countertransference but as a reflection process. According to Searles, the processes at work within client and therapist are reflected in the relationship and communication of counselor and supervisor (1955, p. 135). In analyzing parallel process, we cannot separate the concept without bringing in the literature and information tied to perspective taking, critical thinking, and empathetic resonance as well. It is our belief that the growth from the triple parallel process occurs when client, counselor, and supervisor are in sync, exhibiting authentic, meaningful communications that can be utilized towards deeper meaning, self-understanding, and healing. Normally, the supervisor oversees the teaching and supervising of their CIT in terms of using parallel process. According to Sumerel (1994):

> Supervision can provide an experience for counselors to learn how to use themselves in the counselor/client relationship. By discussing the parallel process in supervision, the counselor will become aware of how oneself is involved in the therapeutic and supervisory relationships. (p. 1.)

Even more fascinating is that not only do you, as the CIT, mirror what is going on in relationship with the client to your CES, but the CES impacts on how you respond in the therapeutic relationship with your clients. When all is working well, the CIT leans into the meaningful connection of desire for growth, learning, and feedback from their CES, which then directly impacts their current and future clients towards health as well. Consider the following fictional blended case study from the CIT perspective.

Case Study

Jenny was struggling with feedback from her site supervisor, who said that she was not able to demonstrate empathy and appeared "cold and disconnected" to her clients. She was, of course, astonished and hurt by the feedback but sought support from her faculty CES to try to grow. While working with Jenny, her CES was able to pull strong applicable metaphors to their relationship and work together with Jenny using the images as metaphors for her personal struggles, which likely led to her apathetic demeanor. The metaphors allowed Jenny to tap into her emotional self and allowed her to express many things that she had previously withheld. While engaging in the process with Jenny, the CES was completely aware of her own strong feelings from her childhood relating to the metaphor image and decided to share them with her CIT to model self-awareness, self-reflection, and finding meaning. This may be one example of appropriate use of self-disclosure, with authenticity, and meaningful connection of the CES to the CIT. It turned out Jenny felt understood, connected, and more open with her CES given their experience together. It is the unique interconnection of client to CIT to CES and CES to CIT to client that allows for all three individuals to experience the parallel process of meaningful connection, themes, and experiences towards ongoing growth and health when each person chooses to be authentic and seeks self-awareness and growth.

So, the process looks like this:

Client impacts CIT, CIT impacts CES *and* CES impacts CIT, and CIT impacts Client

Here are some operational descriptive traits to familiarize yourself with as you seek to implement the Triple Parallel Process within your learning and growth.

- **Insight**: Being able to appropriately self-assess one's own motivation for behavior.
- **Modeling**: Demonstrating professional behavior, thinking, and actions.
- **Knots**: Where the three roles (in the pretzel) meet and may reach an impasse until insight is gained and demonstrated.
- **Messy and Intimate – Dichotomous**: The three roles are inextricably bound together through the desire for change and growth on all parts. The insights gained are anemic when not also assessed through each role. This can make the interactions messy, but, through commitment, authenticity, and tenacity, the process can be a major source of intimacy and, hence, achieve insight and health for all three roles. This also requires immediacy, desire for change, and willingness to be vulnerable with the persons involved.

- **Cognitive Dissonance:** The moment when the understanding that one view cannot exist simultaneously with another opposite view and recognizing that trying to hold on to that position causes more pain than can be tolerated.
- **Authentically Modeling and Sensing It:** Authenticity is measured by others who are in the interaction. As such, each person in this model can sense authenticity, much like as a snake flicks their tongue to determine what is in the atmosphere around them. People who are being asked to be authentic are fine-tuned to each other, can recognize when someone is not being genuine, and have the freedom to confront that based on the modeling in the unit. I (Dr. Lewis), from personal experience, believe that confrontation is one of the most difficult skills for CITs to learn, thus they graduate often lacking this skill, needing more development, and may or may not do so based on the context of their work. This may lead to supervisors, clinicians, and faculty who never learned to be comfortable using confrontation. This model offers opportunity to practice and model that skill for further development by all, remembering that confrontation is not fighting or battling. It is honest and authentic.
- **Vulnerability:** Vulnerability is an aspect of authenticity and humility. To be vulnerable, we must trust the context, be willing to take the risk of being authentic, and be humble enough to allow others to see our imperfections, wounds, and failures. This means we must assess whether it is worth the cost. Ask yourself, is there anything keeping you from being more open, honest and authentic in your meaningful relationship work with your CES?

The model still is applicable even when applied to you as a CIT who has not yet seen clients, as a "pretzel knot" of CIT and faculty/supervisor. Even so, the application continues to impact future clients and colleagues even when they may not be in the picture now. The model visually demonstrates how each ring represents the individual's own developmental experience, while also being in relationship with others in their own developmental process. For example, your CES is responsible for your growth and your client's growth, just as your site supervisor is. While working on remediation issues, your CES must support you in your growth and development while also paying attention to the well-being of your clients. Of course, to grow and understand how you are doing in the process, you as the CIT must be willing to hear and apply feedback.

- How might you as the CIT be prepared to engage in the triple parallel process?
- What thoughts come to mind as you review the image and information pertaining to the "Pretzel" of triple parallel process?
- What are some key professional dispositional elements that would be important to have to engage in the process? Why?
- Journal and take notes about the connection of client to you as CIT to CES and CES to you as CIT to your client. What stands out most about this process and phenomenon?

(See Worksheet 3.4 in Appendix 1.)

Corrective Feedback

Another important part of being in relationship includes the reality that we cannot receive or offer feedback without being in relationship. After immense self-exploration, self-reflection, and ability to look at perspectives, we can begin the wonderful journey of growth through corrective feedback. You may have begun to engage in this process if you asked for another view into your Johari Window. However, it is through relationships that we begin to practice giving and receiving feedback that is geared towards growth and ultimately competency and self-actualization.

Giving and receiving corrective feedback may be a challenge for many CITs. For some, it may feel punitive and some may even feel ashamed. However, in reconceptualizing the process of receiving feedback, we need to remember to first assess our triggers. Following the three-step process (see page XX), where is the root of that trigger about feedback? If we can assume that the person giving the feedback has right and honest intentions, what is the goal they may have? What is your goal, and can your goal be reached through accepting the feedback? Remember, if you have an emotional reaction, it is evidence of a trigger you have. As Eleanor Roosevelt so clearly stated, "No one can make you feel inferior without your consent" (Roosevelt, 2018).

Also, consider that many master's-degree-level counselors are supervisors. If you are not comfortable with accepting feedback, how comfortable are you in giving it? The practice you can gain in receiving it may also help you give it when your turn to supervise comes around. How may you handle that, knowing what you know now?

Corrective feedback is different from critical, constructive, or negative feedback. Corrective feedback has the intent of supporting the receiver towards being the best they can be, focusing on the behaviors and not the person. Corrective feedback can be explored through the Corrective Feedback Inventory Revised (CFI-R) (Hulse-Killacky, Orr, & Paradise, 2006). Through this tool, CITs can consider how they have received feedback from others in the past. In addition, it can be used to open a polite conversation for CES and CITs alike to explore how the CIT best enjoys receiving feedback towards growth. In addition, when considering feedback, sometimes we need to consider what Stage of Change (Prochaska & DiClemente, 1983) you may be in regarding your desire or motivation for growth in the first place. Consider the differences between Corrective Feedback and *critical or constructive* feedback, based on the following CIT experiences.

> "When I hear someone say, 'Can I offer you some critical feedback?' I kind of shut down because I feel like, well that means I failed or something."

> "My parents used to tell me I needed to learn to accept Constructive Feedback, but I always felt like that was just pointing out my flaws."

> "I just reviewed some conceptual differences with the term Constructive and Critical as opposed to Corrective, and I honestly wonder, the corrective piece sounds like its purpose is to make things better, not just focused on my failures."

> (Anonymous supervisee reflections from the CFI-R for CIT self-assessment. See Worksheet 3.5 in Appendix 1 for the full assessment.)

The Corrective Feedback Instrument-Revised (Hulse-Killacky Orr, & Paradise, 2006) helps to guide the process of determining your interpretation of feedback, which may help you to consider alternative perspectives. The definition given for corrective feedback is that it provides information that is intended to encourage thoughtful self-examination and/or to express the feedback giver's perception of the need for change on the part of the receiver. Here is one example from the CFI-R (Hulse-Killacky Orr, & Paradise, 2006) to consider. For more examples see Worksheet 3.5 in Appendix 1 (used with permission from Hulse-Killacky Orr, & Paradise, 2006).

1 – Strongly Disagree; 2 – Slightly Disagree; 3 – Disagree; 4 – Agree Slightly; 5 – Agree;
6 – Strongly Agree

1   I feel criticized when I receive corrective feedback. **1 2 3 4 5 6**
2   I am usually too uncomfortable to ask someone to clarify corrective feedback delivered to me. **1 2 3 4 5 6**
3   I remember corrective feedback as critical when it was delivered to me as a child. **1 2 3 4 5 6**

You may wish to seek permission to use the entire assessment when working with your CES on your ability to use valuable feedback. We will discuss feedback in even more depth in the next quadrant, but, first, we want you to explore your ability in the past and present to receive feedback to support you in this process. We also need to piggyback on the Wounded Healer aspects to truly prepare and continue in ongoing self-growth, while working on our growth process. Is it possible that a lack of self-efficacy in giving and receiving feedback is tied to the wounded healer phenomenon? In addition, refer to The Johari Window (Luft & Ingham, 1955) as this can be used to self-assess, including reflection on the often-cited reasons why you may struggle with hearing, receiving, applying and implementing feedback. Can you reframe feedback, while in your counselor training process, as an amazing experience full of desire, hope, and best intentions from your CES towards your ultimate benefit and competencies? To know if we are ready to consider changing due to feedback offered from our CES, who is speaking deeply into our development, we also must consider if we are ready for change. Consider the following story and the feedback model presented.

Case Study

Jack was in his final year in culinary school and was on his path to success. He was eager and excited to be able to finish his hands-on training as an intern Chef de Partie chef at the *Repas Délicieux & Co*. Jack was confident in completing all his straight A coursework and had only 32 more hours of field experience before graduation. He was given a bit of feedback from the Head Chef in terms of his kitchen etiquette, but, other than that, nothing else was offered. Jack went on to graduate, and get his diploma, and have his party, and all was well. He applied to several four-star restaurants and received a position as a Chef de Tournant, a French vegetarian dining experience focusing on soups for the restaurant. He was nervous, but confident in his abilities since, after all, he graduated with honors. He was given the directive in his first week to make mirepoix (a soup base) and he went about creating his base. Throughout the week he did his job, but the owner received several complaints and feedback concerning the mirepoix as not tasting right. In fact, several customers had left terrible reviews and vowed not to return. Once the Head Chef investigated with Jack, the answer was found. Jack was trained in creating all kinds of soup bases and had always used bacon fat to create this base. He must have created it at least 30 times while in training, and his instructors had never

(continued)

(continued)

mentioned that he had done it incorrectly. Using a meat fat or oil was known as *au gras*; however, the traditional training requires that the chef always specify either *au gras* or *au maigre*, which is considered "without meat". Obviously, the meat base was a poor choice at this establishment to begin with. Jack was astonished to think he had made such a mistake and was dumbfounded when the Head Chef confronted him on the issue. How did things end for Jack?

Consider the following questions:

1   What is the identified problem for Jack and his situation here?
2   How might Jack be feeling?
3   What might be the best response to the Head Chef from Jack?
4   What can Jack do?

Jack responded to the Head Chef stating:
I am so sorry, but my instructors never told me that I needed to specify these features in the soup base and I received straight As throughout my program. I have never been given negative feedback like this nor have I ever made such a mistake! I had no idea I needed to differentiate, or I would never had made such a mistake!

Or

Jack responded to the Head Chef:
I am terribly sorry. Despite not having learned this valuable information, I should have known better in a vegetarian restaurant to not use a meat base. I must have been so eager to complete the task I did not use reason and good judgement. I apologize and will reach out and inquire when something does not make sense or if I need guidance in executing a dish. I am open to continuing to learn and receive the feedback and I am grateful to learn this additional information.

1   What are the differences between these two responses that Jack made to his Head Chef?
2   What might be the differences in how this story plays out simply based on his reaction and response to feedback, and why?
3   What is the moral of this story and example?
(See Worksheet 3.6 in Appendix 1.)

Often the ability to give and receive feedback with authentic genuineness and support is directly tied to not only how we were given feedback as a child or youngster, but also in connection to our own expectation of ourselves. If we see feedback as a criticism and not ultimately for our growth and wellbeing, the feedback, and sometimes the giver of it, can become our *enemy* rather than our *advocate*. This is a cognitive reframing shift that is imperative for you as the CIT to experience to reach your fullest potential as a professional. One story, offered from a former supervisee with permission, fits this beautifully.

In the Army, we learn early on to accept and offer feedback and it is never a personal attack. In fact, when I receive feedback from a Commander, Warrant Officer, or any higher-ranking official to me, it means they took the precious time and effort to focus on me as a subordinate to give and speak into my growth. They could always look the other way, pass by, or ignore my mediocre performance but they choose to give me a precious gift of letting me know where I am at, what my strengths are, and where my growth areas are so as I can truly be the best I can be. (Anonymous, 2017.)

If we consider this reframing we see that feedback is indeed a gift. It is data, knowledge, and information for us to process on how others are experiencing us. Without this, we may live in a vacuum of thinking we know how others are experiencing us, but perhaps that is not totally accurate considering we are looking through only our own worldview lens. What better way to gauge and adjust and learn and grow than through immediacy and the feedback offered to us. For the CIT, this feedback is essential within assessment, evaluation, and in general through the supervisory rapport and relationship. It is part of the entire CIT training, whether informal or formal, and the more we offer it to our CITs, the more comfortable they often get with receiving it, and applying it, and then offering feedback when appropriate to colleagues and others.

Some common attributes CITs report they like to have from their CES when receiving feedback include:

1 existing rapport and understanding of each other's personality;
2 balance of support and challenge;
3 authenticity, genuineness, and humor;
4 cultural competency and humility;
5 the CES asking for feedback on how they are doing in the eyes of the CIT;
6 use of immediacy to build connection;
7 use of creativity in the process to make things more interesting;
8 use of technology to build connection if in a remote/online environment.

Feedback is essential to growth and more growth leads to ongoing feedback with diminishing anxiety and personal stress. The CFI-R (Hulse-Killacky, Orr, & Paradise, 2006) and other experiential activities can assist the CES in supporting their CIT in reflecting, applying, and experiencing ways to reframe feedback, while embracing it as a wonderful gift towards their ultimate growth and success. Feedback is only good when it is received. To ensure it is received, we must also consider assessing the level of readiness for receiving feedback and that includes being ready for change. Consider returning to the activities in Chapter 1 about readiness for change (see pages XX–XX). Review that information one more time as you now may have a different perspective on change than you had at the time you read the previous chapter.

As you have seen, the assignments and process of the UGM begin with self-reflection and analysis of values, worldview, and awareness of self. In addition, we, as your CES, support you in realizing the need for change and growth for all of us and, next, in finding the motivation connected to these aspects to begin that process within relationship. It is through relationship that we can see ourselves anew, and that is exciting towards building our competencies. We encourage you to continue to build trust, authenticity, and rapport within the meaningful relationship of your work with your CES. This is your greatest asset professionally. These facets are imperative as you begin to see your CES, not as the *bad guy*, attempting to take away your passion and dreams of becoming a counselor, but, through reframing the entire process and relationship to one of support, mentorship, and guidance, as your partner towards success and excellence in the profession.

References

American Mental Health Counselors Association (AMHCA) (2015). *Code of ethics*. Retrieved from: https://c.ymcdn.com/sites/amhca.site-ym.com/resource/resmgr/Media/ethics2015FI NAL.pdf.

Bronfenbrenner, U. (1979). *The ecology of human development*. Cambridge, MA: Harvard University Press.

Carkhuff, R. R. (1969). *Helping and human relationships* (Vol. 2). New York: NY: Holt, Rinehart, & Winston.

Coke, J. S., Batson, C. D., & McDavis, K. (1978). Empathic mediation of helping: A two-stage model. *Journal of Personality and Social Psychology, 36*(7), 752–766.

Hulse-Killacky, D., Orr, J., & Paradise, L. (2006). The corrective feedback instrument-revised. *Journal for Specialists in Group Work, 31*(3), 263–281, doi: /10.1080/01933920600777758.

Lambie, G., Mullen, P., Swank, J., & Blount, A. (2016). *Counseling Competencies Scale, Revised (CCS-R)*. Orlando, FL: University of Central Florida, Counselor Education Program. Retrieved from: http://webmedia.jcu.edu/counselingdepartment/files/2016/03/CCS- R-Evaluation.pdf.

Luft, J., & Ingham, H. (1955). *The Johari window: A graphic model of interpersonal awareness*. Proceedings of the Western Training Laboratory in Group Development. Los Angeles, CA: University of California.

Neukrug, E. S., & Schwitzer, A. M. (2006). *Skills and tools for today's counselors and psychotherapists: From natural helping to professional counseling*. Belmont, CA: Brooks/Cole, Cengage Learning.

Prochaska, J., & DiClemente, C. (1983). Stages and processes of self-change of smoking: Toward an integrative model of change. *Journal of Consulting and Clinical Psychology, 51*(3), 390–395.

Rigg, G. (2017). *Essentials of psychomotor therapy and the healing circle model*. Greeley, CO: Author [self-published].

Roosevelt, E. (2018). *BrainyQuotes*. Retrieved from: www.brainyquote.com/quotes/eleanor_roosevelt_161321.

Searles, H. F. (1955). The informational value of the supervisor's emotional experiences. *Psychiatry: Interpersonal and Biological Processes, 18*(2), 135–146.

Seigel, D. J. (2009). *Mindsight: The new science of personal transformation*. New York, NY: Random House, Inc.

Sumerel, M. (1994). *Parallel process in supervision*. Retrieved from: www.counseling.org/resources/library/ERIC%20Digests/94-15.pdf.

4 Lifelong Standards

How to Measure and Keep "IT"

A Look at How to Achieve Competence

This chapter offers CITs an in-depth coverage of the purpose of on-going assessment and the gift it offers of competency. The standards benefit not only the profession, but also personal and professional growth for the CIT, and their future clients and colleagues. The CCS-R (Lambie, Mullen, Swank, & Blount, 2016) is offered as one example of assessment in which CITs can self-assess and obtain faculty and supervisor feedback throughout their program and career. In addition, other assessment tools are explored such as the Professional Disposition Competence Assessment (PDCA) (Garner, Freeman, & Lee, 2016). These and other evaluative tools can facilitate long-term CIT growth towards professional identity and competency.

Competency Quadrant

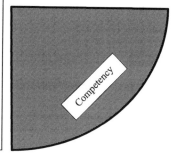

> **Competency Quadrant**
>
> The quadrant of competency invites us to explore our own self efficacy and professional competencies including knowledge, skills, and professional dispositions. We cannot feel that we are competent without being confident in our own power to perform. In this quadrant, for this book, we will be exploring competencies through:
>
> - Review of our skills training in foundational, micro, and macro skills and dispositions, and professionalism
> - Tolerance to Ambiguity
> - PAIR Feedback Model
> - Prior Work Experiences
> - Review of core counseling knowledge

Figure 4.1 Competency Quadrant.

(Modified by the authors with permission from Rigg, 2017.)

Examples of Additional Counseling Competency Assessments

In this book we offer the Counseling Competency Scale-Revised (CCS-R) as one example of an assessment tool that you and your CES can use to evaluate your competencies (Lambie et al., 2016). (**Note:** If you would like to use the CCS-R be sure to contact your Clinical Training Manager for details of how to access and utilize this instrument. *The Counseling Competencies Scale—Revised©* (CCS-R), developed by Glenn Lambie, Ph.D., is available exclusively through *Clinical Training Manager™*, the counselor education software platform developed by Tevera, LLC. For more information, visit: www.clinicaltrainingmanager.com.)

In addition to the CCS-R, there are several other counseling competency assessment tools that may be helpful in assessing your competency in various areas, including:

- The Counselor Characteristic Inventory (CCI) (Pope & Kline, 1999);
- Creating Personal Dispositions for a Professional Counseling Program (Spurgeon, Gibbons, & Cochran, 2012),
- Personal Characteristics Evaluation Form (Frame & Stevens-Smith, 1995);
- The Professional Performance Fitness Evaluation (PPFE) (Lumadue & Duffey, 1999);
- Professional Performance Review Protocol (McAdams, Foster, & Ward, 2007).

For this book, we will be focusing on the CCS-R. However, be aware that other resources are available to you and your CES.

Competency

It is through the reflection and analysis of work on self, and in the dynamic and interpersonal attachment work through relationship, that we see now that the experience of competency can arise. In this quadrant, the CIT can begin to feel competent not only in understanding themselves, but also in how they interact and continue to grow through relationship. Being competent is a concept which may or may not have been developed through childhood. Take some time to consider how you feel when confronted with doing something unfamiliar. Are you ready and eager to learn something new? Or are you filled with trepidation that you will make a mistake or be unable to work through the new task? That may be a clue about how confident you are and how empowered you feel to embark into unfamiliar territory. There may be some personal work to do first, and then you can begin to develop the counseling competencies.

Counseling Competencies

You may have had prior assessment from your CES or your CES may find a need to assess you in this process using the CCS-R or another type of assessment, such as those mentioned to evaluate your foundational counseling skills, professional behaviors and dispositions. Keep in mind, per accreditation standards, that you need to be assessed on knowledge, skills, and dispositions. You have also likely observed and self-assessed through the challenging work of self-evaluation, reflection, and relationships. In this quadrant, you, as the CIT, begin to gain self-efficacy as you practice and engage with the more demanding skills and competencies that are required for all counselors. At this stage of the UGM, you may find you have an additional need for a skills plan to hone your foundational skills after having worked through a development plan addressing dispositions. This is a perfect dovetail experience because it is our belief that to master the foundational skills, one must also have the challenging work of self, relationship, and professional dispositions down. We recommend that this is the time and place for you to continue to sharpen and master your foundational skills towards ongoing competency and success. In addition to sharpening knowledge skills and your dispositions, we must approach the aspect of ambiguity as it ties in to several counselor dispositions.

Tolerance of Ambiguity

The ability to tolerate the ambiguity of the unknown in life is essential to functioning and modeling resilience as a counselor to your clients. There may be a correlation with the fact that many folks enter the profession of counseling wanting to find meaning and purpose in their pain by helping others. From previous wounding such as grief, loss, trauma, etc., there may exist an even deeper dislike of ambiguity than the general population has. This is to be understood as those who have experienced woundings may not feel comfortable in the unknowns of life. Although difficult to endure, tolerating the unknown or ambiguous parts of life is essential for the competent and effective CIT. Tolerance of ambiguity involves dispositional qualities in addition to critical thinking and reflection. As you move from the evaluating, reflecting, and growing of the personal self to relationship with others, you begin to see the connection and need for tolerating ambiguity and are more comfortable in that space. As mentioned, Ronnestad and Skovholt (2003) report that new CITs often are in a phase of wanting to do everything the right way. While the goal of excellence is admirable, the desire to be perfect will counteract growth in the therapeutic relationship. Clients will recognize the CIT's perfectionism, and will then cover up their own inadequacies and failures so the CIT will not think less of them as broken and wounded beings. However, when the CIT can show vulnerability, accept errors and mistakes, and be able to move on, the client is reassured that, with this CIT, it is OK to be imperfect, thus opening the gates for their healing. The CIT who can respect high standards in themselves, yet allow for errors to be growth opportunities, will project that to clients, and, thus, be more effective as a clinician. First, look at the log in your eye before pointing out the speck in the eye of your client. Competence never equals perfection.

Ideally, in the competency stage, you will begin to let go of doing everything "right, perfect, and correct" and instead face the ambiguity with a curiosity for learning and growth. Your CES may choose to offer you the exploration of using the Revised Tolerance to Ambiguity Scale assessment (MacDonald, 1970; see Tolerance to Ambiguity in Appendix 2 and Worksheet 4.1), while engaging with you in conjunction with other experiential activities to help support your growth, comfort, and reflection on how tolerating ambiguity can be a growth experience. Ultimately, letting go of control, of knowing everything, of perfectionism, and of unrelenting standards allows you to reach a new level of freedom in your education and growth. You may start to believe and experience that no question is a stupid question and you start to reach out and enjoy the freedom of not knowing all the answers, while enjoying growth in the process itself. Consider these examples from the Tolerance to Ambiguity Scale (see Tolerance to Ambiguity in Appendix 2) to complete and conduct a self-assessment of your own ability.

Tolerance to Ambiguity Scale (MacDonald, 1970)

1   A problem has little attraction for me if I don't think it has a solution.
2   I am just a little uncomfortable with people unless I feel that I can understand their behavior.
3   There's a right way and a wrong way to do almost everything.

(MacDonald, 1970, p. 793)

As you can tell, if you answer T on the first one, you may dislike ambiguity. The same with answering T on the second one. And if you said T on the third one, you may not tolerate ambiguity as well either. Consider the integration of ambiguity, critical thinking, and the ability to see multiple perspectives in the work you do as a CIT. Let's explore some activities as examples in assessing and building our tolerance of ambiguity.

Consider the *Twilight Zone* episode "Five Characters in Search of an Exit" in Season 3, Episode 14 (Serling, 1961). (See Worksheet 4.1 in Appendix 1.) The film begins with an apparent Army Major awakening in a blank circular room with no idea who he is or how he got there. He looks around and finds four other people in the room with him. A hobo, a ballerina, a clown, and a bagpiper all unaware of who they are or how they got there either. Each has a desire to get up and out of the room in search of an escape. Throughout the entire film you have no idea what is going on or where they are. Consider watching this episode and observing the following.

- What was it like not understanding or knowing what was occurring during the film?
- What feelings came up for you while watching the film?
- What were you thinking during the film?
- What are your thoughts in retrospect, looking back to the film and your experience of sitting in ambiguity?

Consider viewing images or paintings that have hidden two or three pictures in one and then being asked to describe what you see. For example, the witch and the beautiful woman. Which do you see? Consider finding such an image and exploring it with your CES in terms of your feelings, thoughts and experience of finding the "hidden or known" images within it.

Think back to a time you were at an event such as a football game, parade, carnival or circus and someone dressed in an animal or clown suit was there. Imagine that you could not see who was inside and yet they came up to you and pretended to know you. What would be the predominant feeling, thought, etc., that you experienced when this occurred? Describe how you would have experienced this and what you may have disliked about the situation. How does our ability to tolerate ambiguity or the unknown directly impact our work within the counseling field?

PAIR Feedback Model

In compliance with the ACA *Code of Ethics* F. 6. (2014), giving feedback and accepting feedback is required, and F. 9. guides the CES to give continuous feedback to and assessment of the CIT. In addition, your CES provides you with ongoing feedback regarding your performance throughout your training program and the feedback appears to occur in stages.

The **PAIR** feedback model that includes: **P**reparation for hearing feedback, **A**ctually hearing the feedback, **I**mplementing the feedback, and **R**eforming in response to the feedback. In addition, there may be a phenomenon in which you as CITs filter out feedback that does not match your pre-existing schema of self. This is where the disposition of self-reflection and deep desire for growth must supersede the fear and anxiety of potential change to move forward in your development. You may also turn to reviewing the stages of change again (see p. XX) to see if you are at least contemplative in desiring change while entering the field as it requires the ongoing need to self-assess, evaluate, reflect, and implement newfound learning. It is imperative that within your relationship with your CES, you understand the need to exhibit dispositions such as humility, humble professionalism, use of critical thinking, and desire for growth. The process is not easy, but it is so beneficial.

Preparation to Hear the Feedback

This stage is focused on preparation by completing a CIT self-scan to be sure that you are open to hearing and growing in development. In this stage, you as the CIT are reflecting on your biopsychosocial standing in terms of readiness for change and to hear feedback from the faculty or supervisor. You have already taken into consideration the Corrective Feedback Inventory (Hulse, Orr, & Paradise, 2006; see also p. XX) to ensure you are reframing feedback to consider growth and not as chastisement. In addition, you as the CIT must acknowledge the faculty/supervisors' motivation as being on your side and working in alliance with you towards your ultimate growth and well-being. For you to be able to hear the precious information, you must scan your thoughts or feelings of anxiety, worry, or fear to ensure you are in a receptive frame of mind for the information intended for your growth. Here, as the CIT, you are examining your ability to have a humble, professional humility to hear, grow, and learn. It is crucial that you, as the receiver, anticipate receiving feedback as growth. Understanding this process will offer positive outcomes and an understanding that the intention of the CES is one of joining with you in your development, with the goal of your best interests and those of the profession of counseling in mind. Sometimes, when we are in a place of being tired, hungry, or emotionally preoccupied, it can impact on our ability to utilize feedback.

Actually Hearing the Feedback

Your CES will help you to understand that hearing, digesting, clarifying, understanding, and allowing time to process feedback may be uncomfortable. Differentiating personal emotions from a legitimate need to correct a behavior is vital in this phase. The motivation to end the uncomfortable process quickly is a universal desire. We do not like to sit in the discomfort of our own experiences. However, that is exactly what we need to do with clients, and how better to learn how to do this than to walk through that process while in training with our CES on our team? A motivational speaker once presented the perspective that change only happens by inspiration or desperation (Rohn, 2018). Change by desperation may be quick but it is temporary. Change by inspiration tends to take more time but is longer-lasting. One may hear the feedback and vow to change immediately for the better. Often, that is a short-lived change, or what I call "holding your breath." We can only hold our breath so long; at some point we have to breathe again, and that breath takes us back to the old familiar ways we know. Long-term change takes time, dedication, intentionality, and the willingness to continue changing how you do things. When you change the *way* you change, breathing becomes natural and unlabored.

Implementing the Feedback

Being able to apply the feedback is fundamental in your growth process. Deeply consider, what is the substantiation to prove you have implemented your CES's feedback? Do you have evidence of change? If so, be sure to track, document, and offer it to assess the growth process. How do you put into practice what your CES guides you to do? Again, after changing and working through the initial reaction to feedback, then consider what implementing the changes may look like and how it may look to others. Let's just take a simple example. Let's say that you have received feedback about writing. Suppose that, for a long time, you have used the term: *in regards to*. Many people use it, but even the editing tool in Word recognizes that it is incorrect. You hear others using it; you read articles, books, and watch movies with others using it. It seems to you that everyone uses it. So, why should you have to change? That may be the first stepping stone. Why do you need to change that? What reasons can you think of? The suggestion is to use *regarding* instead. Try it out a couple of times. How does it sound? Start replacing it in your mind when you read it in a document. Start thinking silently that each time you or anyone says it, can you substitute the change and have the information still make sense? How easy is it to make the change? What makes it worthwhile? How do you feel when you do implement the feedback? Can you recognize a difference? Do you change and grow, or hold fast to the position that everyone else does it so I will too? How does what you decide to do reflect your worldview?

Reforming in Response to the Feedback

This process results in changes and a reformation of one's identity. The change experienced in this stage is more than holding your breath for a time. It is a permanent conduit to change that becomes a natural response to insight and feedback. The PAIR Model presents a lifelong opportunity to become and sustain the identity of a mature professional. Once you have tried to imagine the changes and to practice them, you can integrate them into what you do on a daily basis. You are transforming who you are, your image, your self-identity, and you are projecting professionalism as you enter the profession. The reformation that occurs after implementing the feedback may not be noticeable at first, but each time you choose to grow, the change is visible in you.

Assignments using PAIR (see Worksheet 4.2 in Appendix 1):

- Consider asking your CES to offer you authentic feedback from your last meeting. Use the PAIR model and log your experience of it. Afterwards, process your learning, understanding and experience with your CES.

- Take each step one at a time and describe in a CIT processing journal how you were able to try them out. Afterwards, consider soliciting feedback from a peer or friend on something to see how to implement the model in that capacity as well.
- Consider offering feedback to someone and gauge to see how well they may or may not exhibit the model.
- Consider reframing corrective feedback for yourself in a couple of statements. What would this be? Share this with your CES and continue to use this as a reframe with feedback to come.

Here is one example of Jessica as the fictional blended CIT using the PAIR Feedback Model in her work with her CES.

Case Study

CES: Hi Jessica, thank you for meeting me so we could go over your last remediation assignment on perfectionism.

CIT: Sure, no problem.

CES: Well, let's start with me asking you what you believe you did very well in the assignment?

CIT: I felt a little lost but . . . I'd say I was pretty honest about how my negative perfectionist thoughts rule my behaviors and self-worth.

CES: OK, good. I hear you saying you made a connection to the assignment and felt you were authentic in your analysis, reflection and assessment of how perfectionism impacts you negatively? Is that correct?

CIT: Yes, that's it! I guess it's embarrassing to say, but I feel like, I have to be honest to grow in it . . . so. . ..

CES: Yes, good. I am glad you feel safe enough to be honest, and you are seeing it in light of a growth experience. That is fantastic! So what part of the assignment did you find you struggled most with?

CIT: None really . . . I think I did everything else up to par.

CES: OK, good . . . well . . . I will offer you a bit of feedback on one area that I think you can take a peek at a little deeper and you can tell me what you think when you are ready. How does that sound?

CIT: OK, ya, I reviewed the PAIR Feedback Model prior to our meeting and I sorta prepared myself for this part but I know you are on my side, and want me to grow, and if you take the time to tell me some stuff I can work on, well. . .I really do want to hear it.

CES: OK, great! So, let's turn to page 23 and look at that section together. You answer the question concerning "unrelenting expectations" as not an issue at all for you. In light of one of the objectives and goals on your remediation plan and the events leading to the plan, can you help me understand the disconnect to this question?

(continued)

(continued)

CIT: OK, I need a moment to think about that (pauses).

CES: That's OK, take your time.

CIT: (Begins to tear up and pauses longer.)

CES: Take your time, how are you feeling right now?

CIT: I started to feel bad for not answering the question correctly, like shameful, then I remembered the intention of the process is not to make me "perfect" or to shun me, so I am leaning into being OK with the feedback and taking it at face value. So, yes, I believe I avoided that question maybe because I still am frustrated for what happened at my site regarding the initial happenings leading up to my plan.

CES: OK, good . . . thank you for being authentic in how you are doing in the feedback process and considering trying this on.

CIT: (Pauses), I avoided that question because, as I think about it, I was angry still about this process, and I think I may have been avoiding altogether having to look at my responsibility in that spot. I think I would like to redo that one if possible?

CES: OK, so I am hearing that when you initially started that question you felt angry, or even now are feeling angry, but, also, I hear it may be painful to approach and apply that question to your situation. But now, I sense you are asking to try it on again, and see if you can process it deeper and make any connections that may be there?

CIT: Yes. Is that OK?

CES: Sounds good to me . . . I really like that you are not rushing to find all the answers in this moment but are taking conscious time to let it soak in to find deeper meaning.

CIT: I think what I just did with avoiding that question, and almost avoiding your feedback, is exactly what led up to my remediation plan at my site. I am starting to make sense of this.

It is through the reflection and analysis of work on self, and in the dynamic and interpersonal attachment work through relationship, including immediacy and corrective feedback, that we see now how the experience of competence can arise. In this quadrant, you, as the CIT, will begin to feel competent not only in understanding yourself but also in how you interact and continue to grow through relationship.

Assessment of Counseling Skills, Knowledge, and Dispositions

We know that through the CACREP *Standards 2016*, CITs are required to exhibit competencies in knowledge, skills, and dispositions. This includes book knowledge, research, skills training, and professional counselor dispositional character qualities. In this quadrant of competency, you as the CIT begin to gain self-efficacy as you practice and engage with more understanding of the skills and competencies required for counselors. At this stage of the UGM, you may have achieved competency in one of the three areas, or two of the three areas, etc., but still wish to continue growth on all aspects. As mentioned, there are several assessments utilized in the field of counseling to assess CIT competency including foundational skills, professional skills, and professional dispositions. We will offer a bit of in-depth analysis into a couple of assessments just as examples. Your program likely may use their own specific assessment, however most cover these same attributes, so consider either using your CES-recommended assessment criteria or what we offered here.

As one example offered in the book, The Counseling Competency Scale-Revised (CCS-R) is a valid and reliable measurement that was created by the Counseling Department at the University of Central Florida (Lambie et al., 2016). This assessment tool is one that offers assessment with developmental considerations in the areas of Counseling Skills, Therapeutic Conditions, and Counseling Dispositions and Behaviors tied to CACREP-required knowledge, skills, and dispositions. Some areas to consider on the assessment include:

Part I: Counseling Skills and Therapeutic Conditions:

Nonverbal skills, Encouragers, Questions, Reflecting, Paraphrasing, Reflection of Meaning, Reflecting with Summarizing, Advanced Reflection with Meaning, Confrontation, Goals Setting, Focus of Counseling, Facilitating Therapeutic Environment (accurate, empathy, care, present, immediacy, and concreteness) in addition to appropriate respect and unconditional positive regard.

Part II: Counseling Dispositions and Behaviors:

Professional Ethics, Professional Behaviors, Professional and Personal Boundaries, Knowledge and Adherence to Site and University Policies, Record Keeping and Task Completion, Multicultural Competencies, Emotional Stability and Self-Control, Motivated to Learn and Grow Initiative, Openness to Feedback, Flexibility and Adaptability, Congruence and Genuineness. (See Worksheets 4.3–4.13.)

Assessment of CIT Dispositions: Professional Disposition Competence Assessment (PDCA) (Garner, Freeman, & Lee, 2016)

This assessment was created in response to the 2016 CACREP Standards requiring CIT evaluation of dispositions. This assessment includes PDCA traits such as: conscientiousness, self-awareness, interpersonal skills, professionalism, self-regulation, character, critical thinking, appreciation of learning, and spirituality. In addition, Garner et al. (2016) offered further clarifications regarding areas of "conscientiousness, critical thinking, and appreciation of learning" (p. 5) as important competencies. Consider the following questions and assess yourself. As you consider these questions, recognize that Garner et al. (2016) identified an appreciation of learning as an important dispositional feature. Further, being open to learning opportunities was clearly stated by a most beloved jazz musician, Louis (Satchmo) Armstrong, who once said, "There's some folks, that, if they don't know, you can't tell 'em" (Armstrong, 2018, para. 7). In addition, we are all familiar with the idiom, "You can lead a horse to water, but you can't make it drink" (Ammer, 2018). One more aspect we want to mention was from Canning (2015), who declared that some people want to be correct even at the expense of losing a relationship and self-growth. There may be several reasons why some people are more *teachable* than others and some of these attributes include the following areas for consideration (see Worksheet 4.14 in Appendix 1):

- Am I conscientious?
- Do I use critical thinking?
- Do I appreciate learning?
- Am I teachable?
- Is my attitude conducive to learning?
- Do I have an open heart and mind in approaching each day as an opportunity to be curious and learn something?
- Is it difficult for me to be the learner instead of the expert?
- Do I have a lifelong beginner's mindset?

Core themes to consider in continuing to be a beginner are offered by Lisa Canning (2015). These include the perspective that I can learn from everybody, each day, and that all learning experiences provide improvement to me personally.

Ongoing Professional Development

Garner, Freeman, and Lee (2016) included "interpersonal skills, self-regulation, and professionalism (encompassing ethics)" (p. 2) as elements required in professional development.

Example 1: Foundational Skills (Neukrug, 2006, pp. 9–10)

Throughout your training, be sure to continue to practice, self-assess, and seek feedback from others regarding your foundational skills.

Example 2: Self-Regulation Five Factor Traits:

Inability to control personal stress. What is your long-standing stress management self-care model for support while you are not only in training as a CIT, but also once you are working full time in the field of counseling?

Consider the Albee Incident Model as a means of forming a stress management plan while working in the field of counseling. Albee and Gullotta (1997) focused on a prevention model looking at: primary prevention, community issues, systemic change, marginalized populations, and psychoeducation. Consider how organic factors and stress need to be balanced with coping skills, self-efficacy, and support.

Example 5: Professionalism (Encompassing Ethics)

What ethical decision-making model have you chosen to implement throughout your training and work in the field? There are many from which to choose. If you have not yet decided on one for yourself, do some research and find one that seems to fit you and your circumstances.

In addition to foundational skills for you, we recommend continuing to review the other areas of counseling competencies as per the ACA website. For example, according the American Counseling Association Knowledge Center, there are the following additional areas of competencies to consider.

1   ALGBTIC Competencies for Counseling LGBQIQA (2012).
2   ALGBTIC Competencies for Counseling Transgender Clients (2009).
3   Animal Assisted Therapy Competencies (2016).
4   Competencies for Addressing Spiritual and Religious Issues in Counseling (2009).
5   Competencies for Counseling the Multiracial Population (2015).
6   Multicultural and Social Justice Counseling Competencies (2015).
7   Multicultural Career Counseling Competencies (2009).

In considering all areas of competency in this quadrant, we also look to consider how building on your prior work experiences can help solidify and build competency and self-efficacy as well.

Prior Work Experiences

Consider how your prior work and career experience can be a powerful tool to help evaluate strengths and ongoing needed areas for growth and development. Once you have worked on self, and relationship, and are now in the competency quadrant, you begin to see the connections of self-efficacy from other areas of life and can apply those as adult learners to the counseling skills you are working on. It can be tricky because often CITs revert to their personal relational histories as their prior experience, which are often tainted with negative experiences. As you solicit and integrate the feedback from your CES, you will also tap into the strengths model of using your existing life experience as an adult learner toward the current experience to offer deeper connection and application. The key is to lean into the education and supervision process while utilizing all your strengths and to gauge your application of such strengths through the feedback you receive. Remember, we are looking at our prior lived experiences through the lens of self-reflection, consideration, and application. What were some of your personal jobs, experiences, roles and responsibilities leading up to your profession in counseling today? (See Worksheet 4.15 in Appendix 1.)

*   Consider the strengths and skills needed to do what you have done in prior jobs or roles. How might they be transferable to counseling?
*   What skills might you have gained already from those experiences that are transferable to the counseling profession and why?
*   What job duties did you have to perform that are assets to the counseling career path?
*   Consider the strengths you had to have in your interpersonal life. How might those be transferable to your counseling career?

In a similar fashion, it is possible that, as a CIT, you will make inappropriate connections to past work that can be detrimental. You may try to place the counseling position into a box created by having worked in something you see as similar or close enough to counseling. Deeply consider the uniqueness of counseling as a profession and review the roles, responsibilities, definitions, and ethical differences to deliberate about your worldview, professional identity statement, and philosophy of counseling. Consider the case of Barb.

Case Study

Barb was a 52-year-old single woman who had been a hairdresser for over 30 years. She stated that she had "pretty much been working as a counselor" the entire time she did hair. She also equated the challenging work she did with working "double" as she was "essentially doing hair and giving advice simultaneously" without getting paid for the mental health work.

- What are your initial thoughts about Barb and her assertion?
- How might your own past experiences compare with the reality of the counselor (CIT) role and responsibilities ethically, legally and professionally?
- How might you, as a peer and colleague, approach this fellow intern?

(See Worksheet 4.16 in Appendix 1.)

In addition to continuing to master foundational counseling skills, knowledge and dispositions, we recommend continuing to review the other areas of counseling competencies per the ACA as mentioned earlier while seeking support from your CES as appropriate for various areas. Additional areas of ongoing professional development may include (see Worksheet 4.17 in Appendix 1):

1 **Current Literature: Reading and Creating**. Consider ongoing research and exploration in the field.
2 **Professional Conferences: Attending and Presenting**. Consider creating a proposal for a local or national counseling conference, or publishing an article or chapter in the field.
3 **Insight and Awareness**. Consider keeping a CIT journal and writing in it on a weekly basis.
4 **Collaborate with Peers**: Solicit and offer corrective feedback.
5 **Open to New Learning**. Set a goal to learn about an area that is different from what you already know.
6 **Theories**. Continue to explore, research and practice case conceptualization in relation to theories. Consider reading about a new theorist each month. Watch a movie and analyze it from the perspective of a different theory each time. For example, read the book or watch the movie *Life of Pi* (Ang Lee) and consider the various counseling theories throughout the storyline.
7 **Resources**. Join the ACA or your state counseling association and receive newsletters, journals, and emails with information including resources.
8 **Techniques**. Consider reviewing a journal article periodically that illustrates a new technique in the field.
9 **Tools**. Be sure to keep the tools from this book handy in addition to adding to your toolbox throughout your coursework, trainings, continuing education, etc., and visiting the tools periodically.
10 **Inter-disciplinary Collaboration**. Consider attending a conference, training or collaboration group in the field of nursing, education, law, or another field that interrelates with counseling.

11   **Supervision and Supervising Feedback**. Consider reviewing supervision models and inquiring with your supervisor or CES about their model of supervision.

12   **Personal Counseling**. Consider either periodically or regularly obtaining your own personal counseling throughout your training program or as needed in your career.

13   **Self-Care**. Create a self-care plan that includes biopsychosocial features and is long-sustaining but also edit it as needed.

14   **Expand Horizons**. Consider a social change initiative in your own community related to something along the lines of counseling and contribute your gifts.

15   **Ethics**. Choose and hold to an ethical decision-making model of your choice.

16   **Local, State and National Legislation Awareness and Influence**.

After reviewing your core counseling knowledge and ongoing continual educational developmental opportunities, consider the element of self-efficacy and how this concept is pivotal when heading into the final quadrant of actualization.

Gaining CIT Self-Efficacy

After exploring the tools and reflective exercises offered so far, there comes a point where the CIT must transition from the old self to the new self in terms of finding the self-efficacy embedded into their Counselor Identity. Through the self-efficacy comes the ability to handle and solicit feedback, to self-assess, as well as to feel the support and encouragement of your CES without fear or worry. We can use learning to ride a bike as a metaphor in applying our CES identity and development process.

Learning to Ride the Bike of CES Competencies

Dr. Lewis's story. I am the youngest of four children, spanning a range of ten years. My older sister is four years older than I, my next brother is six years older, and the oldest is ten years older than I am. They were all riding bikes for some time before my turn rolled around. My oldest brother took an old bike, restored it, and made it a "girl's" bike for me. It was a treasure, but I didn't know how to balance and ride. I spent many a day crashing and burning, scraping knees and elbows, but pushing forward again the next time. Finally, my big sister said she would help me. She held on to the back of my seat and ran with me as I pedaled the bike, urging me on: "Keep pedaling, keep going straight, pedal faster!" she would yell to me. I would respond with, "Don't let go!!!" She assured me she was right there. I remember the last time she helped me learn to ride that bike. We were on the straightaway of a level road at the top of our hill, and she was running, telling me to keep going, to keep pedaling, and, as I began to feel the rush of air through my hair, I thought maybe I can do it! I wanted to tell her, so I looked back to tell her I could do it, and she was about a half block behind me. She let go. I wasn't ready. I crashed and burned. I felt betrayed. She had promised me she wouldn't let go, and still she did. She lied to me; she broke her promise; I could not trust her. I believe that I also extended that to: "If I can't trust my big sister, I can't trust anyone" and "If my big sister betrays me, everyone will!" That was a worldview I gained at the age of about seven, I would guess. That worldview may have guided me unconsciously for many years. However, at some point, we all need to dig in our heels and open these gift-wrapped boxes of our past. I have a whole closet full in my mind. They will continue to influence our daily behavior until we open them up and unpack everything that is in that box, one by one. When I unpacked this one, I saw the dashing of my little heart as I interpreted the actions as a betrayal. She said she would not let go and she did, even though she promised. There seemed to be a thread of betrayal that I traced as I unpacked the bicycle box, seen in relationships throughout my life. By the time I was 25, I realized hidden triggers had interfered with my healthy expressions. Processing the effects of divorce, I recognized my collusion in having a betrayal theme in my life. Once I disarmed the trigger, I freed my healthy self to confidently grow beyond my past! Freedom is far better than shackles.

Dr. McLain's learning to ride a bike metaphor:

I remember it was a perfect late summer day. It was sunny, and warm but not hot out. My aunt and uncle were visiting my parents and they had a little picnic BBQ meal and were likely drinking beer and having their "adult time." I was about nine or ten years old and we had the old family dark green metallic Schwinn bike in the garage. I had been thinking for some time how exciting it would be to get it out of there. I meant to go exploring and leave my dysfunctional family home. The thought of riding a bike gave me a sense of power to be able to go and get away from the chaos of my parents fighting nonstop. So, as I was outdoors playing with my animals, I came across the bike. I looked it over and thought, "I am going to learn to ride this thing today!" I don't think my family ever came out of the house to see what I was doing out in our driveway, which was fine with me. I felt like I could learn best alone, without critical evaluation, without the pressures. I figured out that our driveway was on an incline from the top that met the road to the garage (my safe zone). I felt safe near the garage because I had played there a lot on my little plastic hot rod since toddlerhood. I used to wear an old ball cap, bright red lipstick and chew gum while riding that hot pink Hot Wheels trike, and I felt good doing it! Imagine the feeling I would get from mastering this large metallic green Schwinn monster!

So, there I was standing over the bike at the top of the driveway leading down gently to the garage. I had to go on a right curve and I started off a little scared but knowing I could hop off at any time. No problem. I felt scared. After all, I had on long pants and the gravel wasn't too bad for a scrape. I think, in that moment, I realized learning to ride this bike meant freedom, fun, and happy memories/travels to come but it would come at a cost. I would need to face the fears, and likely get cut up a bit. So, I agreed with the risks that outweighed the costs tenfold to me. I hopped off when I started to lose balance. I went back to the top again and tried all over. I must have done this ten times or more. Once, I did fall, and the bike cut my leg. I didn't care. I was so driven by mastering this thing that nothing could have stood in my way at this point, after tasting a short glide on that thing peddling on my own! I went to the top again, then my family came out and finally noticed me. They asked me "what are you doing out here?" I replied, "I am learning to ride this bike; come back after I got it down and I will show you what I can do!" They agreed and went back to their BBQ. I didn't bother even going back in to tell them when I got it because I was having so much fun riding it around the driveway and even taking it on the road! When they came back out, I showed them, and they seemed indifferent to my success. I didn't seem to care at the time because now I had freedom!

My grandmother ended up buying me my first bike the following spring for my birthday. It was amazing and special. It was white and purple with unicorns all over it and a basket on the front, with streamers on the handlebars. I rode that bike for at least three years and it became my tool for ongoing independence, exploration and freedom!

Some of the core worldview schematic themes that pertain to my CIT development include:

- abandonment and neglect;
- emotional neglect;
- perfectionism.

Now, there are also some positive aspects of these schemas as well, including:

- survival, autonomy and creative flexible thinking;
- deep compassion and empathy for others;
- leadership, commitment to excellence and passion to teach others.

I have felt that for much of my life I was a parentified child who learned how to survive and thrive on my own, just as the bike experience illustrates so perfectly. Although this created a deep loneliness in me, I strived to figure things out and nothing was too big or too intimidating to discover and learn. In that emotional loneliness, I always took time for others, asked about their lives, and learned to deeply connect with advanced empathy, intuitively seeking to understand, read, and pick up on what people felt or needed. In a sense, the wounding led to my ability to desire healthy authentic relationships with others. The problem in often being left to find things out for myself was that I never knew the standard or where the bar was to know if I was on track. This created a perfectionist tendency in never understating what good enough was. In addition, in not having family members there to congratulate me when I mastered riding the bike, I believe this led to me not being able to receive positive acknowledgements in such a way as to truly feel proud of myself for my accomplishments. However, throughout the metaphor lies the beauty that, even in my deprivations, I have always been driven to self-reflection, desire for growth, and a love and passion to be in relationship with others.

In the bike metaphor we can see how our early life experiences can tie into other parts of our worldview. They may have informed our thoughts about self and others in the world, as they lead to our counselor identity, philosophy, and theory. Take some time to consider your own learning to ride a bike metaphor (see Worksheet 2.11 in Appendix 1). Reflect on the 4-F responses (see p. 44) and the prior wounded healer from Chapter 2 as well. You can substitute learning to drive a car if that is more applicable for you.

- Describe the day and time, your age, and even where you were developmentally.
- How did you feel and who was around you?
- Did you have support from others, and leadership, guidance, or bystanders watching?
- What was the process like for you?
- Who congratulated you once you mastered the task? How did that feel?
- Who do you wish would have been present? What do you wish you would have heard?
- How might you integrate this experience into your reflection of your worldview?

We have illustrated the deep need for a CIT to have self-efficacy in their counselor roles and the need for us all to continue in our growth process. Now we can apply our own reflection to our CIT example case study of Stacy.

Case Study

This is the story of Stacy (a fictional blended CIT). Stacy has been referred to have a remediation plan after having made it through her graduate program with a 3.87 GPA. Recently, while in her practicum course, her field experience supervisor reported that her skills and behaviors had become problematic in the last three weeks. Specifically, the supervisor reported that Stacy had been late on several occasions, stating it was because, as she reported, that her husband was not helping pay bills and her water was shut off, causing her to be late. In addition, the supervisor stated that a client was made aware of the student's situation, likely due to the CIT telling her client about it. The supervisor appeared clear that the student was struggling with self-care, boundaries, and ability to hear and accept feedback, and struggled even more with implementing the feedback. The supervisor stated that when she attempted to have a serious conversation with Stacy about self-care, the student simply brushed it off, and stated, "everyone has stressors in life; I am doing the best I can." According to the student, when speaking with her, she said "I do not see what the problem is, I have a 3.87 GPA, and, ya, I am struggling a bit personally but who doesn't?"

What are your thoughts about Stacy's:

- philosophy of change;
- worldview;
- beliefs about feedback and confrontation;
- understanding and training concerning gatekeeping;
- relationship with her supervisor;
- ability to read her non-verbals, verbals and sense emotions;
- CIT's own awareness of how they are experiencing the situation (fear, anger, desire not to get involved, etc.).

As well as giving your thoughts on any other likely areas for learning.

In reviewing this case, we can see a metaphor, perhaps, in using the idea of bringing in a mirror and asking Stacy to consider her reflection. How might reviewing the ACA code of ethics and the CACREP requirement of competencies in knowledge, skills and dispositions apply?

Perhaps this student would have heard, accepted, and understood the metaphor and connection and moved forward . . . or perhaps not. So, what are some potential barriers for students who find themselves receiving necessary feedback from their CES? In conclusion, you can see that a CIT's journey is much more than knowledge, good grades and skills; it also includes counseling dispositions including the desire for feedback and ongoing growth and development. As we mentioned, faculty using the CCS-R, Tolerance to Ambiguity Assessment, Corrective Feedback Inventory-R, Carkhuff Empathy Scale, and other assessments, can help you as the CIT to work with your CES in several ways.

Assessing and Building Self-Efficacy in CITs

Now that we have seen some examples of self-efficacy and evaluated the example CIT case study, how can we assess self-efficacy? There are many self-efficacy self-assessments to choose from. One consideration is for you to explore your own discovery of self-efficacy by choosing ways to consider how you feel about your ability to accomplish and feel competent in your achievements. One example is the Self Efficacy Survey (SES) (Panc, Mihalcea, and Panc, 2012). Self-efficacy is defined as "the belief system that people have regarding their capabilities to produce designated levels of performance that exercise influence over events and situations affecting their lives" (Bandura, 1994, p. 71). According to Bandura's (1994) theory, those with a powerful sense of self-efficacy face and approach difficult talks and continue to work towards mastering tasks, behaviors, etc., to achieve objectives; furthermore, they are able to manage the challenges that come along, despite setbacks as they come up. Those who appear to have a low self-efficacy when faced with an arduous task may perceive themselves as incapable of completing the task, or solving the problem, and lose confidence in their ability, focusing only on failure and the setbacks.

One can argue that self-efficacy in counselor training comes with your CIT worldview, ongoing counselor development, and experiences. Additionally, it comes with excellent supervision and consultation support when you are faced with difficult circumstances. This adds to your ability to gain self-efficacy. There are ways to help assist you in building self-efficacy and one is simply through the mentoring relationship you have with your CES. In fact, many CITs report having a higher self-efficacy once they have completed a remediation development plan, having gone through immense struggle, healing, growth, and learning. Furthermore, they share that they come out on the other side feeling more confident in their skills, dispositions, and abilities. The nature of the supervisory relationship consists of being genuine, authentic, giving feedback, and, of course, laughing and building ongoing rapport. You as a CIT can begin to feel comfortable coming to your CES with immensely deep, ethical, and personal questions that allow you the safety and freedom to work through things rather than hiding or ignoring them. So, whatever area you as the CIT struggle with, practice, and being allowed to practice, fail, make mistakes, and have a safe supervisory relationship to come back to is important. We recognize, of course, that there are some mistakes, especially repeated ones, that have larger consequences and can be markers of needed gatekeeping protocol as indicated in the ACA *Code of Ethics* (2014).

Some CIT activities to boost self-efficacy may include (see Worksheet 4.18 Appendix 1):

1 What was something in your life you felt proud to master or accomplish?
2 What was that like for you? Who was your support network?
3 What strengths did you tap into to accomplish that feat?
4 What fears and weaknesses did you have to combat to achieve your goal?
5 What area do you currently feel a drive to achieve in your self-efficacy as a CIT?
6 What aspects of your worldview coincide with your thoughts and feelings of accomplishment in pursuing difficult tasks?

7 How might you apply your prior experience to this?

8 Who do you need to be your support on this part of your journey?

9 Where do you see yourself ideally regarding mastering this facet in your CIT development? In other words, in your dream of the future, describe who you are and how you have mastered self-efficacy regarding your counselor identity and development.

10 Challenge yourself in something! In the next week or so, choose an activity you haven't done before, or one you haven't done in a long while that you were good at. A few examples are included below.

- Go bowling.
- Go fishing.
- Go roller-skating, ice-skating, etc.
- Go golfing (mini golf counts!).
- Consider any sport and joining a game at your local YMCA or Recreation Center.
- Play a game with your family.
- Pick up and play a musical instrument.
- Ride a bike.
- Go to the local fair, play a game, or go on a ride.
- Go for a walk or hike to a special destination.

You get the picture. You as the CIT are pushing yourself to do something that perhaps you have mastered before, but maybe not have experienced in a long time. Or, become daring in trying something new to master. Consider writing about your experience and sharing with your CES in terms of how you experienced the activity and how it can be a metaphor for the needed area of growth you hope to achieve in your self-efficacy as a counselor.

Summary

This chapter seeks to offer CITs a variety of ways to implement the assessments and tools towards ongoing growth and optimal development. You can evaluate and understand how your own worldview influences everything, including your counselor identity, philosophy of counseling, and your own prior experiences, perhaps of wounded healing. This information also corresponds to the skills and dispositions often cited as potential areas of remediation and gatekeeping concern for CITs. These areas are interconnected and can be approached in a variety of ways, but the main point is that you lean into the growth and competencies through support from your CES in all areas of counseling skills and dispositions.

References

Albee, G. W., & Gullotta, T. P. (1997). *Primary prevention works*. Thousand Oaks, CA: Sage Publications.

American Counseling Association (ACA) (2014). *ACA Code of ethics*. Alexandria, VA: American Counseling Association.

American Counseling Association (ACA) (2018). *ACA knowledge center*. Retrieved from: www. counseling.org/knowledge-center/competencies.

Ammer, C. (2018). You can lead a horse to water, but you can't make it drink. *The American Heritage® dictionary of idioms by Christine Ammer*. Retrieved from Dictionary.com website: www.dictionary.com/browse/you-can-lead-a-horse-to-water-but-you-can-t-make-it-drink.

Armstrong, L. (2018). *Louis Armstrong quotes*. Retrieved from: www.goodreads.com/author/quotes/85528.Louis_Armstrong.

Bandura, A. (1994). Self-efficacy. In V. S. Ramachaudran (Ed.) *Encyclopedia of Human Behaviour*, Vol. 4. New York, NY: Academic Press, 71–81.

Bernard, J. M., & Goodyear, R. K. (2004). *Fundamentals of clinical supervision* (5th ed.). New York, NY: Pearson Publishing.

Canning, L. (2015, September 24). Coachable, teachable, and trainable: The three keys to doing anything [Web log post]. Retrieved from: http://blog.entrepreneurthearts.com/2014/09/24/coachable-teachable-and-trainable-the-3- keys-to-doing-anything.

Frame, M. S., & Stevens-Smith, P. (1995). Out of harm's way: Enhancing monitoring and dismissal processes in counselor education programs. *Counselor Education and Supervision*, *35*(1), 118–129.

Garner, C. M., Freeman, B. J., & Lee, L. (2016). Assessment of student dispositions: The development and psychometric properties of the professional disposition competence assessment (PDCA). *Ideas and Research You Can Use: VISTAS*, *52*, 1–14.

Hulse, D., Orr, J., & Paradise, L. (2006). The corrective feedback instrument-revised. *Journal for Specialists in Group Work*, *31*(3), 263–281, doi: /10.1080/01933920600777758.

Lambie, G., Mullen, P., Swank, J., & Blount, A. (2016). *Counseling Competencies Scale, Revised (CCS-R)*. Orlando, FL: University of Central Florida, Counselor Education Program. Retrieved from: http://webmedia.jcu.edu/counselingdepartment/files/2016/03/CCS- R-Evaluation.pdf.

Lumadue, C. A., & Duffy, T. H. (1999). The role of graduate programs as gatekeepers: A model for evaluating student counselor competence. *Counselor Education and Supervision*, *39*(2), 101–109.

MacDonald, A. P. (1970). Revised scale for ambiguity tolerance: Reliability and validity. *Psychological Reports*, *26*(3), 791–798, doi: 10.2466/pr0.1970.26.3.791.

McAdams, C. R., Foster, V. A., & Ward, T. J. (2007). Remediation and dismissal policies in counselor education: Lessons learned from a challenge in federal court. *Counselor Education and Supervision*, *46*(3), 212–229.

Neukrug, E. S. (2016). *Skills and techniques for human service professionals: Counseling environment, helping skills, treatment issues*. Norfolk, VA: Counseling Books, Etc.

Panc, T., Mihalcea, A., & Panc, I. (2012). Self-efficacy survey: A new assessment tool. *Procedia Social and Behavioral Sciences*, *33*, 880–884.

Pope, V. T., & Kline, W. B. (1999). The personal characteristics of effective counselors: What 10 experts think. *Psychological Reports*, *84*(3), 1339–1344, doi: https://doi.org/10.2466/pr0.1999.84.3c.1339.

Rigg, G. (2017). *Essentials of psychomotor therapy and the healing circle model*. Greeley, CO: Author.

Rohn, J. (2018). *BrainyQuotes*. Retrieved from: www.goodreads.com/quotes/335376-we- generally-change-ourselves-for-one-of-two-reasons-inspiration.

Ronnestad, M. H., & Skovholt, T. M. (2003). The journey of the counselor and therapist: Research findings and perspectives on professional development. *Journal of Career Development*, *30*(1), 5–44, doi: 10.1023/A:1025173508081.

Serling, R. (Teleplay writer) & Johnson, L. (Director) (1961). Five characters in search of an exit. In B. Houghton (Producer), *Twilight Zone*. New York, NY: Columbia Broadcasting System (CBS).

Spurgeon, S. L., Gibbons, M. M., & Cochran, J. L. (2012). Creating personal dispositions for a professional counseling program. *Counseling and Values*, *57*(3), 96–108.

5 Application to Challenging Work
The Lifelong Growth Plan

Counselors in Training are introduced to the Actualization process from the UGM, including the Professional Growth Plan that paves the way, combining skills practice, assessment, newfound meaning, and growth in an ongoing fashion. You can create a growth plan from the beginning of your journey or halfway in, assessing your strengths and areas of challenge, helping to set you up for ongoing growth throughout your professional career. This is a wonderful way to have a portfolio ready when you apply for licensure or apply to jobs as well, in case you want to share your professional development plan and process with others.

In addition, you can explore how you have perceived feedback prior to your counseling training and reflect upon the sometimes-difficult process of self-growth, while studying to help others. The CIT responsibilities are articulated with support from CACREP *Standards 2016* (CACREP, 2015), ACA *Code of Ethics* (2014), and ACES *Best Practices in Clinical Supervision* (2011), as well as with a discussion of key components of professional orientation and professional skills. The growth plan can also serve as a tool if a skills deficit is found, to help guide you towards quality practice and success. You are encouraged to review your growth plan throughout your training and during your career to see the immense growth already achieved, and you can add as needed towards ongoing areas for growth throughout a lifetime. This chapter also summarizes what you have learned throughout this journey, from self through the present, while reiterating how to continue to use this book throughout your longstanding professional careers in clinical mental health, as a developmental guide in your ongoing growth. You will be offered a step-by-step guide showing how to put together a potential final growth plan project and explore post-assessment strategies long into the future of collaboration and supervision.

Self-Actualization Through Metaphor

Self-actualization was described by Abraham Maslow (1943) as the highest level of needs at the top of a pyramid of life needs. It includes morality, creativity, problem solving, etc. To reach this top order of need, it is said that we must have the other levels of basic needs met first. These basic needs may include food, shelter, safety (Self in the UGM), then belonging and connection to others (Relationship in the UGM), esteem (Competence in the UGM) before moving to self-actualization (Actualization in the UGM). In many ways our UGM is like the Maslow hierarchy in that we believe that, for successful development to occur, as CITs follow the quadrants of self-awareness

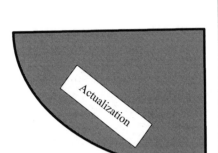

The quadrant of actualization invites us to explore our own deepest growth towards our fullest potential. In this quadrant, for this book, we will be exploring actualization through:

- Self-Actualization Through Metaphor
- Growth in Mistake Making and Through Failure
- New Awareness Applied to Relationships
- Relationship Growth in Authenticity
- The Growth Plan

Figure 5.1 Actualization Quadrant.

(Modified by the authors with permission from Rigg, 2017.)

and exploration, relationship awareness and work, competency, to actualization, their growth will be exponential. The beauty is that as we enter actualization we are then led back into more work on the *self* and so on throughout the circle model.

Sometimes metaphors allow for a unique way that is once-removed to make a connection to the process you are undertaking of self, relationship, competencies, towards actualization. Often, I will ask my CIT to describe to me what the process of self-evaluation, relational focus, and competency was like for them. They report things like:

> "At the beginning, I was so closed off, scared and had walls up, but then once I connected and built trust with my CES, I began to enjoy the process of self-exploration."

Another supervisee reported that:

> "I am excited now, to receive feedback, analyze and try it on, and use it towards immense growth and development. In fact, when I don't receive any feedback from my CES I ask for it because I want to get all I can from the process!"

I offer my CITs various metaphors to illustrate a concept, growth, or process of enlightenment, which can also pave the way for them in their own personal process as well. One CIT explored her process and likened it to remodeling her home. She stated that the house she was living in had been abandoned, neglected, and left to rot for years. Early in the meaningful relationship-building process she had used similar words to describe her own childhood experiences in relation to problems professionally. When she began talking about the house and the need to fix it up, I pointed out the similarity and asked if the metaphor fit for her. She immediately teared up, was quiet and then made the connection and ran with it throughout the process, even creating deeper meaning and introspection in actualization towards the end of the mentorship.

In fact, the use of art, metaphor, and anything creative can be most beneficial for CITs as they seek to make meaning from their experience to repeat the beautiful Universal Growth Model cycle all over again in new situations that occur. Olsen (2013) shared: "deconstruction and reconstruction of the self becomes a possibility through poetic self-expression, resultant epiphanies and recognition of an evolving self that is characterized by self-actualization" (p. 2). In this way, we see how you can use creativity in the use of drawing, painting, building or sculpting, creating a piece of music, poem, or connecting to another piece of art; any option can provide a framework for self-expression and deeper meaning towards growth. According to Olsen (2013) "Metaphor and allegory, as used in artistic expression, can be utilized to create self-permeable boundaries that are nevertheless intact, for both the artist and his audience" (p. 2). To connect everything in self, relationship, competency towards actualization, you must connect to the creative side of yourself. The creative can be anything that makes sense to you, and the beauty of this is that it is personal, and you can tailor fit it towards your unique needs, aptitudes, and interests, and can then also contribute towards the self-understanding and self-reflection, thus repeating the growth cycle and completing the UGM. Actualization is creative, developmental, and cyclical in nature. In other words, once you go through the process you are likely to continue towards ongoing growth. "And self-realization is self-actualization. It has been suggested that it is only the most functional people who are able to achieve being values [sic], resolution of dichotomies, peak experiences and meaning in life" (Olsen, 2013, p. 2).

Here are two examples of "self-realization and actualization" through use of metaphor from a former CES supervisee who summarized her process of counselor education as a personal self-actualized journey and connected it to deeper life meaning.

Case Study: Olaf and the Dissertation

For me the counselor education supervision program and dissertation process was in some ways like a continuation of a master's program and, in other ways, so much more than what I expected. In the end, I realized growing through the program actually changed the way I think. I have no idea when that occurred, but I know that, at some point in the process, my thinking process changed. I often heard "trust the process" and in this case it did work. I trusted the process in my master's and I did it again in my doctoral program. Good programs are designed to influence all of you, not just put information into your mind, or skills at the ready. The program is designed for transformation into the professional we long to be after we enter the field, and forevermore.

(continued)

(continued)

I worked tirelessly on evaluation of myself in coursework, then relationships in my fieldwork. I had passed "competencies" in all areas in my skills, coursework, etc. Next, I needed to complete my dissertation in a fairly short period of time, after having spent what seemed like forever in class after class writing paper after paper. I felt discouraged and pretty concerned about being able to make my deadline. I began to look at the process I had followed thus far, from my very first class in my doctoral program. I thought I had really come a long way. It was fall; I had started years ago in the summer semester. If I was able to accomplish this task, I would be DONE by summer. I thought, I'm going to loooooove summer! That made me think of Olaf in the movie, *Frozen*. That's IT! Olaf loves summer. I love summer. I'm going to let Olaf be my inspiration to change what I was doing, embrace the dissertation process, and finish this!

One of my instructors had cautioned us to not do a dissertation that was our Life's Work. It was an assignment. Five more papers, and I'll be done. OK, Olaf . . . We love summer! I surrounded myself with Olaf to keep focused. He was the first thing I saw in the morning, and the last thing I saw at night. I had an Olaf Pez dispenser on my dashboard. I had an Olaf screensaver on my computer, an Olaf thumb drive to put into my computer, an Olaf lotion dispenser beside my computer, Olaf cards, towels, stuffed figures. I put my focus on Olaf and summer and being done so I could love summer.

That inspiration and focus worked for me and, by February, I completed my final defense, and by May, my dissertation was edited, accepted, signed off on, and submitted to the school. Without Olaf, I would never have been able to complete the job. I graduated in May, and I Loooooved Summer! (Anonymous.)

Case Study: Horse training with the "Red Flag"

I had been working with substance abuse clients for years and was taking a break to self-care out with my neighbor and daughter on a sunny mild beautiful day training her gigantic Percheron/Paint Mare. I knew she was in one of her "moods" and as much as I tried not being frightened of her, it can be hard to have a 2500-pound, 8-foot-tall horse stampeding your way. My neighbor was riding the other gentler well-trained quarter horse and asked if my 6-year-old wanted to join her for a little pasture ride time. I hesitated but my daughter really wanted to get up. I allowed her, and they began walking around a little in the green grass. Out of nowhere, the Percheron bolted towards them, attempting to bite and attack the quarter horse my daughter was on! I tried not to freak out but rapidly went over, got her down, had her run to safety while we calmed the quarter horse down. I asked my friend, "what is her problem! She acts jealous that you two were riding him and not giving her attention?" My friend asked me if I was frightened by her behaviors and I agreed.

What did this remind me of? I was full of fear and triggered! It was like when I had court-ordered clients (some with violent backgrounds) cross boundaries and try to frighten me at the treatment agency. My friend immediately got out her training flag (which is a 3-foot-long thin handle and a vinyl bright red colored flag at the end that makes sound) and she said to me, "well take this, we are going to do some training with her working with boundaries." We walked over, and the horse tried to come towards me and I used the flag and shook it to signify this was my space and she needed to back up. That felt good! My friend asked me, "do you feel safer to have the flag in your hand?" I agreed. In the pasture that day I was processing a lot about what the scary big horse reminded me of and I saw immediately connections to people in my own life that have tried to "stampede" and "bully or scare me." I thought deeply about my need to stay firm, grounded, not run away in fear, but to pick up and find my own "flag" in those professional processes and relationships in life. I realized I was mainly "triggered" during bully situations when working with professionals who attempted to use power and control over me and others, and the ramifications of those professionals angry with me for doing what is ethical, right and just. I went home and painted the flag and took a photo of it and I pull it up on my phone even today if I need to. The flag is my tool to protect me, self-care, and to set limits to tell others, especially clients, to back away if needed. As silly as it sounds, even today when I meet a bully, I can think of that flag and I choose words that represent the flag actions which help protect me and establish a boundary with people. (Anonymous.)

Metaphors can be powerful in creating a deep meaningful relationship towards obtaining self-actualization for CITs, especially when sharing with supervision. This is done through acknowledging a safe place to make mistakes and learn from failures. Many CITs take their metaphor home with them for the duration of their counselor developmental process and even use the metaphor for life-long self-care, safety, and perspective taking.

Consider a couple of metaphors that show your own personal CIT growth or training process. What is a significant event you may have experienced from which you had growth? Consider the elements of that experience and the process you followed to gain deeper understanding (see Worksheet 5.1 My Metaphor in Appendix 1).

Growth in Mistake-Making Through Failure

It is easy to laud one's accomplishments but it tends to be more difficult to share our failures. However, it is through our failures that more growth occurs as we continue to expose our learning opportunities *because* of our failings. Some companies take the position that if employees are not having failures, they are not trying. If we reason through that perspective we see that, if we try and fail, we have learned quite a bit that will then translate towards success. Think of the man, Spencer Silver, who invented post-it notes, now a staple on every desk. The invention was the result of a failure as he was trying to find a kind of glue but his glue allowed a person to put on and take off the note multiple times. What a rotten glue! However, this *failure* resulted in an amazing product that is used everywhere, from covering automobiles to a reminder in a calendar to pick up the children. His failure was a success when he modified the *context*. In addition, consider the following thoughts and experiences from a few great men and women.

As noted in the article on "Successful people who failed" by Sugar, Feloni, & Lutz (2015), many now famous successful people first failed, sometimes several times, before reaching success. Walt Disney had worked hard for years before his success and was even fired from the *Kansas City Star* due to his supervisors' believing he lacked imagination and unique ideas. He apparently also failed at other businesses prior to his success with his cartoon film *Snow White*, which paved the way towards his tremendous success. In addition, Oprah Winfrey was apparently fired from her first television job for appearing to be too emotionally invested in the stories she presented. Now, she is known as the Queen of Television Talk Shows and is successful for the very reasons for which she was earlier criticized. Steven Spielberg was apparently rejected from admission to the University of Southern California School of Cinematic Arts several times. In fact, now, he is considered one of the most brilliant movie directors of all time. He began his distinguished career with *Jaws* in 1975 and has won three Academy Awards and four Emmys.

Remember our previous discussion about a fixed versus a growth mindset and Bandura's self-efficacy? If we begin to change our entire worldview and perspective about what failure even is, and attempts in life towards success, we can begin to see that perhaps failure doesn't really exist. Only attempts at moving closer and closer towards growth and the full potential that is success. "Failure is not an event, but rather a judgment about an event. Failure is not something that happens to us or a label we attach to things. It is a way we think about outcomes" (Ortberg, 2001 p. 22). I suggest you read that last quote one more time. As a CIT, you can reframe the entire experience of counselor development as one that is a gold nugget opportunity to excel, stretch, face your fears, and flourish in the face of change. We, as counselors engaged in ongoing training, must remember that "Fear and growth go together like Mac 'n cheese" (Ortberg, 2001 p. 21). The decision to grow means taking a risk, facing fears, and deciding the growth is worth the risk.

There appears to be a phenomenon some experience once they feel the freedom to make mistakes and use them towards optimal growth and learning. It is described by the youngest and oldest students as liberating or ultimately a new world of seeing leading towards "actualization." CITs no longer are bound by the perfectionistic bondage of black and white thinking or pressures of performing a specific way, or even looking at joining the field of counseling as their identity but rather, the transformation in becoming a counselor helps them find their core center personal identity. The CIT finally can see that in all those mistakes, perhaps they weren't mistakes at all. This new perspective opens the door for living life fully without regrets, looking for deeper meaning, and application in everything they do. The growth then fuels the CIT's desire, thirst, and longing to continue the process. In all honesty, I have had many supervisees ask to keep seeing me for ongoing mentoring long after their remediation plans were accomplished and closed out. I would like to think it was because I am such an amazing CES but, honestly, I believe it is really connected to the bug they were bitten by called *actualization*: realization of new meaning, and a new way of living that excites them. Through meaningful connection, growth can be liberating, and intoxicating. Many may come from environments or lifelong learning situations where they were not aware that mistakes were normal, and instead of being chastised, condemned, and doomed, they could self-reflect, seek supervision, apply feedback knowing it was intended for their optimal growth, practice competencies, and then obtain actualization all over again.

New Awareness Applied to Relationships

The new learning, actualization and connection you obtain appears to elicit a new awaking in that it helps encourage you to look at even other places of ongoing needed growth in life. Some CITs find it compelling to begin to dig more intentionally in areas to challenge themselves and explore new areas of their self, relationships, and competencies, which appears to encourage them to seek feedback from others. In fact, the metaphor that you used, which we discussed earlier, can become the new meaning and theme for growth in your world, which is also a tool towards ongoing feedback and growth. Here are a few ideas to encourage ongoing growth and development through feedback and work on counseling competencies.

- Use your prior metaphor, if it fits still, and build on it continually. Or, create a new metaphor that fits. Consider passions in your life such as hobbies, recreational self-care etc. art, music, etc. as inspiration for your metaphor.
- Consider using a personal CIT development journal. Write in your journal each week to explore growth, needed areas for ongoing growth, self-awareness, reflections and feedback from others. Consider logging how often you practice asking for feedback on how others are experiencing you.
- Consider one self-reflective activity each week that you designate and devote to your own growth process. This could be a meditative experience, exercise, or challenging yourself to go into an area of discomfort.

For example, I had a supervisee once who reportedly had an argument with a staff member at the center she worked at and, after processing the event, she recognized she reacted out of a triggering and was ashamed of it. Once she worked through her response, explored it, and processed it, she felt compelled to still avoid the staff member. She hated feeling this way and wanted to face her fear of having to see and talk to the staff member again, so she volunteered each week to come and lead group in that cottage. After the third time of offering to support, the other staff member asked the CIT, "why do you keep volunteering to help me in here?" The CIT was faced with a choice to be authentic or to "fight, flight, freeze or fawn" (Walker, 2014). She told the staff member, "I am sorry I got upset in our last discussion and I have done a lot of processing about the communication. I realize I reacted out of a personal trigger, but I am aware of it now, and feel badly about it." The CIT went home, journaled it, and continued to work on her interactions with others using this process.

- Practice the use of immediacy and authenticity in daily living while journaling about it and the experiences and results you see after initiating it. Ask yourself, what am I feeling right now? How am I experiencing this process?
- Consider writing out the five core counseling dispositions you believe are most important and why. Integrate this into your professional identity statement as you begin to explore who you are as professional counselors.

Relationship Growth in Authenticity

Using the foundational counseling skill of immediacy and facing fears within situations and relationships, while also reflecting and using self-awareness, can contribute to meaningful connection. There is a deeper level of authenticity that occurs in the actualization phase of the UGM model for the CIT if they are willing to do the challenging work leading to this point. When we look at what the term *authenticity* means, the *Merriam-Webster* dictionary (2017) states that it often refers to the notion of "not false or imitation: Real, actual." In addition, *Merriam-Webster* says, authenticity is to be "true to one's own personality, spirit, or character." And, finally, the dictionary gives the example, "is sincere and authentic with no pretentions" (*Merriam-Webster*, 2017). From the humanistic psychology movement, Rogers noted the strong emphasis towards requiring an "authentic, genuineness of self," coupled with the need for empathy to help personalities grow and form the way they should. In fact, Rogers believed that "for a person to *grow*, they need an environment that provides them with genuineness, which includes openness and self-disclosure, acceptance, or being seen with unconditional positive regard, and empathy, meaning being listened to and understood" (McLeod, 2014, p. 1). We understand this to mean that the CIT must be willing to exhibit authenticity regarding where they are, what they are experiencing, while also engaging in vulnerabilities that they can continue to work on with the support of the CES.

Of course, these types of reactions are not necessarily easy for some CITs, especially if they come from the Fight, Flight, Freeze or Fawn responses we talked about earlier. However, if we indeed agree that the key to health, relationship, growth, and self-actualization includes these dynamics, then it is our responsibility as counselors who work with clients to implement these meaningful life connection tools. Consider the following application. Contemplate reviewing the area of stress responses and continue to consider your own automatic responses.

- Experts can tell counterfeit currency by studying genuine money closely and carefully. There are specific things to look for in true currency, including the sharpness in the details, security threads, hidden ways to discern fake from real. How might you begin to study and be authentic and genuine in your life?
- Who in your own life do you know who exhibits the qualities of authenticity, genuineness, and congruence on a regular basis?
- When someone else is genuine or authentic with you and perhaps uses immediacy and here and now self-disclosure, how do you normally respond? Consider reviewing the 4-Fs presented earlier. In addition, review the foundational counseling skills and consider how your nonverbals, tone and pitch and speed of voice all impact the relationship as well.
- Consider meeting with your CES or work supervisor, etc., and practice common immediacy, openness, self-disclosure, and empathy.

  o Tell me how you have been experiencing me from the beginning of our CES/CIT relationship until now?
  o I have experienced you as XXX in our work together.
  o How might I continue to grow in my counselor developmental process?
  o I am currently feeling XXX as you give me that feedback.
  o I appreciate that you are XXX (use a descriptive word to describe your experience with the CES).
  o One challenge I have within our work together has been XXX.
  o Even in this moment as we discuss XXX, I am experiencing XXX. Or, in this moment, I am experiencing you as XXX in our work together.

- ○ How can I demonstrate a sense of openness within our work together?
- ○ In our last meeting, I don't think I was as genuine with you as I had liked to be. I went home and reflected on ABC and realize I really am feeling XXX.
- ○ In my journal, I have been logging my ability to use immediacy, self-disclosure and openness. I recognize the following XXX.
- ○ I have been thinking about the situation with XXX and realize that, from your perspective, I may have appeared XXX.

(See Worksheet 5.2 Authenticity in Appendix 1.)

Case Study

Assignment Example: Jane Smith served in the military and is currently a student. She posted the following online discussion reply as a response to the question of "how well you receive feedback in your counselor developmental process?"

I have come to reflect on this quite a bit since starting in my training as a counselor. At first, I realized, I was slightly different than other folks in that I was used to getting and giving feedback daily in the military. In fact, it was a part of daily life. My ability to hear and accept and implement feedback meant a matter of life or death in that world. I also had profound respect and admiration for supervisors and leaders who took their time to offer their genuine feedback for how I could be a better soldier. I was honored by that, and, in turn, felt it was my responsibility to do the same for my fellow peers and, someday, my own subordinates. Feedback is a part of growth and, without it, we have no idea how we are doing really. I find that I respect and feel honored by my CES and colleagues who give me feedback and take the time to tell me how they experience me, so I can know what I am working towards. (Personal communication, anonymous.)

Questions to consider:

- How did Jane's articulation of feedback resonate with you?
- Compare how Jane views feedback to what you experience.
- How does Jane demonstrate she is in the actualization quadrant of the UGM towards her growth process?
- What golden nugget did you take away from Jane's articulation of feedback?

(See Worksheet 5.3 The Case of Jane Smith in Appendix 1.)

Jane Smith, the soon-to-be Master's in Counseling graduate, will now share with us her examples for her Growth Plan. (See Worksheet 5.4 in Appendix 1 for a Blank Growth Plan Exercise for you.)

Sample Growth Plan for Jane Smith

My Professional Identity Statement:

I have chosen the field of mental health counseling due to my own prior woundedness, which I will continue to process and work though, throughout my entire life,

(continued)

(continued)

especially while serving others as a counselor. Professionally, I commit to helping clients in any way I can through the adherence to the ACA *Code of Ethics* (2014) and through supporting clients along the way without imposing my own values and worldview onto them; rather, as a companion through the travels they have in self-exploration towards healing, I meet them where they are at in their own worldview. I commit to asking for supervision/help and support as needed and will remain a curious teachable counselor throughout all the days as a professional in this career. I commit to my own ongoing healing trauma work as well. Finally, I commit to self-care, which for me includes therapy, recreation, exercise, eating healthily and having family time with hobbies.

Counselor Philosophy:

I am still refining my foundational theoretical orientation, but I notice from my worldview and giftings, in addition to feedback from others, that I lean towards a humanistic person-centered approach, with a focus on CBT and attachment theory as well. I believe people hurt because of wounds, whether biological, psychological or social, and that healing can also take place through these facets as well.

Background Self Reflection:

As a child I experienced physical and sexual assault. I was also raised in a single-parent home with minimal parenting, so I am a parentified child with some prior abandonment and neglect. I have engaged in ongoing personal treatment extensively and still continue to seek counseling for "tune ups" at least four times a year.

My Short and Long-Term Professional Goals:

My short-term goal includes from now until graduation. How will I complete my degree? How will I then complete my post-graduate hours? Find employment? Find any specialties or training? I plan on finishing my coursework and enrolling in field experience towards graduation. The site I have chosen is not too personally connected, but is, instead, working with adolescents. I wanted to work with veterans with trauma but decided that would come later after I continue my ongoing healing process and have close supervision. After graduation, I hope to work at the agency where I served in field experience, under a supervisor I feel connected to who also has a supervisor model I align well with. If I am unable to work there, I plan on networking with other therapists in my community to find a well-trained supervisor to work with for the two years post-graduation in adolescent counseling, substance abuse, and behavioral management. My hope is to receive certification in substance abuse counseling and to continue to work in trauma training. Then, for my ten-year goal, I want to be certified in addictions counseling and work with veterans with comorbid disorders.

Research/Presentation Ideas:

In the next year, I hope to speak and present at my local state counseling conference with my faculty mentor on the topic of trauma and addiction and the adolescent brain. Within the next three years I hope to put my social change project idea in action within my community by conducting some research at my local community mental health center by partnering with my community college and peers. After that, I hope in the next five–ten years to publish an article or begin writing a workbook on helping teen clients and their counselors within the addiction field.

Clinical Practice:

I plan to continue to work under supervision at my local community mental health agency (Field Experience) eventually becoming licensed as an LPC and Addictions Counselor while moving into a full-time therapist position. In 10–15 years, I hope to work with veterans and to also supervise new counselors in training as well and receive an approved clinical supervisor certification to do so.

Community Service/Social Change Ideas:

Serving my community is deeply interconnected to my research idea to conduct research with my local community mental health agency to collect data on trauma and addiction. In addition, I hope to implement my social change project that includes more community support for those struggling with addiction and trauma, including our veterans. I hope to do this within the next ten years.

Self-Care Plan:

My current self-care plan includes stress management and biopsychosocial and spiritual weekly and daily self-care including: Eating a balanced diet, limiting carbohydrates for at least two meals a day, drinking a gallon of water each day, and exercising at least three times a week through running, hiking or elliptical machine. I also set aside Saturdays to sleep in, read my Bible, and catch up on housework and focusing on doing something relational with friends and family Saturday PM. Sunday morning I clear my schedule to attend church and rest, only doing two hours of homework towards the evening to have the ability to work my Monday through Friday work week and finish all coursework. Once a month I want to meet with my personal counselor to verify I am on track with my own personal healing journey as well. In addition, I hope to keep this plan while obtaining my licensure hours after graduation.

Licensure:

I am seeking state licensure under my supervisor from my field experience who has agreed to take me on as a counselor after graduation to help with individual and group counseling. If something doesn't work out with her, I have a backup plan to work at another agency locally. I will take two years to accumulate these hours and, in the meanwhile, I hope to continue to pursue my addictions licensure as well.

Continuing Education:

I am taking the courses on addiction offered at my agency towards addictions certification. I am also interested in taking additional courses on use of animals

(continued)

(continued)

to assist in therapy or trauma counseling specialist training. I hope to later apply this work in working with veterans using equine assisted therapy.

Ethical Decision-Making Model Choice:

I enjoy using the ethical decision-making model by Kitchener, Stadler, Malouf, Forester-Miller and Rubenstein, which includes the seven steps of ethical decision-making. I have printed this out and saved it on my computer and I bring it to my field experience class and to the site to use in supervision and consultation. In addition, I will print out the ACA *Code of Ethics* and the professional counselor dispositions to self-assess and solicit feedback from others weekly.

Supervisee Needs and Elements:

I have come to find that I need my hour of individual supervision weekly to process my cases under support, learning, and growth from my current supervisor. I do enjoy group supervision (Staffing) every other week as well, but I covet the individual private time I have in supervision. I hope to continue this relationship and, if it changes, I hold that I need the following elements in my supervisor: Trust, authenticity, commitment, scheduled time, ability to make mistakes and learn from them, and to work on my own interpersonal anxiety with working with clients and self-efficacy. I also know about myself that I must continue to work on perfectionist tendencies and reframe feedback offered to me to understand it is about growth and not about being perfect and in control.

Areas of Strength:

Date: 12.12.12. My last evaluation from supervisor/faculty and self-assessment noted my great capacity to execute micro and macro skills. I am great with empathy and connecting to clients. This helps me build trust with clients quickly.

Areas of Needed Growth:

Date: 12.12.12. At my last evaluation from supervisor, faculty, and self-assessment it was determined that I need to work on my ability to write case reports and use case conceptualization. In addition, I struggle with accepting feedback and with feeling anxious about my ability to be an effective competent counselor. I feel I mainly struggle with the "imposter syndrome" as I seek to clarify whether I am indeed competent or not. This is directly related to my perfectionistic tendencies from early on in my life. I have reviewed my tendencies, the 4-F Model, noting my strengths and striving to eliminate the negative aspects, and will continue to incorporate the PAIR feedback model, Johari Window, and other resources as I build relationships with my supervisors and colleagues.

In summary, I hope to not only manage my professional development through graduation but ongoingly after graduation when I seek to obtain a full-time clinical job with supervision to accrue hours towards licensure. I will check in every month with my plan and seek a formal review from my mentor faculty and my site supervisor as well. After graduation I plan on updating my professional development plan and asking my new supervisor to be involved ongoingly.

Table 5.1 Putting it all together

Self	Relationship	Competence	Actualization
Johari Window	Foundational Skills including Empathy CCS-R Foundational Skills	Review of Foundational Skills/ Counseling Competencies	Self-Actualization Through Metaphor
Grief and Loss and Change	Pretzel Model & Triple Parallel Process	Tolerance to Ambiguity	Growth in Mistake Making and through "Failure"
Trauma Model of Counselor Development	Corrective Feedback Inventory	PAIR Feedback Model	New Awareness Applied to Relationships
Disarming the Trigger	Stages of Change		Relationship Growth in Authenticity
Transactional Analysis		Prior Work Experience	The Growth Plan
Cultural and Spiritual Reflection		Review of Core Counseling Knowledge	
Self-Care Stress Management		Self-Efficacy	
Defining Worldview and Counselor Identity			
Myers Briggs Type Indicator			
Conflict Management Style			

Application

The key to getting "IT" is to do exactly what was just done above. Consistently and constantly review the self-awareness that was gained through the assignments and apply it to the experiences you have daily in both personal and professional settings.

Summary

"Every person must choose how much truth he can stand" (Yalom, 2003, p. 277). In the end, your CIT Professional Growth Plan should be honest, authentic, challenging, and supportive to your goals and health as a professional counselor working towards competencies. Ultimately, that means it must be *yours*. If you want it bad enough, you will own it. In reflection on the application of the UGM, we are reminded of some great insights by our own Irv Yalom.

"Only the wounded healer can truly heal" (Yalom, 1996, p. 97). In addition, "Despair is the price one pays for self-awareness. Look deeply into life, and you'll always find despair" (Yalom, 2003, p. 139). In reviewing everything thus far, consider how, after self-actualization, you will eventually go back into the Self quadrant towards evaluating, reflecting and working on the self again. After this, you can move to relationships and competency and back to actualization all over again. Life is the cycle of life, so is the cycle of growth. We are excited for your ongoing journey and believe that this process is a precious and sacred one that, if done, will benefit all your clients to come immensely. Keep your book and don't be afraid to continue to use it for the rest of your professional career as a professional counselor.

References

American Counseling Association (ACA) (2014). ACA *Code of ethics*. Alexandria, VA: American Counseling Association.

Association of Counselor Education and Supervision (ACES) Executive Council (2011). *Best practices in clinical supervision*. Retrieved from: www.acesonline.net/sites/default/files/ACES-Best-Practices-in-clinical- supervision-document-FINAL.pdf.

Authenticity (2017). In *Merriam-Webster online dictionary*. Retrieved from: www.merriam-webster.com/dictionary/authenticity.

Council for Accreditation of Counseling and Related Educational Programs (CACREP) (2015). *2016 CACREP standards*. Alexandria, VA: Council for Accreditation of Counseling and Related Educational Programs.

Maslow, A. H. (1943). A theory of human motivation. *Psychological Review*, 50(4), 370–396.

McLeod, S. (2014). Carl Rogers. *Simply Psychology*. Retrieved from: www.simplyPsychology.org/carl-rogers.html.

Olsen, A. (2013). *The theory of self-actualization*. Retrieved from: www.psychologytoday.com/blog/theory-and-psychopathology/201308/the-theory-self-actualization.

Ortberg, J. (2001). *If you want to walk on the water, you've got to get out of the boat*. Grand Rapids, MI: Zondervan Publishing House.

Rigg, G. (2017). *Essentials of psychomotor therapy and the healing circle model*. Greeley, CO: Author.

Sugar, R., Feloni, R., & Lutz, A. (2015). Successful people who failed at first. *Business Insider* (July, 9). Retrieved from: www.businessinsider.com/successful-people-who-failed-at-first-2015-7#charles-darwin-was-considered-an-average-student-he-gave-up-on-a-career-in-medicine-and-was-going-to-school-to-become-a-parson-15.

Walker, P. (2014). *Complex PTSD: From surviving to thriving*. Lafayette, CA: Azure Coyote Publishing.

Yalom, I. D. (1996). *Lying on the couch* [Kindle Edition]. Retrieved from: www.amazon.com/Lying-Couch-Irvin-D-Yalom- ebook/dp/B00N6WQXE6/ref=sr_1_1_twi_kin_1?ie=UTF8&qid=1495756943&sr=8-1&keywords=lying+on+the+couch+by+irvin+yalom#reader_B00N6WQXE6.

Yalom, I. D. (2003). *When Nietzsche wept* [Kindle Edition]. Retrieved from: www.amazon.com/When-Nietzsche-Wept-Novel-Obsession- ebook/dp/B00ET7IZE8/ref=sr_1_1?ie=UTF8&qid=1495756912&sr=8- 1&keywords=when+nietzsche+wept+by+irvin+d.+yalom.

Appendix 1: Worksheets

This section offers a variety of resources, forms, logs, and other structured record-keeping strategies that assist CITs in program documentation, organization, and long-term professional development organization towards licensure and beyond.

Chapter 1 Worksheets:

1.1   Case Study
1.2   Self-Exploration
1.3   Readiness for Change
1.4   Moving Toward Change

Chapter 2 Worksheets:

2.1   *Life of Pi*
2.2   Critical Thinking Application
2.3   Johari Window Exercise
2.4   Grief and Loss Case Example
2.5   Stages of Grief and Loss
2.6   Woundedness
2.7   Stress Responses
2.8   Disarming a Trigger
2.9   Full Circle Worksheet
2.10 CIT Defining Worldview
2.11 Riding a Bike or Driving a Car
2.12 Why Counseling?
2.13 Review and Reflect
2.14 Steps to Counselor Identity
2.15 Philosophy of CIT Identity
2.16 MBTI Application

Chapter 3 Worksheets:

3.1   Foundational Skills
3.2   Empathy Scale
3.3   Dispositional Self-Assessment

3.4   Pretzel Model
3.5   CFI-R Hulse-Killacky
3.6   Feedback

Chapter 4 Worksheets:

4.1   Ambiguity in the Twilight Zone
4.2   The PAIR Model
4.3   Ethical Decision Making
4.4   Ethical Behavior
4.5   Ethical Boundaries
4.6   Ethics of Policy Compliance
4.7   Ethical Timely Records
4.8   Ethical Multiculturalism
4.9   Ethics of Self Control
4.10 Ethics of Learning Motivation
4.11 Ethics of Feedback
4.12 Ethics of Acclimation
4.13 Ethics of Genuineness
4.14 PAIR Considerations
4.15 Lived Experience
4.16 The Case of Barb
4.17 Additional Areas of Ongoing Professional Development
4.18 Self-Efficacy

Chapter 5 Worksheets:

5.1   My Metaphor
5.2   Authenticity
5.3   The Case of Jane Smith
5.4   My Growth Plan Exercise

WORKSHEET 1.1

Case Study

Based on the information below, find as many of the common comportment issues as possible in this case study. Use the check list at the bottom of the case to indicate areas of concern. Mark all that apply. This case is a fictional blended case example.

Jack is a brand-new student in his counselor graduate-level training program. He appears eager to begin the process of training; he shared since his first day of class that he had come from a very traumatic background of abuse, neglect, and suffered ongoingly his entire life from his own addiction problems. He shares with you that he has been working in a substance abuse clinic, working towards his drug and alcohol certification. In his discussions with peer colleagues he was eager to point out that he would make "the best counselor because he understood what his clients were going through." He also submitted work and made comments often without supporting them with any scholarly research or substantiation. In fact, he commented to a peer in class that "life experience is far better than research." In addition, a peer colleague gently confronted him asking "do you think that you are healed enough to also offer boundaries and self-care in your counseling profession?" Jack quickly retorted, "I take pride in my past struggles and no one is perfect." He paused and remarked, "I already know how to counsel; I just need the degree to say I am fit for licensure." The instructor stepped in and acknowledged that everyone has something to learn in the counselor training process and Jack interrupted stating, "I am sure many do, but some of us have already done all of our personal work."

As a fellow CIT evaluating this case, what areas of concern might you have as a professional colleague to Jack? Check all that apply as concerns:

- Grades are below acceptable standards;
- Seems to display uncontrolled emotions;
- Behavior does not meet standards in the profession;
- Concerns about comportment;
- Not demonstrating skills at the required level of competence.

WORKSHEET 1.2

Self-Exploration

Contemplate the dispositions of those to be on your cheerleading team. Do you want someone authentic, compassionate, realistic, safe, healthy, wise, peaceful, mature, professional and supportive?

Consider the following questions regarding your alignment to counseling as you enter your first course:

1   What compelled you to want to pursue this field and why?

2   What do you believe will be your role, function and duty ethically, legally and professionally to the field? Consider writing a brief professional counselor identity statement to offer a foundation for your developmental process. "I believe a counselor is xxxx."

3   What are your strengths and ongoing needs for growth for this process or role?

4   What are you most concerned about in your developmental process and why?

5   How are you able to consider your ongoing need for self-reflection, self-exploration, to accept feedback from faculty and supervisors, and to commit to ongoing growth and development?

6   What do you need from your CES and how can they best support you in the process? What do you potentially need from your cheerleading teammates? Who can you call in an emergency, or when you have a time crunch? Who do you trust with your children, pets, or home responsibilities? When will you know it is time to call for help?

7   Review the American Counseling Association website and find their definition of a counselor, including roles and responsibilities of a professional counselor; deeply consider this in reflection on your answers above.

WORKSHEET 1.3

Readiness for Change

Take the inventory below to see your own readiness for change in terms of ongoing CIT growth and willingness to accept feedback. Growth inevitably involves change and change often means discomfort for many. Reflect upon the following questions and score each one on a scale of 1–5, where 1 is: This is not true for me at all; and 5 is: this is totally true for me completely.

Where do you land?

1   I am great. Nothing needs to change. I am only here to jump through the hoops to receive my degree and move forward. I am good but thank you.

    1 2 3 4 5

2   I know I need to grow and change. I am uncertain if I am ready to embark on what that exactly entails or means, and it is a bit scary but . . . I do know it is necessary at some point for me to be an effective, ethical counselor. I am working on observing who may be safe to explore with, eventually.

    1 2 3 4 5

3   I want to be ready for change. I am not sure what that means, but I am willing, and will seek support, ask questions, and prepare myself for that process personally and professionally. I recognize it will require work, facing my fears, but I want to grow.

    1 2 3 4 5

4   I am actively in the process of change. I am humble, receive feedback from colleagues, supervisors, faculty and use self-reflection, openness and curiosity for learning, and I am eager to continue to progress towards sometimes painful growth and ongoing change.

    1 2 3 4 5

5   I have been involved in change for some time, and I want to continue to engage in it through the knowledge, skills, and dispositions required of me. I have a plan for how I will continue to do this using my support network, my personal commitment, and through ongoing inquiry for feedback from faculty, colleagues, self-reflection and from supervisors.

    1 2 3 4 5

Total Score: _____

WORKSHEET 1.4

Moving Toward Change

The following stages of change were identified by DiClemente, Prochaska, Fairhurst, Velicer, Velasquez, & Rossi, (1991, p. 1):

1   Pre-contemplative: self-protective, not ready to change
2   Contemplative: thinking about changing; estimate own readiness to change
3   Preparation: getting ready to make the change
4   Action: making changes
5   Maintenance & Relapse: Monitor and stay on track

If you find you are not ready for change, what can you and your CES do to help assist you towards a readiness for change?

- Deeply consider past times in your life when you engaged in positive change and what helped motivate or facilitated growth for you. What do you stand to gain or lose by not moving through the change progression?

- Consider the benefits and costs to you in your current counselor developmental journey. If you are not ready for change, growth, or to move forward in change, have you considered the following?

  o   Taking a break from your training as a counselor.
  o   Obtaining personal counseling and engaging in even more personal healing.
  o   Is this the right field, profession, and career for you? There are many things that counselors do, from School Counseling to Career Counseling to Clinical Mental Health Counseling, to Addictions Counseling. Outside of counseling, there are avenues such as Social Work, Psychology, Life Coaching, Case Management. Are you in the right place?
  o   Reassessing work–life balance and health.

Consider some activities offered by your CES, such as the following, that can help guide you in your motivation towards change and desire for growth.

- Have you experienced a recent crisis or reason for change that has motivated you, and, if so, what is it?

- If you have had a CIT remediation or development referral, what was the issue you experienced and what are your thoughts about the rationale and requirement you now may have?

- Consider engaging in meaningful connection with rapport building with your CES to discuss what occurred. How might you practice being authentic, receptive, engaged, and curious about your own growth process?

- Bear in mind that your CES is not telling you that you need to change. Rather, they will likely be asking you to offer your perspective and experience of what happened to lead to the referral for a growth plan, and how you feel about it. Only you can decide when and if you are ready to embark on *change*.

- Consider what led to the requirement for a growth plan.

- What are the anxieties, fears, and consequences at stake?

- What positive strengths do you have in being in this process currently? Share them with your CES.

- Are you feeling one or more of the following about the act of engaging in CIT growth? Check all that apply and share with your faculty:
  - Hesitant (I am confused as to why I am here, what is going on, or why I would need to change anything).
  - Defiant (I am angry and fear losing control over the process, my profession, my schedule and expectations of what I had planned).
  - Suffering (I feel hopeless about change and overwhelmed by the time and hard work this will take me).
  - Excusing (I have all the answers, and this was not my problem, but theirs).

Feel free to jot down some notes below concerning your experience and your deeper reflection of the questions offered above.

WORKSHEET 2.1

Life of Pi

After you have watched the movie *Life of Pi*, answer the following questions:

- How did you experience the film? What emotions did you experience throughout the film?

- What were the most difficult parts of the movie for you? Why?

- List all you can see in the movie that applies to ambiguity, critical thinking, cultural diversity, and theories in counseling.

- From the *Life of Pi*, which story do you prefer? Why? Which is the correct story? Which story is Pi's? Why does it matter?

- How did the ending resonate with you?

WORKSHEET 2.2

Critical Thinking Application

Review the material below and respond as indicated:

- Application to theories of personality coursework.

  o   Consider case conceptualization and list all the potential theories offered within the work, and how you see the theory playing out within the context of Pi and his family members.

- Application to professional orientation and discussion of social and cultural areas of competency.

  o   Consider all the various religious and spiritual connections and how you experienced them, your personal biases, worldview, and how they may apply to clients you work with.

- Applied to ASERVIC Spiritual Competencies and evaluation of spirituality in counseling.

  o   What are the spiritual competencies to consider that apply to the work?

- Applied to grief and loss, crisis and trauma coursework, and training.

  o   What diagnostic criteria or symptoms did you see? What are the themes of grief and loss and trauma? How might you work with someone who has experienced something such as this?

- Applied to practicum, internship, and beyond in application to working with immense issues surrounding ambiguity, supervision, case consultation, etc., including consideration of counseling theories.

  ○ How can the narrative approach in counseling offer the characteristics necessary for critical thinking? Consider diagnosis, assessment, case conceptualization, ethical decision making, cultural competencies, spiritual competencies, and other tasks as a clinician.

  ○ What possible theoretical applications did you pull from the film? Give examples of which areas you connect to theory and why.

In addition to assessing your critical thinking skills using this experiential activity, you may be interested in exploring measurements that are tailored toward assessing critical thinking. One example is the *California Critical Thinking Dispositions Inventory* (CCTDI), (Facione, et al., 1998). In addition, consider *The Problem Solving Inventory* (PSI) (Heppner, & Petersen, 1982) or others that your CES may recommend as well.

WORKSHEET 2.3

Johari Window Exercise

In the blank box below, fill in your own information based on the description in each of the four boxes in this first sample Johari Window box. Based on the Johari Window (Luft, & Ingham, 1955).

	Known to Self	*Not known to Self*
Known to Others	**OPEN** What are some things you know about yourself, and that others know about you as well? Consider adding items to the square like professional aspects, personal, common things you openly share with others about yourself (you may include gifts, strengths, or even weaknesses). **(Consider the image of an open window.)**	**BLIND** What are some things you may not know about yourself, but that others do know as this comes in the form of feedback from others around you. Remember, to fill this window and reach insight and growth you must be vulnerable to allow others to know you and offer the feedback. **(Consider the image of a window with wooden blinds on it.)**
Not Known to Others	**HIDDEN** What are some things about yourself you know, but keep hidden from others (fears, dreams, politics, religious beliefs, weaknesses, convictions, biases)? **(Consider the image of darkout curtains over the window.)**	**UNKNOWN** These are things you do not know about yourself, and that others may not know as well. This is the future and can be filled by building authentic relationships with others. **(Consider the idea of having a window you did not know existed in your home.)**

	Known to Self	*Not known to Self*
Known to Others	**OPEN**	**BLIND**
Not Known to Others	**HIDDEN**	**UNKNOWN**

WORKSHEET 2.4

Grief and Loss Case Example

Case Study

The CES contacts the CIT regarding a concern. The CIT denies it:

"Hi, Sally. This is Dr. ____, I have some concerns. . . ."

Denial: CIT: "What?? I DID not do that! You must be mistaken."

CES: "Well, let's look at the concerns expressed."

Anger: CIT: *Internally thinking*: "I cannot believe this is happening. It's like everyone is against me and doesn't want to see me succeed. Who do these people think they are? Well, it's not my issue."

Bargaining: CIT to CES: "So, if I make the changes, can I still pass the class?"

Depression: CIT: *Internally when they realize they have a remediation plan*: "I don't know what I'm going to do . . . my whole life plan depends on this degree! I can't lose everything!"

Acceptance: CIT to CES: "Okay . . . maybe I can learn something about myself if I listen to what is being said and make changes that are real. After all, it will make me a better counselor, and that is what I want."

Consider as the CIT:

• Can you relate to Sally? If so how?

• Can you relate to the CES? If so how?

• What are your personal reflections after reviewing the example?

• How might CIT and CES benefit from such work together?

WORKSHEET 2.5

Stages of Grief and Loss

Take a moment to consider if you are indeed in one of the stages of grief and loss as per Kubler-Ross's (1969) model: Denial, Anger, Bargaining, Depression, Acceptance.

- If you are in grief and loss, which stage are you at?

- Who is your support person as you explore this process?

- What do you stand to lose or gain as you enter the process?

- How have you endured and worked through other examples of grief and loss in your life?

- What assets and strengths might you lean into to help you?

- What roles do your CES, colleagues, and mentors play to support you?

WORKSHEET 2.6

Woundedness

Consider the following questions and process with your CES.

- Part of my worldview as a CIT involves being hurt by people or experiences.

- Part of my desire to enter the counseling helping profession is to help others because I understand personally the experience of pain, suffering, and injury.

- I feel a deep desire to contribute to this profession, to give back what was offered to me when I have struggled.

- Although I have personal life wounding, I have and continue to work through those first-hand experiences.

- I believe my own history of wounding can and may influence the counseling work I do with clients; therefore, it is important to continue to monitor, work on, and seek ongoing close supervision and consultation.

- My work or drive to become a helping professional is my entire focus and identity to "help others."

- Helping others makes me feel good and needed. I enjoy "fixing" a problem for people.

- I have been known to respond unprofessionally before, especially when I felt "triggered" by something that caught me off guard.

WORKSHEET 2.7

Stress Responses

After reviewing the 4-Fs, identify your own most often used response style. Then work through these questions to gain insight:

- Which stress response style do you most relate with? Share, when you are ready, with your CES.

- Which positive strengths for each response do you recognize in yourself?

- What other aspects come to mind as you reflect on the model, theory and phenomena of stress response, especially considering perhaps your current work in your counselor developmental process?

- What, in addition, might be helpful to share with your CES concerning your responses and how to move forward in growth and development?

- How might your trauma/stress response be your responsibility to manage while working on other areas of your professional development?

WORKSHEET 2.8

Disarming a Trigger

A three-step process to identify and disarm triggers. Consider the emotional response that was just experienced. Identify the feelings that are associated with the reaction. Then:

1   Think about the last time you felt this same emotion. Who was there, what were you doing, what did you see, what did you hear, what did you smell, how did you feel? Identify the emotions and check out all five senses as you process and reflect on the context.

2   When was the first time you felt this way? Again, process through your senses and context. Look at the similarities and the feelings. Which feelings seemed to align with which events? Look for themes, commonalities, conclusions you may have come to as you review this occurrence through the lens of the event in #1.

3   When was the time before that? Typically, a person will identify the "first" time as somewhere in their early teens. Through experience, many people identify that the true first time was earlier in childhood, and the teenage experience was repeating the pattern. So, go back to the time before that. What was going on? What do you remember about the situation? What were the thoughts and conclusions you came to at that point in time? And process through all that happened at that point, which may reveal a long-held belief that was probably not the truth. You have found your center, and you can now disarm that trigger. As you process through the thoughts, memories, events, emotions, and beliefs, you may be able to find a new understanding of who you are.

WORKSHEET 2.9

Full Circle Worksheet

Consider your thoughts, ideas, beliefs, biases, and experiences of self, others and the world:

Biological: Our selves: Our own body, self in addition to the human body, sexuality, birth, disease, medical, genetics, medicine, treatment, nutrition, science, origin of life, death, etc. An example of Biological worldview: "I believe that mental illness has a genetic factor."

Social/Cultural: Our own lives, in addition to their application to others in terms of: Family, community, culture, ethnicity, biases, tradition, prejudice, privilege, socio-economics, politics, government, freedom, moral and ethical standards. An example of Social/Cultural worldview: "I believe that all people are born into privilege and prejudice of some nature; without connecting with others, we will never dispel those injustices."

Psychological: Our own psychological thoughts, feelings, ideas, fears, concerns, anxieties, passions, understandings. Also, about the brain, cognitive, affective, science of the mind, dreams, thinking, behaviors, morality, ethical standards, etc. An example of Psychological worldview: "I believe that a child growing up in a home with authoritarian parents will most likely rebel."

Spiritual: Higher Power, religion, spirituality, relationship with God, creation, identity, life, death, human condition, meaning, purpose in life, ideas about good, evil, freedom, moral and ethical standards. Spirituality, or relationship with a Higher Power of any kind, can be a deep and meaningful part of identity, including counselor identity and counselor educator supervisor identity, and impacts all the work with clients in the future. An example of Spiritual worldview: "I believe that Jesus Christ came, lived, died for all humanity's sins and that, because of this, there is hope and healing for all who believe in Him."

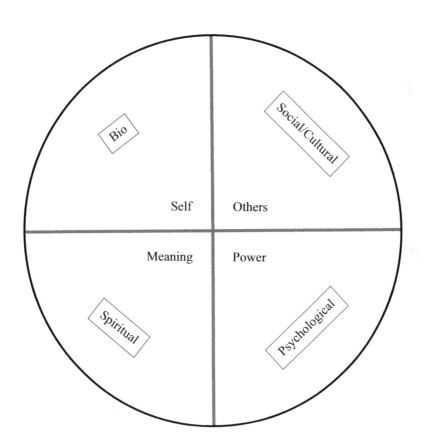

WORKSHEET 2.10

CIT Defining Worldview

Defining your worldview

Process your thoughts as you go through this worksheet and dig deep into your own thoughts, beliefs, and opinions.

- Think back to your recent attending or experiencing of a life rite of passage such as a birth, death, marriage, becoming a grandparent for the first time, etc., and reflect on the integration of values, beliefs, experiences, etc. that now have new meaning for you.

- Review an old movie/music that you listened to or watched at various developmental stages (see Erikson's stages of development (Erikson, 1963)). How have you changed from the person you were years ago? Does the movie and/or music apply across multicultural contexts?

- Consider a current headline in the news. What do you believe about the news event/article and why? Explore what others in an opposing position believe about the headline and consider where are they coming from and why.

- Choose to have a conversation with someone who has a completely opposite point of view than yourself on a particular subject. Challenge yourself to stay present in their stance, listen for clarity in their understanding of the topic, and take notes pointing to the three main themes of what they believe and why. Afterwards, ask them if you captured an accurate understanding of what they believe.

- Consider sharing the riding a bike metaphor examples and offer your own metaphor to help you understand your life experiences and worldview.

WORKSHEET 2.11

Ride a Bike or Driving a Car Metaphor

Fill out the information below as you revisit your own story about learning to ride a bike. You can substitute learning to drive a car if that is more applicable for you. You may gain some insights into how you approach learning new tasks and what your expectations are from this metaphor. Then apply these insights to your learning now.

- Describe the day and time, your age, and even where you were developmentally.

- How did you feel and who was around you?

- Did you have support from others, and leadership, guidance, or bystanders watching?

- What was the process like for you?

- Who congratulated you once you mastered the task? How did that feel?

- Who do you wish would have been present? What do you wish you would have heard?

- How might you integrate this experience into your reflection on your worldview?

WORKSHEET 2.12

Why Counseling?

Process through your own inspiration and the steps you need to take to reach your goal:

1   What is the function, role, and mission of the clinical mental health counselor?

2   What licensure, training, and credentials must a counselor have to be ethically able to work as a professional in the field?

3   What is the difference between a counselor and, say, a social worker, psychologist, or life coach, and why?

4   Who are some of the founding fathers and mothers of the clinical counseling field and what are the core foundational philosophical elements that have helped form the counseling field?

5   What is the American Counseling Association? What benefits are there to joining?

6   What is the Council for Accreditation of Counseling and Related Educational Programs (CACREP) and why do they matter?

7   How does my original mission for pursuing this field align with my research on the preceding questions?

WORKSHEET 2.13

Review and Reflect

Reflect on and respond to these questions as you gain insight into your identity as a counselor and the influences upon you of past and future.

- Review your personal beliefs and values (worldview) from this chapter.

- What are your personal attributes/strengths?

- What are the current roles in which you serve? Mother, father, husband, wife, advocate, teacher volunteer, etc.

- Why did you enter the field to begin with? Here, it is important to explore what led you to becoming a counselor, and to believing this was your calling or the fulfillment of your dream, including how this ties into your worldview.

- Reflect on the mentors and influences that helped shape your experiences. Who was the most influential teacher or mentor you had throughout your life?

- Explore the personal goals that you have for yourself and how you can contribute to social change in mental health/counseling.

- Where do you personally fit into the role of counselor, the field and your responsibilities as a CIT?

WORKSHEET 2.14

Steps to Counselor Identity

Begin by answering each question and diving into the responses (see pages XX-XX in Chapter 2 for guidance). Don't be too quick to just write something in. Pause. Consider. Think. Then write as much as you need to.

1   Define the Roles:

2   Define the Who:

3   Define the What:

4   Define the Where:

5   Define the Focus of Practice:

6   Define the Orientation:

7   Define Why You:

Consider these as well:

• Identity statement

• Worldview

• Standards and Guidelines

• Roles and Responsibilities

• Social and Cultural Aspects

WORKSHEET 2.15

Philosophy of CIT Identity

Activities for Philosophy of CIT Identity: Using creativity to help define your identity is often a very powerful experience. Work your way through these questions thoughtfully.

- According to the summary on page XX of Chapter 2, what other things might the songwriter, myself, or you value or believe in our worldview and philosophy of life?

- How might you relate to these words or compare and contrast them to your own worldview ideas?

- Choose your own favorite poem, short story or song and consider the lyrics and words and how they represent your own worldview, philosophy of living, or even counselor identity traits.

- Consider how worldview, philosophy of life, and beliefs and understandings in counseling, education and prior supervision may impact your CIT philosophy and identity statement.

- In a statement or two, what is your philosophy of counseling? What is a counselor and their purpose? What is your personal belief in your role and responsibility to clients in the field?

- What is your philosophy concerning the online format and the use of technology, or bricks and mortar schooling?

- In a statement or two, what is your philosophy of life? One example is "Hakuna Matata" which means "no worries."

WORKSHEET 2.16

MBTI Application

Consider taking the Jung Typology test at www.humanmetrics.com, retrieving your previous MBTI results, or taking the MBTI online if available. Then apply your typology to this worksheet.

- Write down your preferences and percentages. Explore the summary reflection in the assessment tool with your CES.

- What are the type descriptions that go along with your results? Do you agree or disagree, and why?

- These are all preferences and there are no right or wrong types or combinations. However, what do you see as your greatest strengths and potential weaknesses in terms of communication in evaluating and reflecting on your type?

- What are some key indicators to keep in mind after reviewing your type?

- What are some thoughts about who you work with daily considering your type?

- How might your data and the descriptions help you to better understand yourself?

- How might you combine this activity with others such as the Johari Window, worldview exploration, or others to reflect further and deeper on your self-growth?

WORKSHEET 3.1

Foundational Skills

Consider the following assessment and reflective activities to refine your foundational skills.

• Review a role-play video session to gauge your foundational skills (you can find some role-play videos in a university library, online, etc.). Which foundational skills did you see demonstrated?

• Consider investing in an educational technology tool such as *Acclaim* (see Appendix 2: Resources) that offers you the ability to save videos that are encrypted, so that you can receive feedback from supervisors and faculty alike that is confidential.

• Review your prior techniques, skills, or course assessments to reflect on areas of strength and areas of needed growth in foundational areas.

• After meeting with your CES, ask for an observation or assessment of a video or transcription to inquire about feedback on your skills.

• What are additional ways to grow, assess, and practice your skills towards optimal competencies?

WORKSHEET 3.2

Empathy Scale

Measuring empathy is a process that will be done in your own mind eventually. However, begin by practicing it on paper. Here are the levels from Carkhuff (1969, pp. 174–175), paraphrased. After reviewing, consider your own levels of empathy following any challenging encounters or thoughts you may have. Where do you land?

Level 1: The counselor's verbal and behavioral responses do not meet the needs of the clients or take away from the client's experience significantly.

Level 2: The counselor responds to the client's feelings in a way that subtracts from the client's expression of experience or feelings.

Level 3: The counselor responds to the client in an interchangeable manner so as not to add any depth or breadth of feelings to the client's experience, but meets them exactly where they are at in their communication and conveyance of feelings.

Level 4: The counselor adds notably to the client's expression of feelings or experience and adds a deeper level of awareness and meaning for the client to utilize, one that they would not have had alone.

Level 5: The counselor's response adds significantly to the client's awareness of the meaning of expression and feeling, offering them even more depth and breadth to self-understanding and thus fostering a deep meaningful connection to the counselor.

WORKSHEET 3.3

Dispositional Self-Assessment of Empathy

After reviewing the Carkhuff Empathy Scale, consider your own self-assessment or feedback from others concerning your empathic resonance skills. If this is an area you want to work on, consider the following.

1 Pay close attention to your CES and their own demonstration of empathy as you work together towards your common goals of competency and success in counseling.

2 Consider empathy training techniques and skills while paying attention to the emotional and cognitive types of empathy.

3 Consider the types of empathy including cognitive and affective. Which do you struggle to exhibit and why?

4 Consider videotaping role-play skills sessions, including empathy examples your CES may suggest, to offer opportunities to initiate, practice, and execute deep empathic understanding and review for learning.

5 Consider a short story, poem, fairytale, or lyrics from a song to explore, evaluate, and process in terms of recognizing each character's perspective and potentially what they are experiencing and feeling. Process this with your CES to gauge your understanding and ability to connect to the emotion of others in the art and relationship with your CES.

WORKSHEET 3.4

Pretzel Model

Of course, to grow and understand how you are doing in the process, you as the CIT must be willing to hear and apply feedback. As you consider the Pretzel model, think about how you are influenced by and influencing your CES as well as your clients, and how each of them in return influence you. Considering feedback, both verbal and non-verbal, that you have received from your CES, clients, supervisors, and others, process through these questions:

• How might you as the CIT be prepared to engage in the triple parallel process?

• What thoughts come to mind as you review the image and information pertaining to the "pretzel" of triple parallel process?

• What are some key professional dispositional elements that would be important to have to engage in the process? Why?

• Journal and take notes about the connection of client to you as CIT to CES and CES to you as CIT to your client. What stands out most about this process and phenomenon?

WORKSHEET 3.5

CFI-R Hulse-Killacky

Corrective Feedback Instrument-Revised (CFI-R).

Think back to the groups you have participated in recently and to the corrective feedback that was exchanged among members in these groups. Using the following definition and considering the examples below, please circle the number that best fits your response.

Definition:

Corrective feedback is intended to encourage thoughtful self-examination and/or to express the feedback giver's perception of the need for change on the part of the receiver. Here are some examples of corrective feedback:

I notice that . . .

. . . you almost never talk in group.

. . . you have not shared any of your feelings or experiences.

. . . you keep looking around the room. I'm wondering if you are bored.

. . . you often fight to keep the group focus away from yourself.

. . . your face gets red and you seem angry, but you don't talk about your feelings.

. . . you start to shuffle around when your input in the group is required.

. . . you avoid eye contact whenever the leader turns in your direction.

. . . your tone of voice increases if other members question your comments.

1 I feel criticized when I receive corrective feedback. 1 2 3 4 5 6
2 I am usually too uncomfortable to ask someone to clarify corrective feedback delivered to me. 1 2 3 4 5 6
3 I remember corrective feedback, when it was delivered to me as a child, to be critical. 1 2 3 4 5 6
4 Giving written corrective feedback is easier for me to do than speaking directly to the person. 1 2 3 4 5 6
5 When I need to give corrective feedback, I prefer to write it out. 1 2 3 4 5 6

6 Because my childhood memories of corrective feedback are negative ones, I am very sensitive about receiving corrective feedback now. 1 2 3 4 5 6

7 Receiving corrective feedback as a child was painful for me. 1 2 3 4 5 6

8 I fear conflict because of my negative experiences with corrective feedback as a child. 1 2 3 4 5 6

9 I think negative thoughts about myself when I receive corrective feedback. 1 2 3 4 5 6

10 It is hard for me not to interpret corrective feedback as a criticism of my personal competence. 1 2 3 4 5 6

11 When I receive corrective feedback, I think I have failed in some way. 1 2 3 4 5 6

12 When the norms of the group support the exchange of corrective feedback, I will be open to receiving corrective feedback. 1 2 3 4 5 6

13 I like to hear the leader clearly state his or her support for corrective feedback. 1 2 3 4 5 6

14 Telling someone I have a different view is scary to me. 1 2 3 4 5 6

15 When I reflect on the corrective feedback I received as a child, I hesitate to give others corrective feedback. 1 2 3 4 5 6

16 Verbalizing corrective feedback is awkward for me. 1 2 3 4 5 6

17 I prefer to receive corrective feedback in written form. 1 2 3 4 5 6

18 If I am in a group setting where corrective feedback exchange has been established as a norm, I will be receptive to corrective feedback. 1 2 3 4 5 6

19 If I observed the leader reinforcing the giving of corrective feedback in the group, I would be willing to give corrective feedback more frequently. 1 2 3 4 5 6

20 When I am not sure about the corrective feedback message delivered to me I do not ask for clarification. 1 2 3 4 5 6

21 If I have a part in helping set norms for receiving corrective feedback, then I will probably be open to receiving corrective feedback. 1 2 3 4 5 6

22 I always felt criticized whenever I received corrective feedback as a child. 1 2 3 4 5 6

23 I try to avoid being in conflict with others whenever possible. 1 2 3 4 5 6

24 It is easier for me to write down my corrective feedback than to speak it. 1 2 3 4 5 6

25 Most of the time I am too uncomfortable to say what I really mean to someone else. 1 2 3 4 5 6

26 When I am given corrective feedback, I think my skills are being questioned. 1 2 3 4 5 6

27 I believe that positive experiences with corrective feedback can occur in a group when the leader takes an active role in setting the stage. 1 2 3 4 5 6

28 If I can take part in helping to set norms for giving corrective feedback, I will probably be more open to giving corrective feedback. 1 2 3 4 5 6

29 It is too scary for me to ask other group members to clarify their corrective feedback if it is unclear to me. 1 2 3 4 5 6

30 I worry too much about upsetting others when I have to give corrective feedback. 1 2 3 4 5 6

Small Group Activity*

Consider breaking into groups of 4–6 and then divide the items into clusters of:

- Giving, receiving, and clarifying feedback.
- Which clusters are the most difficult for you? Which do you believe you enjoy most?
- What could you do to develop and assist with the areas you may struggle with?
- How will this assessment and what you have learned contribute to your development as a counselor?

*Addendum added by Dr. McLain (2011).

WORKSHEET 3.6

Feedback

Consider the following story and the feedback model presented.

Case Study

Jack was in his final year in culinary school and was on his path to success. He was eager and excited to be able to finish his hands-on training as an intern Chef de Partie chef at the *Repas Délicieux & Co.* Jack was confident in completing all his straight A coursework and had only 32 more hours of field experience before graduation. He was given a bit of feedback from the Head Chef in terms of his kitchen etiquette, but, other than that, nothing else was offered. Jack went on to graduate, and get his diploma, and have his party, and all was well. He applied to several four-star restaurants and received a position as a Chef de Tournant, a French vegetarian dining experience focusing on soups for the restaurant. He was nervous, but confident in his abilities since, after all, he graduated with honors. He was given the directive in his first week to make mirepoix (a soup base) and he went about creating his base. Throughout the week he did his job, but the owner received several complaints and feedback concerning the mirepoix as not tasting right. In fact, several customers had left terrible reviews and vowed not to return. Once the Head Chef investigated with Jack, the answer was found. Jack was trained in creating all kinds of soup bases and had always used bacon fat to create these bases. He must have created it at least 30 times while in training, and his instructors had never mentioned that he had done it incorrectly. Using a meat fat or oil was known as *au gras*; however, the traditional training requires the chef always to specify either *au gras* or *au maigre*, which is considered "without meat." Obviously, the meat base was a poor choice at this establishment to begin with. Jack was astonished to think he had made such a mistake and was dumbfounded when the Head Chef confronted him on the issue. How did things end for Jack? Consider the following questions:

1   What is the identified problem for Jack and his situation here?

2   How might Jack be feeling?

3   What might be the best response to the Head Chef from Jack?

4   What can Jack do?

Jack responded to the Head Chef stating:

I am so sorry, but my instructors never told me that I needed to specify these features in the soup base and I received straight As throughout my program. I have never been given negative feedback like this nor have I ever made such a mistake! I had no idea I needed to differentiate, or I would never had made such a mistake!

Or

Jack responded to the Head Chef:

I am terribly sorry. Despite not having learned this valuable information, I should have known better in a vegetarian restaurant to not use a meat base. I must have been so eager to complete the task I did not use reason and good judgement. I apologize and will reach out and inquire when something does not make sense, or if I need guidance in executing a dish. I am open to continuing to learn and receive the feedback and I am grateful to learn this additional information.

1   What are the differences in these two responses that Jack made to his Head Chef?

2   What might be the differences in how this story plays out simply based on his reaction and response to feedback, and why?

3   What is the moral of this story and example?

WORKSHEET 4.1

Ambiguity in the *Twilight Zone*

Consider watching the Episode 14 "Five Characters in Search of an Exit" in Season 3 of the *Twilight Zone* as a learning assignment and observing the following things. Provide your responses and thoughts:

- What was it like not understanding or knowing what was occurring during the film?

- What feelings came up for you while watching the film?

- What were you thinking during the film?

- What are your thoughts in retrospect, looking back to the film and your experience of sitting in ambiguity?

WORKSHEET 4.2

The PAIR Model

Work through these steps using the PAIR Model to explore your experience of giving and receiving feedback. Write your responses below.

1   Consider asking your CES to offer you authentic feedback from your last meeting. Use the PAIR model and log your experience of it. Afterwards, process your learning, understanding and experience with your CES.

2   Take each step one at a time and describe in a processing journal how you were able to try them out. Afterwards, consider soliciting feedback from a peer or friend on something to see how to implement the model in that capacity as well.

3   Consider offering feedback to someone and gauge to see how well it aligns with the model.

4   Consider reframing corrective feedback for yourself in a couple of statements. What would this be? Share this with your CES and continue to use this as a reframe with feedback to come.

WORKSHEET 4.3

Ethical Decision Making

Review these situations, which are examples of ethical violations that occur leading a CIT to a remediation or development plan. After reviewing, respond to the questions.

- Susie was trained at her site and instructed not to see clients at home or to communicate with them on any other device than the work-issued phone. She chose to violate this policy, which was not only a site policy concern but also an ethical concern as well. How so? Consider agency and university policy and procedures, and the specific potential ACA codes that were violated.

- Max was working at a residential facility as an intern in field experience and decided to do a Skype internet video session with a client who was on home pass. He was not trained in internet-based therapy and the agency did not allow the use of video conferencing systems with clients. He used Google hangout and the video was accidently recorded and published online. What are the agency, university, state legal and ethical potential concerns here?

WORKSHEET 4.4

Ethical Behavior

Review these examples regarding ethical behavior and answer the questions posed below.

- Betty, who was reported by her site supervisor, was caught smoking with clients at the agency and going into the client bedrooms to "chat." The agency was an alcohol and substance treatment center and they discouraged counselors from smoking with clients because, in their minds, it was not good role modeling and blurred professional boundaries. In addition, she often came to work dressed in jeans with holes in them, and dirty shirts. What are the potential agency, legal, and ethical concerns?

- Jack, who worked at a community mental health hospital, often decided to curse with clients, even those who didn't use cursing in their repertoire of normal communication. What concerns might this bring?

- Mary arrived at her internship site with low-cut blouses, short skirts, tight pants, or other clothing that drew attention to her figure. She did not change her manner of dress after several comments and warnings from her site supervisor and was terminated from the field placement. She maintained that she had the right to wear whatever she liked. What are the agency, university or ethical and legal concerns?

WORKSHEET 4.5

Ethical Boundaries

Review the situations below and respond to the questions posed. Ethics is often rather gray but dig into the cases and think outside the box.

- In the case of Susie, she blurred boundaries with her clients by going outside and smoking with them despite the agency protocol and rule. In addition, she potentially violated the clients' private personal space by going into their bedrooms. Even if nothing inappropriate occurred, how is it our responsibility to avoid even "appearance of doing something inappropriate?" This impacts boundaries with the client and supervisor on several levels.

- Jenny is working under supervision in her final semester of Internship and begins to give orders to other new interns despite it not being her job responsibility. She often takes over their roles, projects, and even intervenes with their clients. When confronted by a peer, she stated that she knew more and had been there longer, so it was her responsibility. What are the potential concerns here?

WORKSHEET 4.6

Ethics of Policy Compliance

These situations are about following and complying with policies. Your agencies, practices, locations, etc., all have rules by which they are run. Reflect on how well you comply.

- In the case of Susie (as in Worksheet 4.3), she violated the site policy in addition to blurring boundaries and causing concern for an ethical violation.

- Amy reports never having time to do her clinical DAP notes on the company office residential unit computer. She finds a workaround and accesses her client's data file on her personal laptop while on campus at the agency and enters them from there. She has no permission from the agency or her supervisor to do this and does not have any password protection on her laptop. What are the concerns here?

WORKSHEET 4.7

Ethics of Timely Records

A CIT's ability to complete record-keeping and other tasks on time and effectively is imperative as a professional in the field. As a professional, the intervening life experiences are less accepted as the investment in the timely records is critical for the client and the agency.

- Kari worked for about a year as a postgraduate at a residential treatment facility and, although she led groups and had three assigned clients, she was behind on her DAP notes, from three months back. She reported that she kept attempting to get caught up after her shift on the weekends, and never got around to it. What are the potential ramifications and concerns?

- Fred worked with mandated clients. He neglected to complete his monthly treatment summary reports to both the Probation Officer and the Case Workers, which led to a county investigation. What are the various concerns here?

WORKSHEET 4.8

Ethical Multiculturalism

Critical thinking is also a large part of obtaining cultural competency, as we have stated from the quadrant of Self, and we will review these skills time and time again. Continue to review and respond to these examples.

- Tammy, a biracial female CIT, worked in a clinical mental health hospital as an intern. While there, she assessed, evaluated, and offered diagnostic impressions for the lead therapist. When assessing anyone of biracial ethnicity as herself, she opted to offer only z codes to try to help them avoid a potential *stigma*. When Tammy's supervisor asked her about her biases, she reported, "I am fine, I have none." What are the potential ramifications or concerns with this?

- Mark is a Caucasian male aged 41 who sees clients of diversity. He reportedly struggles to work with female African-American clients as offered by reports from his clients and colleagues. When in supervision, he reported that he feels uncomfortable and unsure of how to relate to these clients. His supervisor asked him about his white privilege and the power differential and he had no idea what these terms meant. What are the concerns here? Consider the related ACA codes.

WORKSHEET 4.9

Ethics of Self Control

Consider these examples, especially through the lens of the Pretzel Triple Parallel Process Model (see p. 83). Respond to the situations.

- Jen reported that she simply does not like her client who is, in her words, "emotionally draining." When Jen's CES asks her more about the client relationship, Jen gets very reactive and moody, blurting out "I want to refer her to my peer, I just don't like her." The CES notes that she too feels "emotionally drained" when working with the CIT.

- Jack is a CIT who has a military background. Jack reported to his CES that he escalated in session the other day and felt highly anxious, having to step out of the session. His CES asked more about what triggered the departure and he reported it was due to the client reminding him of someone he had fought while serving in war.

WORKSHEET 4.10

Ethics of Learning Motivation

Review these situations about learning, growing, and the motivation to learn and improve counseling competencies across the board. Write your thoughtful responses.

- Mary has just completed her Master's program in counseling and has decided to pay for external supervision while she continues to serve as a volunteer at a youth shelter. She noticed that she feels triggered by the client's stories sometimes, and she hopes that, with immense supervision and her own counseling, she can soon work through these triggers to be effective in the field to work with clients as a primary therapist.

- Jason has been on a remediation plan for one semester. He seems to be stagnant in his growth and learning; when his CES checks in with him, he reported, "I simply don't have the urge, nor see the value in tracking my own processes, or self-reflecting." In addition, he reported that he thought that, once he completed all the coursework, he was done with education. He is upset by the notion of having to take continuing education credits throughout his career.

WORKSHEET 4.11

Ethics of Feedback

Review these incidents and think very critically about your own willingness to accept feedback and also your interpretation of it.

- Ralph has been approached by his CES to explore his reaction to feedback. The CES has noted that anytime an assignment is returned to him, his first response is to write to the CES and explain all the intervening issues that prevented him from doing what was asked in the assignment, including blaming the instructions and his faculty. The concern is that his defensiveness will hinder his ability to embrace and incorporate any feedback being offered, thus preventing any advancement in his skills.

- Colleen continued to resubmit assignments without making corrections. The assignments were designed to be progressive through the course, eventually comprising the final assignment. By not incorporating the feedback, she will not pass the course. When approached about her lack of progress, she commented that she was writing the way she always wrote, and didn't feel the need to do thing differently, such as supporting her beliefs and assertations regarding her case conceptualization process.

WORKSHEET 4.12

Ethics of Acclimation

CITs will need to learn to go with the flow and handle ambiguous situations. Part of this skill is the ability to acclimate to client's diverse needs or to situations that may happen. How well do you manage ambiguity? Reflect and respond to these paragraphs.

- Sam was hired at an agency to work with middle-aged clients who reported substance-abuse histories and trauma. However, halfway through her first year, they added an adolescent unit. She was offered a position in that unit and, although anxious about the shift, took it with the intent of growing and learning to be more flexible.

- Jessie led a weekly transitional-living counseling group, but at the last minute was told by his supervisor that they needed to do a debriefing with the milieu since a client at the center had committed suicide. He was asked to help plan this new project instead since the entire agency was deeply impacted.

WORKSHEET 4.13

Ethics of Genuineness

To be genuine is to be authentic and real, and that what you do is congruent with those expectations of you. Being honest, real, and true in all ways is the expectation of a professional.

- Jane's supervisor experienced her as thoughtful and curious, with a desire to learn and grow. Her clients, however, reported to her supervisor that, when in session, Jane appeared standoffish, full of power, control, and judgmental. This was incongruent in terms of how the CIT presented with colleagues and her supervisor versus how her clients experienced her.

- Mike has a diverse client load and was recently offered an opportunity to teach a new group on sexual identity. Recently, his clients and supervisor reported that in his individual sessions he appears more genuine and consistent with his style, leadership, theoretical orientation, and relationship dynamics than in his group sessions, where they feel he isolates, is much more restrictive, and puts on a different professional face.

- As mentioned, in each of these foundational dispositional themes, we see the importance of continuing to maintain competency, while also considering how the themes often interconnect.

WORKSHEET 4.14

PAIR Considerations

Consider these questions as you work through the self-reflection to gain insight and assess your readiness to grow further into the professional you long to be. The action of self-assessment and reflection is a continuous, lifelong process.

- Am I conscientious?

- Do I use critical thinking?

- Do I appreciate learning?

- Am I teachable?

- Is my attitude conducive to learning?

- Do I have an open heart and mind in approaching each day as an opportunity to be curious and learn something?

- Is it difficult for me to be the learner instead of the expert?

- Do I have a lifelong beginner's mindset?

WORKSHEET 4.15

Lived Experience

What are some of your personal jobs, experience, roles, and responsibilities that may help you strengthen your professional performance? What things happened in the past that you wish you could do differently, and what do you think the changes would have been had you been able to do so? Reflect:

- Consider the strengths and skills needed to do what you have done in prior jobs or roles. How might they be transferable to counseling?

- What skills might you have already gained from those experiences that are transferable to the counseling profession and why?

- What job duties did you have to perform that are assets to the counseling career path?

- Consider the strengths you had to have in your interpersonal life. How might those be transferable to your counseling career?

- What were some difficult experiences you encountered and how did you resolve these interpersonal conflicts in your prior work/life experiences? How might this apply to counseling work?

WORKSHEET 4.16

The Case of Barb

Case Study

Barb was a 52-year-old single woman who had been a hairdresser for over 30 years. She stated that she had "pretty much been working as a counselor" the entire time she did hair. She also equated the challenging work she did with working "double" as she was "essentially doing hair and giving advice simultaneously" without getting paid for the mental health work.

- What are your initial thoughts about Barb and her assertion?

- How might your own past experiences compare with the reality of the counselor (CIT) role and responsibilities ethically, legally and professionally?

- How might you, as a peer and colleague, approach this fellow intern?

WORKSHEET 4.17

Additional Areas of Ongoing Professional Development

1 **Current Literature: Reading and Creating.** Consider ongoing research and exploration in the field.
2 **Professional Conferences: Attending and Presenting.** Consider creating a proposal for a local or national counseling conference, or publishing an article or chapter in the field.
3 **Insight and Awareness.** Consider keeping a CIT journal and writing in it on a weekly basis.
4 **Collaborate with Peers:** Solicit and offer corrective feedback.
5 **Open to New Learning.** Set a goal to learn about an area that is different from what you already know.
6 **Theories.** Continue to explore, research and practice case conceptualization in relation to theories. Consider reading about a new theorist each month. Watch a movie and analyze it from the perspective of a different theory each time. For example, read the book or watch the movie *Life of Pi* (Ang Lee) and consider the various counseling theories throughout the storyline.
7 **Resources.** Join the ACA or your state counseling association and receive newsletters, journals, and emails with information including resources.
8 **Techniques.** Consider reviewing a journal article periodically that illustrates a new technique in the field.
9 **Tools.** Be sure to keep the tools from this book handy in addition to adding to your toolbox throughout your coursework, trainings, continuing education, etc., and visiting the tools periodically.
10 **Inter-disciplinary Collaboration.** Consider attending a conference, training or collaboration group in the field of nursing, education, law, or another field that interrelates with counseling.
11 **Supervision and Supervising Feedback.** Consider reviewing supervision models and inquiring with your supervisor or CES about their model of supervision.
12 **Personal Counseling.** Consider either periodically or regularly obtaining your own personal counseling throughout your training program or as needed in your career.
13 **Self-Care.** Create a self-care plan that includes biopsychosocial features and is long-sustaining but also edit it as needed.
14 **Expand Horizons.** Consider a social change initiative in your own community related to something along the lines of counseling and contribute your gifts.
15 **Ethics.** Choose and hold to an ethical decision-making model of your choice.
16 **Local, State and National Legislation Awareness and Influence.**

WORKSHEET 4.18

Self-Efficacy

Use this sheet to explore the activities and ideas to build your competence and ability to learn and improve to boost self-efficacy. Write your answers in the space provided and feel free to use additional paper as needed.

1 What was something in your life you felt proud to master or accomplish?

2 What was that like for you? Who was your support network?

3 What strengths did you tap into to accomplish that feat?

4 What fears and weaknesses did you have to combat to achieve your goal?

5 In what area do you currently feel a drive to achieve in your self-efficacy as a CIT?

6 What aspects of your worldview coincide with your thoughts and feelings of accomplishment in pursuing difficult tasks?

7 How might you apply your prior experience to this?

8 Who do you need to be your support on this part of your journey?

9   Where do you see yourself ideally regarding mastering this facet in your CIT development? In other words, in your dream of the future, describe who you are and how you have mastered self-efficacy regarding your counselor identity and development.

10   Challenge yourself in something! In the next week or so, choose an activity you haven't done before, or one you haven't done in a long while that you were good at. A few examples are included below:

*   Go bowling.
*   Go fishing.
*   Go roller-skating, ice-skating, etc.
*   Go golfing (mini golf counts!).
*   Consider any sport and joining a game at your local YMCA or Recreation Center.
*   Play a game with your family.
*   Pick up and play a musical instrument.
*   Ride a bike.
*   Go to the local fair, play a game, or go on a ride.
*   Go for a walk or hike to a special destination.

You get the picture. You, as the CIT, are pushing yourself to do something that perhaps you have mastered before, but maybe have not experienced in a long time. Or, you become daring in trying something new to master. Consider writing about your experience and sharing with your CES in terms of how you experienced the activity and how it can be a metaphor for the needed area of growth you hope to achieve in your self-efficacy as a counselor.

Comments:

WORKSHEET 5.1

My Metaphor

Consider a couple of metaphors that show your own personal CIT growth or training process. What is a significant event you may have experienced from which you had growth? Consider the elements of that experience and the process you followed to gain deeper understanding. Use this space to process through your own experience.

- A favorite movie, novel, or character that you feel deeply attached to.

- A process or experience that shaped you significantly (often bringing strong emotion). Examples could be: a trek, a backpacking trip, a mission trip, a rite of passage, training for a sport/musical instrument, belonging to a group, etc.

- A developmental aspect in time (often could be a self-efficacy experience) that significantly shaped your life.

- A hobby, creative art activity, or even a prior job occupation/career role or position you held.

- A role you have served in the past, present, etc. that has new application and meaning in your CIT development.

Continue below as you begin to process and explore your personal metaphor.

WORKSHEET 5.2

Authenticity

Consider the following application. Contemplate reviewing the area of stress responses and continue to consider your own automatic responses and reactions to stress.

- Experts can tell counterfeit currency by studying genuine money closely and carefully. There are specific things to look for in true currency, including the sharpness in the details, security threads, hidden ways to discern fake from real. How might you begin to study and be authentic and genuine in your life?

- Who in your own life do you know who exhibits the qualities of authenticity, genuineness, and congruence on a regular basis?

- When someone else is genuine or authentic with you and perhaps uses immediacy and here and now self-disclosure, how do you normally respond? Consider reviewing the 4-Fs presented earlier. In addition, review the foundational counseling skills and consider how your nonverbals, tone, pitch, and speed of voice all impact the relationship as well.

- Consider meeting with your CES or work supervisor, etc., and practice common immediacy, openness, self-disclosure, and empathy.

  - Tell me how you have been experiencing me from the beginning of our CES/ CIT relationship until now?

  - I have experienced you as XXX in our work together.

  - How might I continue to grow in my counselor developmental process?

  - I am currently feeling XXX as you give me that feedback.

  - I appreciate that you are XXX (use a descriptive word to describe your experience with the CES).

- ○ One challenge I have within our work together has been XXX.

- ○ Even in this moment as we discuss XXX, I am experiencing XXX. Or, in this moment, I am experiencing you as XXX in our work together.

- ○ How can I demonstrate a sense of openness within our work together?

- ○ In our last meeting, I don't think I was as genuine with you as I had liked to be. I went home and reflected on ABC and I realize that I really am feeling XXX.

- ○ In my journal, I have been logging my ability to use immediacy, self-disclosure and openness. I recognize the following XXX.

- ○ I have been thinking about the situation with XXX and realize that, from your perspective, I may have appeared XXX.

WORKSHEET 5.3

The Case of Jane Smith

Jane Smith served in the military and is currently a CIT. She posted the following online discussion reply as a response to the question of "how well you receive feedback in your counselor developmental process?"

> I have come to reflect on this quite a bit since starting in my training as a counselor. At first, I realized, I was slightly different than other folks in that I was used to getting and giving feedback daily in the military. In fact, it was a part of daily life. My ability to hear and accept and implement feedback meant a matter of life or death in that world. I also had profound respect and admiration for supervisors and leaders who took their time to offer their genuine feedback for how I could be a better soldier. I was honored by that, and in turn, felt it was my responsibility to do the same for my fellow peers and someday, my own subordinates. Feedback is a part of growth, and without it, we have no idea how we are doing really. I find that I respect and feel honored by my CES and colleagues who give me feedback and take the time to tell me how they experience me, so I can know what I am working towards. (Personal communication, anonymous.)

Questions to consider:

- How did Jane's articulation of feedback resonate with you?

- Compare how Jane views feedback to what you experience.

- How does Jane demonstrate she is in the actualization quadrant of the UGM towards her growth process?

- What golden nugget did you take away from Jane's articulation of feedback?

WORKSHEET 5.4

My Growth Plan Exercise

Fill in each section as you work through this process of development and growth. Use as much space as you need to complete this exercise.

My Sample Growth Plan

My Professional Identity Statement:

My Short- and Long-Term Professional Goals:

Research/Presentation Ideas:

Clinical Practice:

Community Service/Social Change Ideas:

Self-Care Plan:

Licensure:

Continuing Education:

Ethical Decision-Making Model Choice:

Supervisee Needs and Elements:

Areas of Strength:

Areas of Needed Growth:

Appendix 2: Resources

(**Note**: While the authors have made every attempt to offer up-to-date accurate links and information, neither the publishers or authors assume any responsibilities for changes that occur after publication.)

Acclaim: www.getacclaim.com (video, storage, transcript, and commenting).

Andrew Jobling story: *The Girl in the Green Dress* http://andrewjobling.com.au/home-1/girl-in-green-dress.

Counseling Competencies Scale, Revised (CCS-R): (Lambie, Mullen, Swank, & Blount, 2016). Retrieved from: http://webmedia.jcu.edu/counselingdepartment/files/2016/03/CCS-R-Evaluation.pdf.

(**Note**: *The Counseling Competencies Scale—Revised*© (CCS-R) developed by Glenn Lambie, Ph.D. is available exclusively through *Clinical Training Manager*™, the counselor education software platform developed by Tevera, LLC. For more information visit: www.clinicaltrainingmanager.com.)

Cross Cultural: AMCD Multicultural Counseling Competencies, 1996: www.counseling.org/Resources/Competencies/Multcultural_Competencies.pdf

Ethical Decision Making Model to consider: www.counseling.org/docs/default-source/ethics/practitioner's-guide-to-ethical-decision-making.pdf?sfvrsn=0.

Johari Window Model and worksheet: www.humanresourcefulness.net/CypressCollege/docs/HUSR224/Johari_Window_Questionnaire-package.pdf. Or www.cls.utk.edu/pdf/ls/Week2_Lesson12.pdf.

Jung Typology (MBTI) worksheet: www.humanmetrics.com and www.humanmetrics.com/cgi-win/jtypes2.asp.

Killan & Thompson presentation: MBTI insights:

www.cpp.com/en-US/Resources/Impactful-Influencing-Harnessing-the-Power-of-the-MBTI-Assessment-Webinar

www.skillsone.com/Pdfs/CopingResourcesInventory.pdf

www.criticalincidentstress.com/what_is_your_stress_index_

www.criticalincidentstress.com

http://stresscom.net/index.asp?mod-16

www.ecu.edu/cs-dhs/rehb/upload/Wellness_Assessment.pdf

www.counseling.org/wellness_taskforce/PDF/ACA_taskforce_lifepie.pdf

www.behavioralhealth.army.mil/prt/PROQOL_vIV_English_Oct05.pdf

Meyers Briggs Type Indicator: www.myersbriggs.org/home.htm?bhcp=1 and www.myersbriggs.org/my-mbti-personality-type/mbti-basics/home.htm?bhcp=1.

Paul & Elder (2013): Critical Thinking Exam: www.criticalthinking.org/data/store/store_393734382.800x800.jpg.

Perceived Stress Scale (Cohen & Williams, 1988):
www.mindgarden.com/documents/PerceivedStressScale.pdf

Thomas-Kilmann Conflict Mode Instrument: One Per Person: www.kilmanndiagnostics.com/catalog/thomas-kilmann-instrument-one-assessment-person.

Tolerance to Ambiguity (MacDonald): www.sgha.net/library/pr0%252E1970%252E26%252E3%252E791.pdf.

Trailer to Life of Pi: www.youtube.com/watch?v=_J3cNY929k4.

Twilight Zone: Five Characters in Search of an Exit: www.dailymotion.com/video/x4yk2g8; http://www.imdb.com/title/tt0734569.

Glossary

Operational Definitions

(For references, see Chapter 1.)

Counseling as a Profession "Professional counseling is a professional relationship that empowers diverse individuals, families, and groups to accomplish mental health, wellness, education, and career goals" (ACA, 2017).

Counselor Educator Supervisor Those who train and enter the counseling field are professionals who are educated in the art of teaching others to be counselors and supervising both at the student and professional level. The education includes a doctoral degree in Counselor Education and Supervision from an accredited university. A CES can have various licensure but also adheres to the ACES *Best Practices in Clinical Supervision* (2011) and ACA *Code of Ethics* (2014) as well as following CACREP *2016 Standards* (2015). In addition, they may shift from roles including therapist, teacher, and consultant (Bernard & Goodyear, 2004). However, the CES is not in the role of giving therapy to the CIT.

Student Remediation Supporting a student to gain professional competency in all areas, while also maintaining a gatekeeping function for the field of counseling. This may include but is not limited to retaining the CIT in the program, dismissing them from the program, recommending a leave of absence, transfer to a non-counseling program if warranted, or continued guidance, support, and teaching to reach competence (Foster & McAdams, 2009; Homrich, DeLorenzi, Bloom, & Godbee, 2014).

Student Recidivism Students who repeat remediation processes more than one time. The changes that were gained may not have been effective enough for long-term changes; thus, the CIT either continues with the same unprofessional interactions, or when they reach one area in competence and another issue arises in a different area.

Student Support Support that can be done in a variety of ways to assist students in their growth process, through remediation, short-term support for life-events, and mentoring or training. Support can include helping with skills, knowledge, or dispositions. Student development, comportment or remediation is considered a form of student professional support as well.

Personal Counseling for Supervisees

Counseling for Supervisees   If supervisees request counseling, the supervisor assists the supervisee in identifying appropriate services. Supervisors do not provide counseling services to supervisees. Supervisors address interpersonal competencies in terms of the impact of these issues on clients, the supervisory relationship, and professional functioning. (F. 6. c., ACA *Code of Ethics*, 2014.)

Evaluation

Per the CACREP *2016 Standards* (2015), formative evaluation examines the development of professional competencies, with a focus on identifying strengths and deficiencies and corresponding learning interventions. Summative evaluation focuses on outcomes and is used to assess whether desired learning goals are achieved consistent with a professional standard (p. 45).

- **F. 9. a. Evaluation of Students**   Counselor educators clearly state to students, prior to and throughout the training program, the levels of competency expected, appraisal methods, and timing of evaluations for both didactic and clinical competencies. Counselor educators provide students with ongoing feedback regarding their performance throughout the training program (ACA *Code of Ethics*, 2014, p. 15).
- **F. 9. b. Limitations**   Counselor educators, through ongoing evaluation, are aware of and address the inability of some CITs to achieve counseling competencies. Counselor educators do the following   1. assist students in securing remedial assistance when needed, 2. seek professional consultation and document their decision to dismiss or refer students for assistance, and 3. ensure that students have recourse in a timely manner to address decisions requiring them to seek assistance or to dismiss them and provide students with due process according to institutional policies and procedures (ACA *Code of Ethics*, 2014, p. 15).
- **F. 9. c. Counseling for Students**   If students request counseling, or if counseling services are suggested as part of a remediation process, counselor educators assist students in identifying appropriate services (ACA *Code of Ethics*, 2014, p. 15).

Defining Competency

Comportment Issues   "Inability to insightfully understand and resolve their [student's] own issues so that these issues do not interfere with the therapeutic process" (Bemak, Epp, & Keys, 1999, p. 21).

Counseling Knowledge   Per CACREP, CES are to monitor and evaluate the CIT's knowledge, skills, and professional dispositions towards competency in these areas. In addition, knowledge is defined by Merriam-Webster as "the fact or condition of knowing something with familiarity gained through experience or association, or acquaintance with or understanding of a science, art or technique" ("Knowledge," 2017). It appears that knowledge involves understanding and application, or confirmation of that knowledge, as evidenced by assessment towards optimal competencies by CES.

Counseling Skills Foundational counseling skills at the micro, mezzo, and macro level; these include basic and advanced counseling skills. These skills are also categorized in the field in looking at what are known as "helping skills" according to Neukrug (2016).

Professional Counseling Behaviors and Dispositions Desired traits that were identified by Spurgeon, Gibbons, and Cochran (2012) as "commitment, openness, respect, integrity, and self-awareness" (p. 103, Table 1). Further, the CACREP 2016 *Standards (2015)* defined "The commitments, characteristics, values, beliefs, interpersonal functioning, and behaviors that influence the counselor's professional growth and interactions with clients and colleagues" (p. 43).

Professional Development Plan It appears most professionals hold to the standards of practice such as looking to reliable and valid assessment tools, evaluation processes, developmental remediation action plans, and ongoing assessment protocols that have been working in the field. This applies to all CITs in training.

Professional Growth Plan also referred to as Professional Development Plan, Remediation Plan etc. Assessment, evaluation, support, and developmental processes to allow the CIT opportunity to demonstrate competencies in areas of required need, support or growth to fulfil CES Gatekeeping responsibilities and obligation in the field of professional counseling.

Student Deficiencies Counselor trainees who do not meet professional standard competencies for skills, dispositions, or professional behaviors. The term was implemented to distinguish deficiencies from *impairments*, which could have implications through the Americans with Disabilities Act (Bryant, Druyos, & Strabavy, 2013; Gaubatz & Vera, 2002).

Student Professional Development

Analytical Thinking Analytical thinking is a thinking process or skill in which an individual can scrutinize and break down facts and thoughts into their strengths and weaknesses. It involves thinking in thoughtful, discerning ways, to solve problems, analyze data, and recall and use information (Warner, 2014, para. 2).

Assessment Through the Entire Program Evaluation process per the program of choice, often beginning with admissions process, throughout coursework; may be based on criteria and CACREP standards and objectives and formal and informal assessment process.

Critical Thinking Critical thinking is the intellectually disciplined process of actively and skillfully conceptualizing, applying, analyzing, synthesizing, and/or evaluating information gathered from, or generated by, observation, experience, reflection, reasoning, or communication, as a guide to belief and action. In its exemplary form, it is based on universal intellectual values that transcend subject matter divisions clarity, accuracy, precision, consistency, relevance, sound evidence, good reasons, depth, breadth, and fairness (Scriven & Paul, 2015).

Due Process Providing notice to students and an opportunity to be heard and/or appeal the action being proposed; action being proposed or taken is not motivated by bad faith, ill will, or is made arbitrarily or capriciously (McAdams, Foster, & Ward, 2007); following prescribed procedures to ensure rights are respected and consideration given throughout the process of remediation (Kerl, Garcia, McCullough, & Maxwell, 2002).

Gate Slipping Counseling student trainees who are deficient in professional competence, yet who complete a counseling program without successfully completing remediation or leaving the program (Gaubatz & Vera, 2002).

Gatekeeping "The process whereby a counselor or education program intervenes when candidates and students are not equipped with the requisite knowledge, skills, and values for professional practice" (Ziomek-Daigle & Bailey, 2009, p. 14).

Goodness of Fit assessment from the program and CIT concerning the quality of fit to the specific program and profession based on experience, desire, and ability.

Motivational Interviewing "MI is about arranging conversations so that people talk themselves into change based on their own values and interests" (Miller and Rollnick, 2013, p. 4).

Pre-admission The period when a CIT investigates the program, profession, commitments, and has understanding, disclosures and consent to understand an agreement to enter the program and the profession.

Professional Identity As professional counselors, our identity is multi-faceted. It begins with our professional and personal beliefs, commitments, understanding, and definitions of our roles and responsibilities. We are professionals at all times, and therefore bear a dedication to our profession. There is great responsibility in how we carry ourselves, behave, and the impact we have on others. As professionals, we have expertise that others do not have. That is a grave and serious responsibility.

Professional Identity Development Ongoing commitment from the CIT towards ongoing training, continuing education, and supervision, feedback and assessment. Often includes ongoing developmental growth plan the CIT maintains on their own.

Professionalism The act of behaving professionally as indicated by following the ethical and legal standards and codes of the profession, membership in professional organizations, continuing with development of skills, knowledge, and appropriate interactions with others through continuing education, training, and recent research, and holding oneself to a standard above that of a non-professional; maintaining professional boundaries; engaging in self-examination, mitigating assumptions and biases, and conducting oneself in a manner befitting the profession to which the person belongs (ACA *Code of Ethics*, 2014; Bodner, 2012).

Synthesis deductive reasoning; the dialectic combination of thesis and antithesis into a higher stage of truth ("Synthesis," 2017).

Index